1969

This book may be kept

HORACE
&
HIS LYRIC POETRY

BY

L. P. WILKINSON, M.A.

FELLOW OF KING'S COLLEGE
AND READER IN LATIN LITERATURE IN
THE UNIVERSITY OF CAMBRIDGE

Hoc paces habuere bonae uentique secundi

CAMBRIDGE
AT THE UNIVERSITY PRESS
1968

Published by the Syndics of the Cambridge University Press
Bentley House, 200 Euston Road, London, N.W. 1
American Branch: 32 East 57th Street, New York, N.Y. 10022

Standard Book Numbers:
521 07403 7 clothbound
521 09553 0 paperback

First edition 1945
Reprinted 1946
Second edition 1951
First paperback edition 1968

First printed in Great Britain by Balding and Mansell, Wisbech
Reprinted in Great Britain
at the University Printing House, Cambridge

CONTENTS

PREFACE

HORACE has the distinction of sharing with Homer a special volume in the Catalogue of the Cambridge University Library. The stream of writing about him continues to flow, swollen recently into spate by the bimillennium of his birth in 1935. The Bursian review covering the years 1929–36 deals with over three hundred books and articles. Yet substantial contributions to our knowledge and understanding of him can still be made. In 1918 Richard Heinze, who transformed Kiessling's edition until it became virtually his own, advanced a theory of Horace's metre which has driven from the field the old theory of Wilhelm Christ.[1] Shortly after the war of 1914 three works of first-rate importance on his sources appeared, Jensen's *Neoptolemos und Horaz* (1919), which has reopened the whole question of the plan of the *Ars Poetica* and its bearing on contemporary literature, Fiske's *Lucilius and Horace* (1920), a useful if rather indigestible contribution, and Pasquali's delightful *Orazio Lirico* (1920). Source-hunting has at least a negative value; it puts a check on false speculation.

Rediscoveries are commoner than discoveries. An interpretation of the end of Epode II recently advanced[2] had already its supporters in the sixteenth century, but was rightly rejected by Lambinus in 1561. It is well-nigh impossible to be sure that you are first in the field; sooner or later you find that your cherished *trouvaille* has been catalogued for years in some more or less remote museum; whereupon you may weep tears of joy, as Porson did when he found that his emendations had been anticipated by Bentley, or you may curse more humanly with Donatus, 'Pereant qui ante nos nostra dixerunt'. The great mass of our common knowledge about Horace is due to Renaissance scholars. Gratitude to them would be more suitably expressed in a general service for the Commemoration of Benefactors than in footnotes which would each be the meagre product of laborious research; there is a limit to the claims of the dead. Nor, again, can one ever be sure that one's happy thought of to-day is not one's reading of last year. But where I am conscious of a debt

1 *Berichte d. Sächs. Ges.*, Bd. 70, Heft 4. See p. 11.
2 N. Salanitro: *L' Epodo secondo di Orazio* (1935).

Preface

to any particular writer, I hope I have acknowledged it. And here at the outset I should mention how much I learnt from Housman's lectures on the text.

Horace's life and character and his relation to his times have been the subject of several recent works, such as D'Alton's *Horace and his Age* (1917), Tenney Frank's *Catullus and Horace* (1928), Turolla's *Orazio* (1931), Bione's *Orazio e Virgilio* (1934) and Zielinski's *Horace et la Société Romaine* (1938). But the work which I have found as stimulating (not to say, provoking) as any is Campbell's *Horace: A New Interpretation* (1925). For the historical background Syme's recent work *The Roman Revolution* (1939) is especially valuable, a welcome corrective to the uncritical panegyrics of Augustus to which we had become accustomed.

Though primarily written for classical students who are not Horatian specialists, this book is intended to be within the scope of anyone who can read Latin, or who could once read it. For the benefit of this last class I have given in footnotes a plain prose translation of most of the passages I quote. I make no apology for quoting familiar passages at length; few readers will know them by heart and not many would take the trouble to look them up. I make no claim to add much to what is known by experts on the subject (a feat which is in any case difficult enough at this stage), being more concerned with putting forward opinions than with establishing facts. In many matters reading and conversation have convinced me that mistaken ideas about Horace are widespread. What is needed is largely a readjustment of emphasis and the extension to a wider public of the increased understanding that time has given us. Where new light has recently been shed, I hope I have profited by it and passed it on. In particular, I have tried to do justice to Horace's poems as poetry, the more so because this side received little attention from Sellar in what is still, after fifty years, our standard account of him.

Most of this book has had to be written on odd evenings after days of war work, and at a country inn remote from libraries. I have been unable myself to check the numerous references, but have been fortunate in securing the scholarly help of the Rev. J. W. Earp, who, under the direction of Dr W. H. S. Jones, has spared no pains in this onerous task, and in that of making the indexes.

Preface

My especial thanks are due to Professor W. B. Anderson, whose most generous help and fastidious scholarship removed many inaccuracies and some misapprehensions. Those that remain are my fault.

My thanks are also due to my University and College, for studentships which enabled me some years ago to do most of the spadework; to the Society of Authors as the representatives of the Trustees of the estate of the late Professor A. E. Housman, and Messrs Jonathan Cape, the publishers of his *Collected Poems*, for permission to print his translation of *Diffugere niues*; to Professor F. E. Adcock, Mr F. L. Lucas, Mr D. W. Lucas and Mr G. H. W. Rylands, who read the typescript and made valuable suggestions; and to other friends who have given me encouragement, among whom I would particularly mention the Provost of King's (Mr J. T. Sheppard), the late Mrs Arthur Strong, Mr Kenneth Fawdry and Mr Brian Treverton-Jones.

L. P. W.

THE DUNCOMBE ARMS
GREAT BRICKHILL   *February 1944*

For the Second Edition I have made a number of modifications and corrections.

L. P. W.

June 1950

In this reprint of the Second Edition, I have only made slight alterations. But it is gratifying that the Syndics of the Cambridge University Press should have felt justified in undertaking a new issue, and I should like to express my thanks to them.

L. P. W.

March 1968

CHAPTER I

INTRODUCTORY

HORACE'S reputation since the Renaissance has been secure in spite of some ups and downs, but it has survived changes of fashion less by the universality than by the variety of his appeal. Some poets have pleased all the people some of the time, such as Pope and Tennyson; others have pleased some of the people all the time, and among these is Horace. He had many moods, his character was not entirely consistent, his words do not necessarily represent his views, and he changed as he grew older. The result is that he said and did many irreconcilable things, and his devotees, charmed by his personality and his verse, have had no difficulty in selecting for emphasis what has pleased them and neglecting the rest, each one quoting scripture to his purpose, each one re-creating Horace in his own image.

> Quaerit in hoc libro pariter sua dogmata quisque,
> inuenit et pariter dogmata quisque sua.

We English think of him as one of us; but it appears that no less to the French he is one of them, and even to the Germans one of them.[1] That is why he has proved inexhaustible; in each generation some section finds him particularly sympathetic; to each he will present a new aspect; for each he requires, and deserves, re-interpretation.

For my own part I feel that many Victorians, and writers like Professor Fraenkel as their latter-day representatives, have laid too much stress on his political significance and on the Stoic side of his character. To them he is essentially the *uates*, and they value most highly the poetry he wrote in this vein. The editor of the Loeb

---

[1] But here I must quote the remark of a perceptive German, Karl Büchner, on Glover's *Horace, A Return to Allegiance* (Bursian, Bd. 267, p. 33): 'It is with astonishment that one notes again and again how congenial Horace's nature is to the English.'

edition of the Odes, C. E. Bennett, writing in 1924, reflects this view clearly in his Introduction (p. viii): 'In content also many of his odes represent the highest order of poetry. His patriotism was genuine, his devotion to Augustus was profound, his faith in the moral law was deep and clear. Whenever he touches on these themes he speaks with conviction and sincerity, and often rises to a lofty level.'[1] It may be so; but is that the whole story? If it were, Horace would have lost many of his admirers in the present generation. What of all those other odes, which deal with the eternal platitudes—the brevity of youth, the vanity of human ambitions and the finality of death? Are these not sincere? Do these not 'rise to a lofty level'? And what of the many odes whose intangible beauty cannot be expressed in terms of subject-matter?

No less one-sided is the all too common view of Horace as a genial but rather superficial character whose most typical activity was drinking wine and uttering proverbial wisdom under a tree.[2] To give a balanced account of his personality is to walk the tight-rope,[3] and one approaches the attempt with diffidence. His life story has often been told,[4] but I have decided to restate so much of it as is certain or generally accepted, because this is necessary as a background, and also because there is a rich layer of fanciful conjecture, and a certain amount of definite misconception, to be cleared away. From consideration of his personality I shall pass on to my main subject, his lyric poetry.

Roger Fry spent a large part of his life in preaching to a fascinated but somewhat bewildered public that the only thing that really mattered about a picture was its formal qualities. He was driven to this by the insensitivity of his contemporaries to form, and himself achieved such aesthetic purity that he once astonished his audience

---

1 Cf. E. E. Sikes, *Roman Poetry*, p. 15; R. K. Hack, *Harvard Studies*, XXVII, 1916, pp. 31–2; and many others. For a more balanced view see Verrall in *Companion to Latin Studies* (1921), pp. 622–3.

2 'Fat, beery, beefy Horace' was a phrase constantly on the lips of one who was (otherwise) one of the best Classical teachers in England.

3 No one, to my knowledge, has walked it so dexterously as T. R. Glover in his two lectures entitled *Horace, A Return to Allegiance*.

4 Tenney Frank's account in *Catullus and Horace* is perhaps the fullest and most readable.

at a lantern lecture by pointing to the central figure in an Entomb-
ment and beginning, 'This important mass here...'. But towards
the end of his life he pronounced a notable palinode.[1] He had
come round to the view that there was every degree in pictures.
At one extreme was the purely narrative or descriptive, moving us,
if at all, by its subject alone, and lacking any formal merit. Here he
showed a slide of Poynter's 'Faithful unto Death'. At the other
extreme was the abstract, or nearly so, illustrated by a still life of
Cézanne, a picture strangely moving for some reason connected
with the subconscious which it was for the psychologist, if anyone,
to investigate. Between these there was every degree of combination, pictures which included most of the 'Old Masters', whose
effect was due to a blend of form and content. And he finally
announced his intention of atoning for the past by writing a book
on 'Rembrandt as a Dramatist'.

Each of these kinds of picture has its admirers. In much the same
way poems and their readers may be distinguished, though the
analogy is by no means to be pressed. Some people read poetry
primarily to enlarge their experience, or to see into the poet's mind
and get to know his personality, or to find their own views better
expressed than they could ever hope to express them, or to understand the mentality of past ages: in any case what most concerns
them is the subject-matter. These, if they care for Horace at all,
will probably say that they prefer the Satires and Epistles to the
Odes and Epodes. It is surprising how many people do say so.
De gustibus non est disputandum; but it must surely be conceded that
serious poetic art has a *prima facie* claim to superiority over versified
talk however witty.

On the other hand there are those who are especially susceptible
to sounds and rhythms; who expect from poetry a more specifically
aesthetic pleasure, and like poems that excel in this respect. There is
(apart from odd experiments) no abstract poetry corresponding to
abstract painting, though there is plenty of evidence of people being
charmed by literature in an unknown tongue.[2] But in some poems
form plays a larger part in relation to subject-matter than in others;

1 In his Sidgwick Lecture at Newnham College, Cambridge, in 1931,
if not also elsewhere.
2 As the boy Petrarch by Cicero, the boy Schliemann by Homer.

Introductory

Latin Elegy is a conspicuous example,[1] and the Horatian Lyric perhaps the most conspicuous of all. This is, indeed, a characteristic of all Latin Poetry, and the reason is not far to seek; not only were the Romans an uninventive race as regards literary subject-matter, but it was these formal qualities which they specially learnt to study and admire at their most impressionable age, as part of their careful training in rhetoric. They were obsessed by the beauty and strength of the Latin Language, and it may be doubted whether anyone who does not share this feeling will care greatly for the Odes; or, further, whether anyone who has not some taste for rhetoric will care for Latin Poetry as a whole, apart from a few authors who are not typical, such as Catullus and Lucretius.

Yet explaining why one likes an ode of Horace is as hard as explaining why one likes a picture. Art critics, unwilling to talk about the subject-matter of a picture where it is the form that they feel to be important, have taken refuge in not very illuminating metaphors—'plasticity', 'rhythm', even 'orchestration'. A similar helplessness afflicts the champion of Horace. And it may be that after all the only useful course is for the former to point to the picture, the latter to declaim the poem. Of attempts to characterise the Horatian ode the best known to me is that of Nietzsche: 'To this day I have got from no poet the same artistic delight as from the very first a Horatian ode gave me. In certain languages what is here achieved is not even to be thought of. This mosaic of words, in which every word by sound, by position and by meaning, diffuses its influence to right and left and over the whole; the minimum in compass and number of symbols, the maximum achieved in the effectiveness of those symbols, all that is Roman, and, believe me, of excellence unsurpassed.'[2]

But I do not wish to seem to be countenancing the old fallacy, that 'ingenium' and 'ars' are really separable; Horace himself was sound enough on that point, and those of his poems in which the two are not inseparably mated are dead. I am only insisting that 'ars' may be the dominant partner in some poetry. For this reason I have devoted considerable space to the question of how Horace

1 Cf. M. Schuster, *Tibull-Studien* (1930), pp. 57 ff., where he suggests that Tibullus is a composer rather than a poet.

2 x, 343. Quoted by Heinze, *Die Augusteische Kultur*, p. 111.

4

gets his effects. I do not think that for most people the discussion of technique destroys the poetry, as Keats thought science had destroyed the rainbow; on the contrary it may increase the enjoyment, as I have found, for instance, in reading Robert Bridges' analysis of Keats' own poetry.[1]

It will be evident by now that for me Horace is the poet of the Odes and Epodes. That is not all, however. As a character I find him most sympathetic; I enjoy (or to be honest, I *quite* enjoy) reading the Epistles, when they are really letters, and the Satires when they approximate to the Epistles. I enjoy, in moderation, the parts of both that deal with literature. If Horace had written only his hexameter verse, I should prefer him to most Latin authors. But the greater part of the Satires presents obstacles to our enjoyment which are not mainly Horace's fault and which are almost insuperable. In the first place they are extremely difficult; and few readers who are not patient devotees can carry in their heads that knowledge of contemporary customs and gossip, even so much as is available, without which many of the allusions mean nothing. Here is a simile (Sat. II, 3, 60):

> Non magis audierit quam Fufius ebrius olim,
> cum Iliónam edormit, Catienis mille ducentis
> 'mater, te appello!' clamantibus.

I choose this example because the situation is quite amusing; but how many of those who only read Horace now and then will understand the reference? And then again, how many unfamiliar words there are in the Satires! What is meant to read like rapid and amusing chatter can barely survive a single peep at the notes or dictionary, let alone continual consultation. Besides this, there is nothing that changes more than taste in jokes. No reputable modern could write a piece like Satires I, 7, leading up to a rather feeble pun, nor would anyone now read it if it were not part of 'The Classics', a document of Roman social history. The unfortunate banquet of Nasidienus in II, 8 is less amusing than embarrassing to our sensibility, and the behaviour of Servilius Balatro, a Gratiano of whom Horace seems to approve, jars much more than his host's

[1] Bridges' love of poetry began, significantly, with reading Ovid as a small boy at Eton. He always approached it from the artistic side.

vulgarity amuses. Above all, both Satires and Epistles presuppose that interest in moral questions which, initiated by Socrates, pervaded the Graeco-Roman world. We can only relish such fare if it is of the lightest and served in very small helpings. Thus the First Satire, a 'diatribe' on avarice and discontent, is no longer very pleasurable reading.

For these reasons, though I shall often have occasion to refer to the hexameter poems, I have made the subject of this book 'Horace and his Lyric Poetry'.

CHAPTER II

LIFE AND WORKS

I N the brief account of Horace's life that follows, I have kept to established facts as far as possible; but there is one topic included which is more a matter of conjecture, the way in which his works were given to the world and received by it; as this is important for understanding them, I have thrown it somewhat into relief.

His father had begun life as a slave, but obtained his freedom and worked as a *coactor* (perhaps an auctioneer's assistant), finally settling down with a small property at Venusia, a military colony near the heel of Italy. Here his son was born on 8 December, 65 B.C. We hear nothing of the mother or of any other relatives, and perhaps it was freedom from family ties that enabled the father, impressed by his own rise in the world and by the obvious abilities of the child, to remove him from the rough company of the centurions' sons at the local school of Flavius and take him to Rome for his higher education.

The teachers there engaged for him were, if Orbilius is representative, the most eminent in the Capital. Under them he would read the early Latin poets, whom he came to regard patronisingly with a mixture of affection and contempt,[1] and he would perfect his knowledge of Greek, of which, as a South Italian, he probably possessed already at least a smattering; he would also study the rhetoric which contributed so much to his poetic style.

But no less important for his education was the influence of his father, who himself undertook the duties of 'paedagogus'. On their walks through Rome the shrewd countryman would comment on the absurdities which are taken for granted in a city where long tradition has made them seem natural, and point out one well-known figure as a warning, another as an example. There is no reason to doubt Horace's assertion that it was this experience which planted in him that interest in human character and conduct which so greatly influenced his choice of subjects when he discovered that he had poetic gifts.[2]

1 *Ep.* II, 1, 69–75. Quintilian recommended that all boys should be taught Greek before Latin, which they would pick up in any case: 1, 1, 12.
2 *Sat.* I, 4, 103–26; 6, 81–8.

The freedman who had thus made his only son his principal interest in life was not content to do things by halves; schooldays at Rome completed, he sent him to Athens for what we should call a University education:

> Scilicet ut uellem curuo dinoscere rectum
> atque inter siluas Academi quaerere uerum.

But into the pleasant social life of Athens and the sequestered calm of the Grove broke the news of Caesar's murder. Not long after came Brutus himself, who received a great welcome and settled down in all appearance to an academic life. The silent influence had its effect. All the Roman youth studying in Athens rallied to the companion of their lectures when the moment came to decide.[1] While some, like young Marcus Cicero, may well have been confirmed tyrant-haters, Horace's decision may be ascribed as plausibly to herd-instinct as to reasoned conviction. He accompanied the Republican army, it seems, to Macedon and Asia,[2] and by the time the rival forces clashed at Philippi he had been given the rank of military tribune. But in one of the several routs during the battle he made good his escape, and thereafter, instead of joining Sextus Pompeius with the die-hards, he returned to Italy 'with wings clipped', desiring only, we may suppose, to escape from the vortex into which he had so unsuitably been sucked.[3] His father was apparently dead, his inheritance was confiscated, and he was left at the age of twenty-three with the sole advantages of his own wits and the best education the world could provide. In the hope of collecting pence or patronage he now took to writing verse.[4] As models he chose Archilochus, the seventh-century iambic poet of Paros, who, besides being unappropriated as yet by any other Roman, had a pungent realism that would suit his mood, and Lucilius, the second-century Roman satirist, whose wide human interest and caustic wit would be no less congenial, while his artistic shortcomings invited competition. The Epodes and Satires occupied him during the next decade.

1 Plut. *Brutus*, XXIV.

2 *Sat.* I, 7. *Ep.* I, 11 mentions some of the places which Horace may have visited at this time.

3 *Odes*, II, 7; *Ep.* II, 2, 49 f.

4 *Ep.* II, 2, 51 f.

8

Life and Works

The general amnesty of 39 B.C. no doubt improved the situation; at any rate Horace procured the modest post of clerk in the Treasury. Meanwhile he was obtaining repute, and in some quarters notoriety, by his mordant verse. So promising a poet could scarcely escape the notice of Virgil, who would also be naturally sympathetic to any Meliboeus who had lost his land in the troubles. Virgil and Varius introduced him to Maecenas about the spring of 38 B.C.,[1] and nine months later he was invited to join their circle. He did not however abandon his clerkship, for seven years later he represents himself as maintaining a not undistinguished, if unlaborious, connection with the Treasury.[2] Nor did he go to live in Maecenas' house; for he tells of the frugality of his own table at Rome, and several years later he still dines with his patron only, it appears, by invitation.[3]

In the meantime he was reading extensively, if not deeply, from all periods of literature. He was fond of sleeping late, playing games, and wandering about the City to watch the strange characters of all sorts who congregated in the poorer quarters. There were also stormy love affairs, if the Epodes may be taken as evidence. About 35 B.C. he collected and published ten of his satires in book form. This does not mean that they were now made public for the first time, for in the Fourth he defends himself against accusations of malice and in the Tenth against the affronted admirers of Lucilius. Nor need we suppose that these were all the satires he had written.

A political lull followed the defeat of Sextus Pompeius in 36 B.C. It was during this period that Horace was presented by Maecenas with the famous farm and estate in the valley of the Digentia among the Sabine Hills, about fourteen miles beyond Tibur.[4] Eight slaves

---

1 *Sat.* I, 6, 55 ff. This delay of nine months may have been partly due to Maecenas' absence in the South, where he was sent as Octavian's envoy to Antony, rather than to any design.

2 *Sat.* II, 6, 36.

3 *Sat.* I, 6, 114–18; II, 7, 32–5. Gardthausen's statement to the contrary seems incorrect (*Augustus und seine Zeit*, I, p. 782). Augustus' suggestion mentioned in the Suetonian *Life* that Horace should leave Maecenas' 'parasitic table' to be his secretary is not to be taken too literally, and probably belongs in any case to a later period.

4 See G. Lugli, *Horace's Sabine Farm* (1930), pp. 45–6.

9

were employed on the farm, and when one remembers that there were also five tenant-farms attached,[1] one takes with a grain of salt the remarks Horace makes about the modesty of his circumstances.

Those who thought peace was now assured were too sanguine. An acrimonious correspondence between Octavian and Antony led to a definite rupture in February, 32 B.C., and war was declared against Egypt in the name of the Roman State in the summer of that year. Horace was naturally on the side of Maecenas and his leader. Despite assertions to the contrary, it is unlikely that either he or Maecenas was present at the battle of Actium. The result of that battle and the capture of Alexandria made lasting peace a possibility, provided that Octavian refrained from reprisals.

Not only the dawn of peace, but also a personal triumph, must have made the year 30 a happy one for Horace. The mood that had made Archilochus sympathetic to him had passed with the improvement in his fortunes. Already in some of the Epodes a milder spirit was beginning to show itself, and finally he turned to other sources of inspiration, or, at any rate, of metre—to the early lyric poets of Greece, Alcaeus and Sappho.[2] The first task was to adapt their metres to the Latin ear. He did not, as some have thought, consult a metrical handbook; but he did introduce a considerable number of rules: thus he made Asclepiads, Glyconics, Pherecrateans, and usually Alcaic hendecasyllables begin with a spondee; he made the fourth syllable of the Sapphic and the fifth syllable of the Alcaic hendecasyllable almost invariably long; and above all he introduced regular caesuras into several types of line. Detailed analysis suggests that his object was to eliminate from his Aeolic verse anything that might suggest iambic, trochaic or dactylic rhythm. Now in so doing he was not making any startling innovation. We are apt to forget that these metres had been used by Hellenistic poets whose work has been almost completely lost. From the surviving fragments it appears that he was simply regularising what had already

1 *Sat.* II, 7, 118; *Ep.* I, 14, 1–3.

2 He did not attempt to *imitate* Sappho. Nor did he have much in common with Alcaeus as a man; but he would appreciate his personal note, his style and his metres. See Wilamowitz, *Sappho und Simonides* (1913), p. 309.

become marked tendencies in Hellenistic lyric. In the case of one metre we can trace the process; for Stobaeus has preserved for us a Sapphic Hymn to Rome in five stanzas, written probably in the first century B.C. by a poetess named Melinno, and we have also the two Sapphic poems of Catullus.[1] Both show as marked tendencies what Horace later established as rules.

In carrying these Hellenistic preferences to their logical conclusion Horace realised, no doubt, that he was at the same time creating measures peculiarly suited to the genius of the Latin language; that the lengthening of doubtful syllables had given weight and dignity, while the caesuras, by emphasising the regular blocks of words they divided, produced a monumental effect. His pride at having introduced Aeolian lyric to Italy is very likely due, not to the phrases or ideas, nor even to the small amount of spirit, which he derived from Alcaeus and Sappho, but to his success in mastering and adapting their metres. I believe that this came to him with the excitement of a discovery, and that it was this which inspired a peculiarly happy and spirited ode, I, 26:

> Musis amicus tristitiam et metus
> tradam proteruis in mare Creticum
>   portare uentis, quis sub Arcto
>   rex gelidae metuatur orae,
>
> Quid Tiridaten terreat, unice
> securus. O quae fontibus integris
>   gaudes, apricos necte flores,
>   necte meo Lamiae coronam,

1 Stob. *Fl.* I, z, 13 (Meineke); Cat. 11 and 51. We may compare the regularisation by Ovid of the growing tendency to end pentameters with a dissyllable. The fact that Horace modified his metres in some respects when he came to write the *Carmen Saeculare* and *Odes* IV suggests in itself that he was an experimenter, not the slave of a handbook.

The conclusions given above are those of Heinze. Following lines suggested by P. Maas (*Berl. Phil. Woch.* 1911, pp. 707 ff.) he put the theory of Horatian Lyric Metre on a new basis, and superseded the views of Christ and Kiessling that had held the field before (*Die lyrischen Verse des Horaz*, in *Ber. der Sächs. Ges.* 1918, Bd. 70, 4 Ht.). He summarises the results of his inquiry on pp. 90–1. They have been widely accepted. (See K. Büchner, *Bursian* 267, p. 118.)

Piplei dulcis! nil sine te mei
prosunt honores: hunc fidibus nouis,
    hunc Lesbio sacrare plectro
        teque tuasque decet sorores.[1]

This poem has been variously interpreted. Some suppose that Lamia has done something to deserve the Muses' crown, something which has not been revealed to us: it has been suggested that Horace was celebrating his first success as a poet.[2] But that hardly allows unity of intention even to so short a poem; for what should Horace's sudden feeling that politics are of no importance to himself, the Muses' friend, have to do with Lamia's success? As Wickham frankly says, 'It is difficult to see the connection between the first and last parts of the Ode unless, indeed, as has been suggested, Horace is holding up his own cheerfulness and its source for Lamia's imitation'. But the difficulties disappear if we take the whole poem to be in celebration of *Horace's* success in mastering the Lesbian metres and adapting them to suit his ear.[3] *Musis amicus* strikes the keynote: he has made the discovery to which he later reverts, as though it had taken him by surprise, that he is indeed a poet, that the Muse has given, even to a dumb fish, the voice of a swan.[4] For the moment all else seems trivial; he is preoccupied with his new medium, and his words recall the similar exaltation of Lucretius:[5]

iuuat *integros* accedere *fontes*
atque haurire, iuuatque *nouos* decerpere *flores*
insignemque meo capiti petere inde *coronam*
unde prius nulli uelarint tempora Musae;

and with

hunc fidibus *nouis*,
hunc *Lesbio* sacrare plectro...

1 'The Muses' friend, I will throw sadness and fears to the wanton winds to carry to the Cretan sea, supremely careless who is dreaded as king of the frozen shore beneath the Bear, or what is frightening Tiridates. O thou that rejoicest in springs untouched, weave sunny flowers, weave a wreath for my Lamia, sweet maid of Piplea; without thee the honours I confer are of no avail; him shouldst thou and thy sisters consecrate with the new strings, him with the Lesbian quill.'

2 Kiessling, *ad loc.*   3 Cf. Pasquali, *op. cit.* p. 30.
4 *Odes*, IV, 3, 19–20. Cf. I, 17, 13–14.   5 I, 927 ff.

he makes it doubly clear that his thoughts are all upon his new instrument, the Lesbian lyre of Sappho and Alcaeus. It is not necessary to suppose that Lamia had done anything; he was simply the first person at hand upon whom the excited poet could exercise his new power of 'conferring honour' and 'consecrating'. He may have been his guest at the time, or his host, as in Odes III, 17.[1]

It is generally and plausibly assumed, since no datable Epode or Satire was written after, and no datable Ode[2] earlier than, the year 30 B.C., that before Horace settled down in earnest to writing the Odes he collected and published the Epodes and the Second Book of Satires in this year. That would then be the date of his earliest attempts in Lesbian metre, and such a date for Odes I, 26 is supported, rather than not, by the reference to Tiridates in line 5. Our authorities are confused, but it seems that Tiridates expelled Phraates from the throne of Parthia in the summer of 31 and ruled until late in 30, when Phraates recovered the throne. He then fled to Syria, where Octavian allowed him sanctuary.[3] What, therefore, could

---

1 That I, 26 is one of the earliest odes was long ago deduced by Lachmann on metrical grounds. He pointed out that l. 11, *hunc Lesbio sacrare plectro*, is unique in the 317 lines of this type in Horace in having a break after the fourth syllable when this is not a monosyllable. Other lines too, 7 and 12, have breaks which Horace generally avoided. (C. Franke's *Fasti Horatiani*, 1839, p. 238 f.). Heinze (*Die lyrischen Verse des Horaz*, p. 79) rejects Lachmann's conclusion; but he gives a weak reason, that this licence is no evidence of immaturity because we do not find it in the Cleopatra ode, I, 37, which must have been written as early as the autumn of 30 B.C. In poems so short the non-occurrence of a feature is no evidence. I, 37 has a licence of its own in l. 14, *mentemque lymphatam Mareotico*, a rhythm unparalleled in *Odes* I–III, which is probably a sign of immaturity. Heinze's own explanation, that the laxity of metre is due to the impromptu nature of the poem, is rather feeble.

2 Some would place I, 14 (*O nauis*) earlier, finding no occasion sufficiently grave after 30 B.C. But see my article in *Hermes* 1957, 495–9.

3 Dio, LI, 18; Justin, XLII, 5, 6–8; *Cambridge Ancient History*, X, p. 79. Tiridates seems to have made a second attempt, fleeing again to Augustus on being driven out in 26–25 B.C. Heinze thinks that on this occasion he may have held the throne as early as 29, to which date he refers this poem. But the earlier attempt fits just as well, and it is very doubtful whether he recovered the throne again as early as 29, if at all. See *C.A.H.* X, p. 261.

be more natural than that in 30, when he had been on the throne for some months, he should have appealed to Rome to defend him against Phraates' counter-offensive; so that *quid Tiridaten terreat* would be typical of the latest political gossip in the City at that time?

The next seven years were probably the happiest in Horace's life. His pleasure in the Sabine farm was still fresh, and the circle of Maecenas still intact. Internal peace was at last assured, bringing with it a feeling of national revival. Above all, he was engaged continually in creative work of whose lasting greatness he was well aware. Much of his time was spent at Tibur, the modern Tivoli. (There is no indication when he obtained the house there which was pointed out to visitors in Suetonius' day near the grove of Tiburnus.)[1] At other times he would be at cool Praeneste on its hill, or at sunny Tarentum, or at the seaside resort of Baiae near Naples. Other poets were to be found in the neighbourhood of Naples; Virgil had a small estate at Nola, and the nucleus of the circle of Maecenas may still have frequented Campania as it did in the days of Philodemus.[2]

Nearly all the odes are addressed to some individual, who no doubt received the first copy. They would then attain a certain publicity by being recited in the circle of Maecenas, where friends like Quintilius Varus might suggest improvements. The state poems may have been circulated more widely. It is most unlikely that they were intended to be sung; the poet singing with his lyre was a mere convention in Roman as in English poetry.[3] By the summer of 23 B.C. Horace had written nearly a hundred odes and the time

1 R. L. Dunbabin, *C.R.* May 1933, does not believe that he had one at Tivoli. G. Lugli, *op. cit.* pp. 14 ff., suggests that the delightful villa of S. Antonio opposite the falls of the Anio may have belonged to Maecenas, but not, as its late owner, Mr G. H. Hallam, believed, to Horace.

2 For the plausible supposition of a circle of poets existing in Campania in Horace's early days, who were also disciples of the Epicurean philosophers Siro and Philodemus, see Tenney Frank, *Vergil*, pp. 48–54; Rostagni, *Arte Poetica di Orazio*, pp. xxv–xxviii. It includes Virgil, Varius, Varus, and possibly Tucca and Horace. Its connection with the villa at Herculaneum in which the Philodemus papyri were found is hypothetical.

3 Cf. R. Heinze, *Vom Geist des Römertums* (1930), pp. 207 ff. Hymns such as 1, 10 and 21 may be exceptions.

had come to give them to the world.[1] Three rolls would be necessary, and for some reason he decided to make the second smaller
than the others. Faced with the problem of arrangement he no
more thought of chronological order, which would have been
illuminating to us, than did any other Roman poet, but seized on
any stray principle that suggested itself. Thus in Book I the first
nine odes, the 'Parade Odes', are all in different metres, beginning
honoris causa with poems addressed to Maecenas, Caesar, Virgil,
Sestius the consul of the year, and Agrippa.[2] In Book II the first
eleven are alternately in Alcaics and Sapphics, and moralising poems
predominate. Book III opens with six long Alcaic odes. These have
been given the name of 'The Roman Odes' by modern scholars
and there has been a tendency to presume that they were written
as a cycle; they have then been forced by elaborate 'interpretation'
to fit theories that they represent, for instance, the several cardinal
virtues, or the virtues of Augustus. It is much more likely that
Horace collected here five great odes on state subjects that he had
written in Alcaics and set before them another long Alcaic poem
whose first stanza (*Odi profanum uolgus* etc.) serves to introduce all
six.[3] By way of relief the rest of this book contains chiefly light
poems. Here and there odes are put next to one another for some
common factor; thus I, 14 and 15 appear to be political allegories,
I, 27 and 28 are dramatic monologues, I, 34 and 35 are both about
Fortuna. Any idea, such as Verrall's, that the Odes are anything
but a miscellaneous collection, is chimerical. We may presume that
it was to round them off that Horace composed two poems in a
simple metre he had not otherwise used, a prologue soliciting
approval from Maecenas and an epilogue demanding a crown from
Melpomene. The collection was dedicated to Maecenas, but a copy
was sent, by the hand of one Vinnius, to Augustus himself.[4]

Horace was clearly disappointed with the reception given by the

1 This date, ascertained by Lachmann and Kiessling, is generally accepted.
For the arguments against Verrall's attempt to advance it to 19 B.C. see
Wickham's Introd. I, 2.

2 No. 5, to Pyrrha, was no doubt inserted for variety and relief.

3 Cf. R. Heinze, *Vom Geist des Römertums*, pp. 213 ff. But for an interesting
suggestion that III, 24 contains the germ of the Roman Odes and points the
connection between the first of these and the other five, see F. Solmsen,
A.J.P. LXVIII (1947), pp. 337–52.

4 *Ep.* I, 13.

public to his 'monument more lasting than bronze'. We must not indeed attach too much weight to odd references in Roman poets to the 'inuidia' or 'liuor' of rivals and critics; these were a convention inherited from Callimachus,[1] who genuinely had to combat a recognised opposition. But the Nineteenth Epistle (addressed significantly to 'Maecenas *docte*') implies that Horace was criticised as lacking in originality by people who did not realise what the world has realised since, that only Horace could write Horatian odes. Besides, the metres were unfamiliar, the verbal points were subtle, the restraint and fastidiousness would only appeal to refined taste; and the standards and sensibility of the circle of Maecenas, to which he had become accustomed, were rare in the world outside. The fact that one who had written a hundred odes in seven years wrote none, so far as we know, in the next six, is significant; it can hardly be explained entirely by his ostensible absorption in moral philosophy. His simultaneous turning to literary criticism may also be partly due to disappointment as a poet.[2]

There were other troubles too. Already in 24 B.C. a shadow had been cast by the death of Quintilius Varus, who had been invaluable as a friendly critic of his poetry. Worse was to come. Late in 23 a conspiracy against Augustus was nipped in the bud, but not before its discovery had become known to the friends of the conspirators. The leakage was traced to Maecenas, who had confided in his wife, the beautiful Terentia; Terentia was a half-sister of Licinius Murena, one of those executed for complicity. There was no question of dismissal or of an open breach between Augustus and Maecenas, for the knight held no official position; but a breach there was, and it was never healed except on the surface. Maecenas ceased to count, and his circle must have felt it deeply.[3]

The epistles of Book I, written between 23 and 20 B.C., are cheerful enough in general tone. The middle-aged poet enjoys the soporific surroundings of his farm, and writes in an avuncular

1 Prologue to Αἴτια, l. 17: Ἔλλετε, Βασκανίης ὅλοον γένος. *Hymn* II, 105 ff.: ὁ Φθόνος Ἀπόλλωνος ἐπ' οὔατα κ.τ.λ. *Ep.* XXIII, 4: ὁ δ' ἤεισεν κρέσσονα βασκανίης. Cf. *Odes*, II, 20, 4: 'inuidiaque maior'; IV, 3, 16: 'et iam dente minus mordeor inuido.' Also *Sat.* II, 1, 76 ff.

2 See *Ars Poetica*, 304–8.

3 Dio, LIV, 3–4; Suet. *Aug.* 19, 1; 66, 3; Vell. II, 91, 2; 92, 3; Tac. *Ann.* III, 30.

manner to young friends in many parts of the world. But his health, never good, has begun to encumber his freedom, and rheumatic trouble keeps him from his friends at Baiae.[1]

Not long after, another blow fell, the death of Virgil. Tibullus died too; and Propertius, a rising star in the poetic world, was alien to him temperamentally quite apart from any question of jealousy. In the three years 20–17 he wrote only one work, the Epistle to Florus (II, 2), unless the Epistle to the Pisos ('Ars Poetica') was, as is possible, also occupying him then.[2] His general tone is weary and bored:

> Singula de nobis anni praedantur euntes;
> eripuere iocos Venerem conuiuia ludum,
> tendunt extorquere poemata.[3]

He only wants to be left alone. Clearly he was on the way to stagnation unless something positive occurred to redeem him.

Redemption came, in 17 B.C. In that year Augustus, after a judicious consultation of the Sibylline Books, declared that the Secular Games were due to be held. Rome was to figure as the Capital of the World, in token of which all free citizens of any land were eligible to partake. Part of the ceremony was to be a hymn sung by a chorus of boys and girls, and the high honour of composing it devolved on Horace. The success of the Carmen and the world-wide publicity of the occasion gave him a new lease of life. He had consented at last to do what he had never definitely done before, to put his lyre at the service of his patrons. Instead of priding himself, as once he did, on the selectness of his audience, he now revelled in the sunshine of popular fame.

It is impossible to say when his personal relationship with Augustus ripened into the friendship reflected by the excerpts from the Emperor's letters in the Suetonian Life. I am inclined to think that it was comparatively late.[4] It is easy to forget that of the fifteen years between Horace's introduction to Maecenas in 38 and the

---

1 For his poor health cf. Suet. *Vita Hor.* par. 5: 'si per ualetudinem tuam fieri possit'; *Epod.* I, 16; *Ep.* I, 7 and 15.

2 C. O. Brink, citing 'nil scribens ipse' (306), inclines to date it after 14/3 B.C.; *Horace on Poetry*, p. 217. But N.B., no ref. to *Aeneid* on epic.

3 *Ep.* II, 2, 55–7.

4 Cf. Wiamowitz, *Sappho und Simonides*, p. 313, n. 1.

publication of Odes I–III in 23 Augustus spent two-thirds on campaign, while on his scattered visits to Rome he would be overwhelmed with business.[1] But the fact that at some time he asked Maecenas to let him have Horace as private secretary is sufficient testimony to the opinion he formed of the poet's worth.

About the year 14 Augustus, on reading 'sermones quidam' of Horace, perhaps the Epistles to Florus and the Pisos, complained that he had not dedicated such a work to him. Horace replied with a long Epistle (II, 1) on the state of poetic taste at Rome. The Emperor also commissioned him to write laureate odes on the victories of his stepsons, Drusus and Tiberius. These, with thirteen other odes, Horace published as Book IV, in 13 B.C. or later.[2]

We hear no more. In 8 B.C. Maecenas died. One of his last injunctions to Augustus was 'Remember Horatius Flaccus as you will remember me'; but within a few weeks Horace fulfilled his own prophecy and followed him to the grave, aged nearly fifty-seven. He had just strength enough at the end to indicate the Emperor as his heir. They buried him beside Maecenas on the Esquiline.

1 From Rice Holmes, *The Architect of the Roman Empire*, vol. I, I gather that he was in Rome for the following periods:
  (1) Nov. 36 to middle of 35 (pp. 119, 130–1).
  (2) A few days in the winter of 34 (p. 134).
  (3) A few months at the end of 33 (p. 135).
  (4) Spring 32 to spring 31, preparing to fight Antony (pp. 141–7).
  (5) One month 31–30 (pp. 159–60).
  (6) Summer 29 to spring 27, reconstructing the state (pp. 173 ff.).
  (7) After the spring of 24, when he returned from Spain.
One of Augustus' letters at least seems comparatively late: Septimius, mentioned in it as a common friend of Augustus and Horace, can hardly have known the Emperor well before the period of the *Epistles*, as he applied not to him, but to Horace, for an introduction to Tiberius (*Ep.* I, 9).
  2 Suet. *Vita Hor.* par. 5.

CHAPTER III

CHARACTER AND VIEWS

I T is difficult for us, who use words primarily as a means of
conveying what we believe to be the truth, to penetrate the
mind of Roman writers, who, like the Italians of to-day, often
used them primarily 'for effect'. To obtain insight into the real
mentality of Horace in particular it is not sufficient to collect
testimonia from the pages of his works. We must take into account
the social and literary climate in which he wrote, and our resultant
impression of him may be one against which his own words may
often be quoted. Those who take him at his face value have a superficial advantage in argument, but they leave an uneasy feeling in
the mind that they have got things out of focus.

The distorting influences are of three kinds, literary, political and
individual. Roman literary education, apart from reading, consisted
largely of rhetoric, the art of making out a case regardless of strict
veracity. And not only were boys thus allowed to say with conviction what they did not think: they were also not encouraged to
think for themselves on fresh lines. Originality was not highly
valued: the favourite exercise was the re-dressing of commonplace
themes (*communes loci*).[1] This doubtless sharpened their wits, but
it confined the range of their minds and kept them to beaten tracks.
Roman poetry itself, having originated as translation, rarely dispensed
with the aid of Greek originals. It was also permeated with understood conventions. Thus when a poet says 'uidi ego', that is no
evidence of autopsy.[2] Even the subjective love-poets Propertius and
Tibullus wove traditional themes and situations into the record of
their experience. These considerations may suffice to illustrate the
danger of taking Roman poetry too literally as evidence for the
poet's life and opinions.

On the political side also there were causes of distortion. It was
widely held by eminent Romans, as by eminent Greeks, that some
beliefs, though admittedly false, were useful as 'dope for the people'.
Again, the Augustan poets' connection with the principate naturally

1 See H. Nettleship, *Lectures and Essays*, pp. 111–2.

2 Prof. M. L. Clarke quotes to me Hazlitt *On Great and Little Things*:
'Some of the poets in the beginning of the last century would often set out
on a simile by observing, "So in Arabia have I seen a Phoenix".'

tempted them to stretch a point at times; for the protégés of
Maecenas would be anxious to say what their patron approved, even
granting that, as seems likely, no compelling pressure was put upon
them; and the extravagances of flattery, familiar from Alexandrian
Court poetry, were inevitably evoked by the person of the Emperor
It may well be that where we suspect insincerity in Horace he was
unconscious of it at the moment of writing, in some cases at least; for
in such an atmosphere we can hardly wonder if a man's sense of the
distinction between sincerity and insincerity became a little blurred

Finally, Horace had individual characteristics which make under
standing of him by no means a straightforward matter. His love
of irony, expressed both in mock-modesty and in mock-solemnity
is liable to escape the unsympathetic or humourless. And the daily
changes in his mood are reflected by his poems, records of his
experiences which he had not the pedantry, nor perhaps the ability
to harmonise for his collected edition.

Yet his works are so full of himself that every reader is bound to
form a strong impression of his personality, subjective though it
must be to a large extent. Some people hold that only perfect
sincerity can produce good poetry, so that where a poem comes to
life it reveals the 'real self' of the poet. Unfortunately what rings
true to one reader rings false to another; but in forming an individual estimate the test has some value, and it is especially applicable
to Horace. In his political poems (and religion belongs partly to
the sphere of politics) I believe him to have been sometimes in-
sincere; and where he seems so, even in some of his most famous
poems, to me his verse is not poetry but only accomplished rhetoric

In the succeeding pages I shall give first a brief sketch of his
character as I see it and then a fuller discussion of various aspects,
particularly the more controversial.

CHARACTER

Horace cannot be called an abnormal character, as so many poets,
even Roman poets, can. He has nothing comparable with the
mysterious other-worldliness of Virgil, the neurotic morbidity of
Propertius, the passionate obsession of Lucretius. Affection rather
than interest is the feeling he evokes; for he is a type, admirably
self-revealed, to which a large proportion of mankind feels itself

o be akin. Yet it is the greatest mistake to think of him, as so many
do, as shallow or superficial. For, endowed with a happy temperament, he achieved in himself a degree of harmony which few can
afford not to envy. He knew himself and applied that knowledge
to the understanding of others.

Apart from his father the chief formative influence on his character
was Greek culture; he was educated in a Greek 'academy', steeped
in Greek poetry, especially Aeolic and Alexandrian Lyric, and in
Greek ideas, more particularly the Hellenistic philosophies of life.
Emphasis laid in recent years on his Roman side should not divert
our attention from this all-important fact. Both the old Lyric poetry
and the Hellenistic philosophy were almost entirely individualistic,
and Horace himself was fundamentally an individualist. Like Cicero,
he was eclectic in his views—he may even have belonged officially
to the eclectic New Academy of Antiochus at Athens[1]—and he
reflected his own personality, not someone else's ideal, in his philosophy of life. With the Epicureans he shared a strong tendency to
rationalism and a keen enjoyment of the more gentle pleasures of
life, friendship, feminine society, literature, wine, and idling in the
town or country; with the Stoics, a sense of the fundamental importance of morality and an adequate, but not excessive, public
spirit; with the Peripatetics, a belief in the value, moral and artistic,
of appropriateness (τὸ πρέπον), and above all, in the Doctrine of
the Mean. Now this last doctrine was simply a characteristic
formulation by Aristotle of the great ideal of Greece, the spirit of
σωφροσύνη, the spirit of Apollo; and it is embodied, more humbly
but no less clearly, in the life and lyric poetry of Horace than it is
in the masters and masterpieces of the fifth century. Yet this Greek
love of form and restraint is strangely accompanied in him by a
Roman strain of informality and exuberance, exemplified in his
works by the engaging inconsequence and vitality of the Satires
and Epistles. The remarkable thing is that he knew so well how to
keep each of the two sides of his nature from interfering with the
other's separate expression in literature.

One manifestation of Horace's feeling for the Mean is his admirable sense of humour, displayed not so much in jokes as in his

[1] See O. Immisch, *Horazens Epistel über die Dichtkunst* (1932), pp. 26 ff.
(*Philologus*, Supplementband XXIV, Ht. 3).

general attitude to life. Ultimately it is a sense of proportion between the importance of the individual to himself and the unimportance of all individuals *sub specie aeternitatis*. This is the lighter aspect of realism that would not allow him to be romantic in love or to aspire to an after-life. His affections were set on things on the earth and he had a double portion of that specially Roman quality *humanitas*—the word covers both interest in and sympathy for one's fellow-men at large. The interest led him to Satire, but the sympathy took the sting out of that satire once his days of bitter experience were over; while friendship played as large a part in his life as it did in that of the Epicurean 'Wise Man'.

Yet his *humanitas* was not universal, like Virgil's. He liked educated and refined people such as he found in the circle of Maecenas, and unassuming rustics with homely wit, such as Ofellus and the *uernae procaces* of his Sabine farm. But he despised equally the self-important centurions' sons of Venusia and the *malignum uolgus* of the City. To these neither his ideals nor his art were likely to appeal. He was proud of his humble birth, because by his own efforts and his father's character he had risen so far above it; and his boasting about the company he kept was pardonably unabashed for he naturally enjoyed looking down on the people who had once looked down on him:[1]

Hoc iuuat et melli est, non mentiar.

At times the melancholy of the Greeks can be felt in his poetry. For all his enjoyment of the present he was sometimes oppressed by consciousness of the brevity and vanity of human existence and the fading of youth and beauty. But refusing facile consolations he faced these facts with a dignified acceptance, and in this mood of perfect sincerity produced his most moving poetry, which could not have been better expressed than in the stately, slow-moving metres he had moulded from Greek models. His attitude to religion is extremely hard to diagnose; probably he thought, like most of his contemporaries, that belief was expedient for the masses, and ritual for the state; but his personal feeling must be left for fuller discussion.

1 *Sat.* I, 6, 45–8; 10, 81–90; II, 1, 74–8; 6, 29–32.

His patriotism, in the better sense of the word, was his own, not merely a product of the Augustan revival, like that of Propertius. Several years before Actium he had felt that he had a right and a desire to address his countrymen at large in time of crisis.[1] But it received stimulation and direction from his contact with Maecenas, and later with Augustus. It is a complete misconception to think of him as tool of a propaganda-bureau. He declined suggested themes, criticised policy, and himself made suggestions, with complete freedom.

As he grew older he changed somewhat, but only by explicable development. After the public triumph of the Carmen Saeculare in 17 he became more of a laureate, anxious to please the Emperor, proud of recognition by a wider public than he had hoped for, and interested in glory of a rather more commonplace kind than before. He also became more anxious to find a philosophic basis for his strong moral feelings, and although he failed to do so (for besides being no philosopher he was too sensible to accept half-truths), such thoughts absorbed him more, as we see in the Epistles, now that he had lost the spontaneous gaiety of his earlier years. To me he is most attractive in the period between his thirty-fifth and forty-second years, when he was writing the Odes of his first collection.

He has left us a meagre sketch of himself at forty four—short, grey before his time, fond of sunshine, irritable but soon appeased.[2] I wish we had never been told that he was fat. There is no reason to assume that he was so before middle-age;[3] and the information is partly responsible for the schoolboy's idea of him as an easy-going wine-bibber, an idea as lop-sided as that which represents him as primarily an earnest patriotic moralist; whereas the most important things about him are his artistic awareness and his sanity of outlook.

> Ne te souvient-il pas d'Oraces,
> Qui tant ot de sens et de grâces?[4]

*   *   *   *   *   *

1 Unfortunately, after endless discussion, it is still impossible to be sure of the date of *Epode* XVI, which was probably his first state poem.

2 *Ep.* I, 20, 24–5.

3 Apart from *Ep.* I, 4, 15–16 (*Me pinguem...Epicuri de grege porcum*), the evidence is all from Suetonius, who is relying on a letter of Augustus which may well be quite late.

4 Jean de Meung, 2nd *Roman de la Rose*, l. 6470.

In this brief sketch of Horace's character there is much tha requires amplification and defence. I have divided what follow under the headings 'Religion', 'Life and Death', 'Morality', 'Lov and Friendship', 'The Country', 'Humour' and 'The State', re serving his view of poetry for a separate chapter.

* * * * * *

RELIGION

In the last years of the Republic Hellenistic philosophies replace the spiritual and intellectual sides of religion for most educate Romans, and of these the one which gained most ground wa Epicureanism.[1] It promised peace of mind to men tired of th turmoil of civil wars; it liberated those who were conscious o religious oppression; it attracted also by its rationalism men wh were by no means quietists, such as Cassius, the intellectual states man, and Atticus, the man of affairs. The Atomic Theory explaine everything so neatly, and with such apparent water-tightness, tha it bred a self-confidence analogous to that of the Victorian scientists The Mysterious Universe was not Mysterious after all: it ha become, potentially at least, *maiestas cognita rerum*.

As is well known, the ruling class at Rome accepted the Stoi division of religion into three kinds, mythical, political an philosophic.[2] The Gods were traditional literary subject-matter Euripides, when he wanted to attack the Apollo of tradition brought Apollo on to the stage as a god, whether or no he believe him to exist. The Hymns of Callimachus hardly suggest that th author was religious. For Hellenistic poets Hymn and Dedicatio had become conventional literary forms.

Philosophic religion, a man's true beliefs and speculations, wa his own affair; but the lawyer Scaevola gave a warning agains allowing the debates of the philosophers to escape from the school into the market-place; for, he said, 'it is expedient that states shoul

1 Cic. *Tusc. Disp.* IV, 3, 6–7.
2 See St Augustine's references to Varro's *Antiquitates Rerum Humanarum et Divinarum* (*De Civ. Dei*, VI, 5). On the whole subject see B. Farrington *Science and Politics in the Ancient World*, esp. chs. 13–15. Cf. T. S. Jerome *Aspects of the Study of Roman History*, pp. 151–9.

e deceived in the matter of religion'. The theory that lies behind
ais dictum had been frankly laid bare by Polybius in a well-known
assage: 'I will venture the assertion, that what the rest of mankind
eride is the foundation of Roman greatness, namely fear of the
apernatural (δεισιδαιμονία). This element has been introduced
ato every aspect of their private and public life, with every artifice
) awe the imagination, to a degree that could not be improved
pon. Many possibly will be at a loss to understand this; my view
that it has been done to impress the masses. If it were possible
) have a state in which all the citizens were philosophers, perhaps
e might dispense with this sort of thing. But the masses in every
ate are unstable, full of lawless desires, of irrational anger, and
iolent passion. All that can be done, then, is to hold them in check
y fears of the unseen and other shams of the same sort. It was not
r nothing, but with deliberate design, that the men of old intro-
uced to the masses notions about the gods and views on the after-
fe. The folly and heedlessness are ours, who seek to dispel such
usions.'[1] Cicero himself was in favour of duplicity. 'With regard
) divination', said this augur to his brother, 'I think it ought to be
ept up for reasons of state and public religion. But we are alone,
) we can inquire into truth without offence, especially as I am on
aost points a sceptic'—this in a work intended for publication![2]
ven the Epicureans sacrificed regularly, and the Sceptics and Cynics
greed with the orthodox view.[3] Lucretius alone stands out as the
nemy of established religion.

Such was the state of opinion in classical Rome, and it is common
nough in modern Europe. There were, of course, many educated
eople to whom the State religion was not merely a pious fraud.
here were people whose minds were in water-tight compartments,
vho acknowledged 'two kinds of truth', like Cotta, the Pontifex
Maximus of Cicero's *De Natura Deorum*. More important, there
vere Stoic syncretists to whom all the traditional deities were

1 VI, 56, 7; tr. Farrington, *op. cit.* p. 166 f. (he renders δεισιδαιμονία
uperstition'). Cf. Diodorus, I, 2.

2 *De Div.* II, 28. Cato wondered that augur could pass augur without
smile. *De Div.* II, 51; cf. *De Nat. Deor.* I, 71.

3 Plutarch, *Non posse suauiter uiui secundum Epicurum*, 21; Sextus Empiricus,
yp. I, 24. 'Diogenes, consultus an Dii essent, "nescio", inquit, "nisi ut
nt expedire"'; Tertullian, *Ad Nat.* II, 2.

48/2

manifestations of one divine power.[1] Nor must we overlook th
wave of irrationalism that swept over Rome in the failure of nerv
caused by the Civil War; in this the early Augustan Age differe
from the Ciceronian[2] as the nineteen-thirties from the nineteer
twenties. Augustus himself was no rationalist: his pathetic trust i
dreams, omens and astrology is widely attested; he published h
astrological 'thema', and struck a silver coin bearing his birth
emblem, Capricornus.[3]

Let us grant, then, that when the new *Princeps* instituted a gre
religious revival, restored defunct priesthoods, repaired old temple
and lavished money on new, the great majority of educated peopl
agreed that this was a necessary concomitant of national regenera
tion; it was not only cynics like Ovid who thought,

> Expedit esse deos, et ut expedit, esse putemus.[4]

But while many convinced themselves that the Gods had somehov
some reality, shall we not also suppose that there were many wh
remained sceptical? The very failure of the Augustan 'revival' i
evidence enough.

Virgil, I believe, belonged ultimately to the former class, Horac
to the latter. For the generation in which these two grew up th
appeal of Epicureanism was immeasurably reinforced by the geniu
of Lucretius. One can readily imagine the impact a first reading o
his poem must have made on natures sensitive to poetry. Who ca
doubt that it was partly this that impelled Virgil to give up h
oratorical studies and set sail for 'the haven of the blest',[5] the Gul
of Naples with its Epicurean Society? From Lucretius too th
youthful Horace derived the confident scepticism with which h

1 We may note that Horace, in *Odes*, I, 34, treats Fortuna, th
Hellenistic Τυχή, as synonymous with Jupiter, the word 'deus' makin
the transition.

2 See Norden, *Aeneis*, VI[3], Introd. pp. 3 ff. The coincidence of the ap
pearance of a comet, afterwards named the *Iulium Sidus*, during the funer:
games of the Dictator must have given a great impetus to superstition
Pliny, *N.H.* II, 93.

3 Dio, XLVIII, 14; LIV, 35; Suet. *Aug.* 91 f.; 94; Pliny, *N.H.* II, 24; XXXI
58.

4 *A.A.* I, 637.

5 *Catalepton*, v.

greeted the pagan predecessor of the Miracle of St Januarius as practised by the priests of Gnatia in South Italy:

> Credat Iudaeus Apella,
> non ego, namque deos didici securum agere aeuum
> nec, siquid miri faciat natura, deos id
> tristes ex alto caeli demittere tecto.[1]

Virgil was by nature on the side of the Stoics, and his unnatural Epicurean phase did not last long. From the sturdy rationalism of his answer in the First Georgic to the question 'Why do rooks caw when rain is coming?' he passed insensibly in the Fourth to a transcendentalism suggested by the marvels of the bees' kingdom, and thereafter never looked back. But Horace, although he was eclectic, piecing together a philosophy of life that suited his own temperament, found Epicureanism the most congenial of the moral philosophies. He was not religious in our sense of the word. I do not believe that the much quoted ode I, 34 (*Parcus deorum cultor*) marks a fundamental change in his attitude. Horace had heard 'thunder in a clear sky' (perhaps a seismic explosion such as are not uncommon in Italy). Strange to say the occurrence of such a phenomenon was a recognised omen among the believers, its non-occurrence an argument of the sceptics![2] Lucretius, denying the divine manipulation of the thunderbolt, had asked ironically: 'Why does Jupiter never cast his bolt on the earth or pour out his thunder from a clear sky?'[3] The thought might naturally flash across Horace's mind, 'What if Lucretius is wrong in everything as in this, and the gods do interfere with the world? There are more things in heaven and earth, Horatio—.' How seriously we take this ode is a subjective matter; but the Epistles, written a few years later, certainly do not give the impression that he has had anything

---

1 *Sat.* I, 5, 100: 'Tell that to the Jew Apella, not to me; for I have learnt that the gods live a carefree life, and that, if nature produces anything remarkable, it is not that gods send it down in displeasure from the high vault of heaven.' Cf. Lucr. v, 82: 'bene qui didicere deos securum agere euum'.

2 As omen, Varro, *Sat. Men.* fr. 103; cf. Ennius, *Ann.* 527 V; Cicero, *De Div.* II, 39, 82.

3 VI, 400 f.

like 'a conversion to Stoicism';[1] we find him there quite undeter
mined, inclined to admire Aristippus the arch-hedonist as much a
anyone,[2] and not noticeably interested in religion. Lucretius himse
had moments of doubt, as he tells us, simply through contemplatin
the order of the heavenly bodies, and he speaks once of 'som
hidden power'[3] which seems to trample on mankind in cru
sport; but it is a great mistake to deduce from this admission an
serious wavering in his opinion on the validity of Epicurean scienc

As for the forms of religion, the name of the Gods, both singl
and collectively, were indeed often on Horace's lips. To some exten
this is due to the fact that already at Alexandria Hymns and Prayer
had become secular literary forms.[4] Odes like i, 10, a Hymn t
Mercury based on Alcaeus, or iii, 22, a dedication of a pine-tree t
Diana in imitation of Hellenistic epigram, tell us nothing about hi
own beliefs. The Olympian gods had long been poetical figure
valued for their legends or their symbolic meaning, evoking i
sophisticated people much the same feelings as they evoke in u
Horace delighted especially in the gods and festivals of the country
as Virgil did; in the humble offering of Phidyle; in Faunus, *nym
pharum fugientum amator*; in the sacrifice of a kid to his Bandusia
spring at the Fontanalia, or the celebration of the Neptunalia wit
Lyde.

Fortunatus et ille deos qui nouit agrestes.

All Hallow E'en, Christmas Trees and Easter Eggs are not peculia
to believers any more than conventional phrases such as 'Than
God!' or 'God knows!' And perception of the beauty of a religion
its ritual, its gods and its mythology, may always be achieve

1 Campbell, *op. cit.* p. 122, says that this ode 'announces in part allusively
but in effect unmistakably, his conversion from Epicureanism to Stoicism'
2 *Ep.* i, 1, 18; 17, 17. In *Ep.* i, 4 he sides with Epicureanism agains
Stoicism.
3 v, 1204–40 (*uis abdita quaedam*, 1233).
4 See Kroll, *Studien zur Verständnis der römischen Literatur* (1924), p. 22
Rostovtzeff, *Augustus* (*Univ. of Wisconsin Studies*, 1922), p. 136, asks whethe
we can believe that Horace was 'a mere liar' in his hymns. The term seem
harsh for one who did what so many good men before and after him hav
done. Laurence Housman has warned people against thinking that th
hymn his brother wrote for his funeral implied any recantation. Cf. A
Oltramare, *Horace et la Religion de Virgile*, Rev. E.L. 13 (1935).

independently of belief. One of the most moving of Christian pictures, the Pazzi Crucifixion, was painted by the infidel Perugino.

Horace certainly shared the orthodox view that the State religion should be kept up. He anticipates by several years the edict of 28 B.C. for the repairing of temples; for in Satires II, 2, 103 he asks the rich man

> Cur eget indignus quisquam te diuite? *quare*
> *templa ruunt antiqua deum?*

It was presumably in connection with that edict that he wrote the ode III, 6:

> Delicta maiorum immeritus lues,
> Romane, donec templa refeceris
>   aedesque labentes deorum et
>   foeda nigro simulacra fumo.
>
> Dis te minorem quod geris, imperas.
> hinc omne principium, huc refer exitum.
>   di multa neglecti dederunt
>   Hesperiae mala luctuosae.[1]

Did Horace believe all this? If so, he had changed rapidly indeed from his Epicurean standpoint. Cicero again indicates the real view of enlightened Romans: 'It is the universally accepted opinion of all philosophers...that God is never angry, never hurtful.'[2] Horace, in supporting a religious revival he approved, gives reasons which privately, as a philosopher, he would probably have disowned. This ode sounds like hollow rhetoric to me until the ninth stanza, when the poet turns from his Jeremiads to what he really did care about, the life and character of the Sabine peasants:

> Non his iuuentus orta parentibus
> infecit aequor sanguine Punico
>   Pyrrhumque et ingentem cecidit
>   Antiochum Hannibalemque dirum,

1 'You will pay undeservedly for the failings of your forefathers, Roman, until you restore the temples and ruined shrines of the gods and their images blackened with smoke. It is because you submit yourself to the gods that you hold sway. To them ascribe every beginning, to them the end. Neglect of the gods has brought many woes upon suffering Italy.'
2 *De Off.* III, 102.

2-2

Sed rusticorum mascula militum
proles, Sabellis docta ligonibus
uersare glaebas et seuerae
matris ad arbitrium recisos

Portare fustes, sol ubi montium
mutaret umbras et iuga demeret
bubus fatigatis, amicum
tempus agens abeunte curru.[1]

What of the divinity of Augustus? 'That Horace also thought o
his Augustus as a living god', says Pasquali,[2] '...will appear natura
to anyone who considers the spiritual conditions of the Augusta
Age.' Now it is true that Messianic ideas were abroad at this tim
and prominent men inspired 'numinous' feelings; Sextus Pompeiu
had claimed to be son of Neptune and almost come to believe i
and Antony was hailed at Athens and Ephesus, not inappropriately
as Dionysus.[3] But is there any reason to suppose that Epicurean
and other men of sceptical temperament were affected by thes
'spiritual conditions' to the extent of believing in a divinity activ
in the world? It would be possible for a Stoic to believe in Augustus
divinity, since he would hold that every man had some spark c
the divine, and the god-emperor was simply a man with a doubl
portion, a superior δαίμων or *genius*. But Horace does not give th
impression of being a Stoic in such matters. Pasquali proceeds t
the length of thinking that when Lucretius, reviewing the benefi
his hero has conferred on mankind, exclaims (v, 8),

deus ille fuit, deus, inclute Memmi,

1 'Not from such parents sprang the youth that dyed the sea with Puni
blood and smote Pyrrhus and mighty Antiochus and dread Hannibal; bu
the manly offspring of rustic yeomanry it was, brought up to turn the cloc
with Sabine mattocks and at the bidding of a stern mother to cut and carr
firewood while the sun was changing the shadows of the hills and takin
the yokes from off the tired oxen, bringing on the welcome hour with h
departing chariot.'

2 *Orazio Lirico*, p. 179. Cf. M. Poplawski, *L'Apothéose de Sylla et d'August*
in *Eos*, 1927.

3 Plut. *Ant.* XXIV, 2; XXVI, 2. Cf. the experience of Paul and Barnaba
at Lystra.

he really believed that Epicurus had been a *praesens diuus*—a signal instance indeed of *l'Anti-Lucrèce chez Lucrèce*! Surely all he meant was that if anyone deserved divine honours, Epicurus did; for he went on to show how his benefits surpassed those of Hercules and Bacchus.

There is only one place in which Horace definitely countenances a belief in the present deity of Caesar.[1] In the second ode of the First Book he affects to be looking for a Messiah. What God, he asks, will come incarnate to redeem the State? Apollo or Venus or Mars—or Mercury in the form of a young man? In the last word of the ode he reveals the identity of the god—Caesar.[2] About the same time (29 B.C.) Virgil, who had allowed his rustics to speak of Caesar Octavian as divine, paid him divine honours himself in the fulsome proem to the *Georgics*. These outbursts were occasioned by the feeling of relief after the conclusion of the Civil Wars. The sense of gratitude was genuine enough, but we need not suppose that Virgil really believed that the Scorpion was drawing in its claws to leave room for Caesar in the sky! Such flatteries were a legacy of Hellenistic baroque, and he would expect his educated readers to recognise them as such.

The extravagances of 29 B.C. did not recur. When Octavian was confirmed in his supremacy two years later as Augustus he 'most pertinaciously' forbade his own worship in the City.[3] It has been noted that Virgil's compliments became less extreme in the *Aeneid*; there Augustus is no longer a god, but *diui genus*. And Horace too, if we look closely, will be seen to have withdrawn discreetly. *Odes* III, 5 begins: 'We have believed that Jupiter reigns thundering in heaven; Augustus *will be held to be* a god on earth *when he has added the Britons and Parthians to the Empire*.' That is hardly the language of belief, and in fact it gives the clue to the writer's real opinion.[4] In several places he compares Augustus to the deified heroes or demi-gods; there was a regular list of these: 'Deos...

1 Apart from the oblique reference at *Odes*, III, 25, 19.

2 Mercury-Augustus never became a public cult; but on a Bolognese altar Mercury has Augustus' features. F. Altheim, *A History of Roman Religion*, E.T. p. 365.

3 Suet. *Aug.* 52.

4 As to this I agree with Campbell, *op. cit.* pp. 61 ff., and J. F. D'Alton, *op. cit.* p. 116.

colunto', says a law quoted by Cicero, 'et ollos quos endo caelo merita locauerint, Herculem Liberum Aesculapium Castorem Pollucem Quirinum.'[1] It is with these that Augustus is compared at the beginning of Epistles II, 1, with these that he will drink nectar hereafter according to Odes III, 3, 11.[2] If we can ascertain Horace' attitude to their 'divinity', we can deduce his attitude to that of Augustus.

Now in several places Horace shows a partiality for the common Greek and Roman practice of rationalising mythology. Danaë's shower of gold becomes a bribe; Orpheus and Amphion were said to have moved stones by their song because they civilised men and inspired them to join in building cities.[3] The line in the *Bacchae*,

λύσει μ' ὁ δαίμων αὐτὸς ὅταν ἐγὼ θέλω,

which should be taken literally, is reinterpreted on Stoic lines to refer to suicide.[4] The view that all the gods were simply men worshipped for their services to mankind was formulated in Hellenistic times by Euhemerus, and had been introduced to Rome by Ennius.[5] It is plainly applied in Odes IV, 8 to the demigods mentioned above. Horace claims for the poets the power to 'immortalise' in this sense. Significantly he mentions Ennius (*Calabrae Pierides*) and the fame of Romulus in this connection; for Ennius the Euhemerist, had sung of the apotheosis of Romulus, 'deferring to the tradition' as Cicero said.[6] And he sums up:

> Dignum laude uirum Musa uetat mori;
> caelo Musa beat: *sic* Iovis interest
> optatis epulis impiger Hercules...,

1 Cic. *De Leg.* II, 19. Pasquali ascribes the origin of this canon to Posidonius' περὶ θεῶν; *op. cit.* p. 685.

2 Cf. *Odes*, IV, 5, 33–6. 'Bibet', not 'bibit', is the true reading at III, 3, 12.

3 *Odes*, III, 16; *A.P.* 392–6. Cf. F. Solmsen, *Hermes*, LXVII (1932) pp. 151–4.

4 *Ep.* I, 16, 73–9; Eur. *Bacch.* 492–8.

5 Varro, *R.R.* I, 48, 2; Cic. *De Nat. Deor.* I, 119; Augustine, *De Civ. Dei* VII, 26.

6 Ll. 19–24. Ennius, *Ann.* 115 V; Cic. *Tusc. Disp.* I, 12, 28. Elsewhere (*De Off.* III, 25) Cicero says that it was 'hominum fama beneficiorum memor' that had given Hercules a place in the assembly of the gods.

which may be baldly rendered, 'It is the Muse that forbids the man who is worthy of praise to die; the Muse that bestows a place in heaven; it is by her doing that tireless Hercules has won a place at the delectable feast of Jove'; and with Hercules are mentioned three of the other four in the canon, the Tyndarids and Liber. With the same idea of a poet's power to 'immortalise' Horace speaks of Augustus in Odes III, 25, 3:

> quibus
> Antris egregii Caesaris audiar
> aeternum meditans decus
> Stellis inserere et consilio Iouis?[1]

All that he means is that the Emperor, in return for certain services, will be honoured as a deity on earth and classed with the demi-gods after death; just as, while alive, he had his statue placed by decree of the Senate among the Lares.

Once or twice Horace uses 'Jupiter' as a pseudonym for Augustus, as Ovid does.[2] In the eastern provinces, and especially in Egypt, it was common to honour him as Ζεὺς Σωτήρ or Ζεὺς Ἐλευθέριος Σεβαστός, and the idea of a mortal being intimately connected with Jupiter was not foreign to Rome itself, for it is thought that 'triumphators' dressed up to impersonate the King of the Gods.[3] In Epistles I, 19, 43 the disappointed poets to whom Horace has refused to recite are represented as complaining 'Iouis auribus ista seruas', referring probably to Augustus. I believe that we should see the same nuance in Odes II, 7, 17. There the poet is welcoming back one Pompeius, who fought with him at Philippi and, proving less reconcilable, has only just been restored to citizenship:

> Ergo obligatam redde *Ioui* dapem
> longaque fessum militia latus
> depone sub lauru mea, nec
> parce cadis tibi destinatis.

1 'In what caves shall I be heard devising to set the eternal glory of Caesar amid the stars and the council of Jupiter?' Minos, Διὸς μεγάλου ὀαρίστυς, is in Horace's mind.

2 *Trist.* I, 5, 78; III, 1, 38; II, 62.

3 E. Strong, *Apotheosis and After-life*, p. 64.

Obliuioso leuia Massico
ciboria exple....[1]

The words in line 3, '*Quis* te redonauit Quiritem', have already
suggested Augustus, so that

Ergo obligatam redde Ioui dapem

becomes an easy metaphor for making one's peace gratefully with
the omnipotent ruler, and *obliuioso* is thus not merely a stock epithet.
The fact that men were used to hearing 'Jupiter' used as a flattering
name for the Emperor should be in our minds when we consider
other passages, Odes III, 1, 6 and III, 4, 49. It has clearly nothing
to do with religious belief. As for Horace's later years (if not his
earlier), could any sophisticated person, such as he certainly was,
continue to believe in the divinity of a familiar friend, however
exalted, who addressed him in letters by indelicate nicknames and
twitted him with his corpulence?[2]

LIFE AND DEATH

Belief in survival after bodily death is commonly considered part
of religion because it has always been connected with the idea of
the soul as a portion of the divine spirit.[3] This belief spread rapidly
at Rome when she came under Greek influence, and particularly
in the troubled times of the Revolution, when the unbearable horrors
and injustices encouraged a wishful belief in a compensation hereafter. The *Phaedo* of Plato, the transcendental Stoicism of Posidonius
and the Neo-Pythagoreanism of Nigidius Figulus had great influence. Cicero in the *De Legibus*[4] represents himself as speaking to
his brother and Atticus of the *spes melior moriundi* afforded by the
mystery religions. Even Ovid contrives to end his elegy on Tibullus
with a hopeful note:

1 'Then render to Jupiter the feast you owe him, and lay your limbs
tired with long warfare under my bay-tree, nor spare the flagons reserved
for you. Fill the smooth goblets with Massic wine that brings forgetfulness....'
2 Suet. *Vita Hor.* 5–6.
3 E.g. already in Pindar, fr. 131.
4 II, 36; and in general see Norden, *Aeneis* VI, pp. 3–4.

Si tamen e nobis aliquid nisi nomen et umbra
    restat, in Elysia ualle Tibullus erit.
Obuius huic uenias hedera iuuenalia cinctus
    tempora cum Caluo, docte Catulle, tuo.[1]

The repeated assertions of Horace that death closes all, while
ley agree with the common view of Classical Greece, are thus
ontrary to the trend of contemporary feeling. The famous ode
, 24) on the death of Quintilius Varus is like most threnodies in
s general form;[2] it begins with the first natural outburst of grief:

> Quis desiderio sit pudor aut modus
>   tam cari capitis?

id continues with memories of the dead friend and complaints
f the injustice of things (σχετλιασμός). But the consolation of the
alist is not a recommendation to 'faintly trust the larger hope';
is simply a dignified resignation:

> Durum. sed leuius fit patientia
>   quicquid corrigere est nefas.

On the subject of burial Horace held a similarly realistic view.
Ve have only to remember the plots of the *Ajax* and *Antigone* to
mind ourselves of the significance once attached to it in Greece,
hich probably outlived the beliefs that gave rise to it. Socrates
und it hard to persuade the common man, Crito, that it did not
atter. But the disciples of Socrates, the wandering philosophic
iars of the Hellenistic age, were at pains by word and deed to
adicate such superstition; Diogenes characteristically asked that
is body should be cast out unburied; οὐδὲ ταφῆς φροντιεῖν τὸν σόφον
as a maxim of Epicurus.[3] Yet in spite of this, though largely for
:her reasons, there were many educated Romans in Horace's day
ho cared inordinately about burial. Think of the morbid anxiety

---

1 Ovid, *Am.* III, 9, 59 ff. Cf. Servius Sulpicius to Cicero on Tullia's
:ath; *ad Fam.* IV, 5, 6. In the time of Seneca (*Ep.* 63, 16) and Tacitus
Agric. 46) belief in personal survival was the orthodox view of philosophers.
2 E.g. Ovid's on Tibullus, Milton's *Lycidas*, Shelley's *Adonais*. Dion.
al. *Ars*, VI. M. Siebourg, *N. Jahrb.* 1910, p. 271.
3 Plato, *Phaedo*, 115, C–E. For Aristippus and Bion the Borysthenite see
:les, *On Exile*, p. 29 f. (Hense); for Diogenes and Theodorus see Cicero,
usc. Disp. I, 102 and 104; for Epicurus, Diog. Laert. X, 118.

of Propertius;[1] think of the vast tombs erected for Caecilia Metell
for Gaius Cestius, for the baker Eurysaces, for Augustus himsel
But there must have been many also who shared the rationalist
view. Seneca has preserved for us the opinion of Maecenas him
self (Ep. 92, 35),

> Nec tumulum curo: sepelit natura relictos;[2]

and that Horace would have endorsed it may perhaps be gathere
from that strange mixture of beauty and gentle irony, Odes 1, 28
The transience of human life and the vanity of human wish
were never far from the thoughts of Greek writers;

> οἵη περ φύλλων γενεή, τοίη δὲ καὶ ἀνδρῶν

said Homer through the mouth of Glaucus, and one poet at lea
thought it his finest line.[4]

> μὴ φῦναι τὸν ἅπαντα νικᾷ λόγον

was a commonplace of Greek literature.[5] And Horace, too, in
degree unusual among the practical and energetic Romans, di
'think by fits and starts' about life and death, and make poetr
of his thoughts. On these occasions there can be no question of h
sincerity. The thoughts were as old and universal as those whic
came to Gray in Stoke Poges Churchyard or to Lamartine besio
the Lac du Bourget; but the depth of feeling they aroused enable
him, like Gray, to express them in language whose beauty an
absolute rightness are as moving as any 'originality' of thought:

> Linquenda tellus et domus et placens
> uxor, neque harum quas colis arborum
> te praeter inuisas cupressos
> ulla breuem dominum sequetur.[6]

1 II, 8, 17 ff.; 13, 17 ff.; III, 17, 21 ff.; IV, 7, etc.
2 What a contrast with Virgil's pathos!

> 'Nudus in ignota, Palinure, iacebis harena',

Aen. v, 871, and the sequel, vi, 327–36; 363–81.
3 For discussion of this poem see p. 108.
4 *Il.* vi, 146; Semonides, fr. 29 D: ἓν δὲ τὲ κάλλιστον Χῖος ἔειπεν ἀνήρ.
5 Soph. *O.C.* 1225 ff.; Theognis, 425; Bacchylides, v, 160–2. Cf. Home
Il. xvii, 446–7; Pindar, *Pyth.* iii, 81–2.
6 'Leave you must your land and home and pleasing wife, nor of the
trees you grow shall any save the dreaded cypress follow their short-liv

> For them no more the blazing hearth shall burn,
>   Or busy housewife ply her evening care;
> No children run to lisp their sire's return,
>   Or climb his knees the envied kiss to share.

Gray, it is true, was more concerned with the poor than the rich, and in this is closer to Virgil; Horace addresses himself to the wealthy class with whom he was continually in contact:

> Cedes coemptis saltibus et domo
> uillaque, flauus quam Tiberis lauit,
>   cedes, et exstructis in altum
>   diuitiis potietur heres.
>
> Diuesne prisco natus ab Inacho
> nil interest an pauper et infima
>   de gente sub diuo moreris,
>   uictima nil miserantis Orci.
>
> Omnes eodem cogimur, omnium
> uersatur urna serius ocius
>   sors exitura et nos in aeternum
>   exilium impositura cymbae.[1]

The last stanza is particularly impressive. The lots are shaken in the urn, and the round monosyllable '*sors*' is held in suspense, to fall out at the beginning of the next line. The long '*o*', '*er*' and '*ur*' sounds give solemnity, as do the elisions in *aeternum exilium impositura*, which make a *rallentando* in the rhythm and somehow heighten the effect of inevitability.

master.' *Odes*, II, 14, 21. *Placens* is the perfect epithet for *uxor*, and is very hard to translate. It dwells on her special appeal to the man himself, whereas Gray's 'busy' merely describes what any onlooker could see. Gray here recalls not so much Horace as Lucretius' famous passage, III, 894 ff., which Horace too must have had in mind.

1 *Odes*, II, 3, 17. 'You will leave the pastures you have bought up, and your home, and your villa washed by the yellow Tiber, you will leave them and the riches you have piled up high shall pass to an heir. It matters not whether as the wealthy descendant of ancient Inachus or as poor and of humblest family you dwell beneath the sky, you are a victim of pitiless Death. One way we all are driven, for all there is shaken in the urn a lot that sooner or later will fall out and place us on the bark for eternal exile.' *Sub diuo moreris* hints at the custom of letting *uictimae* out into the fields for a while when they were due for sacrifice.

'Memento mori' was indeed the message of many Roman work
of art, and many poems too;[1] but these conventional reminder
seldom have anything of the refined beauty of Horace's words.

> Eheu fugaces, Postume, Postume,
> labuntur anni, nec pietas moram
> rugis et instanti senectae
> adferet indomitaeque morti.[2]

The grim spectacle of the underworld is treated in this ode (II, 14
impressively enough, but the effect is due to the sound of th
words—*inlacrimabilem, enauiganda*; where he describes it in the pre
ceding ode the imagination too is awake:[3]

> Quam paene furuae regna Proserpinae
> et iudicantem uidimus Aeacum
> sedesque discretas piorum et
> Aeoliis fidibus querentem
>
> Sappho puellis de popularibus
> et te sonantem plenius aureo,
> Alcaee, plectro dura nauis,
> dura fugae mala, dura belli.
>
> Utrumque sacro digna silentio
> mirantur umbrae dicere, sed magis
> pugnas et exactos tyrannos
> densum umeris bibit aure uolgus.

---

1 E.g. the skeletons on the mosaic pavement in the vestibule of the Muse
delle Terme at Rome and on the cup in the Boscoreale Treasure in th
Louvre. Trimalchio (Petr. *Cena*, 34, 8) had a model of a skeleton on hi
table which inspires him to verse:

'Eheu nos miseros! Quam totus homuncio nil est.'

Cf. Lucr. III, 914, and the last line of the *Copa*:

'Mors aurem uellens "uiuite", ait, "uenio".'

2 'Ah, Postumus, Postumus, the fleeting years glide by, nor ca
devotion call a halt to wrinkles and oncoming age and unconquerabl
death.'

3 There is, of course, no likelihood that Horace believed in the traditiona
underworld; see *Odes*, I, 4, 16; Cic. *Tusc. Disp.* I, 48; *De Nat. Deor.* II, 5
Norden, *Aeneis*, VI, p. 3.

Quid mirum ubi illis carminibus stupens
demittit atras belua centiceps
    auris et intorti capillis
        Eumenidum recreantur angues?

quin et Prometheus et Pelopis parens
dulci laborem decipitur sono
    nec curat Orion leones
        aut timidos agitare lyncas.[1]

We can appreciate the merits of Alcaics for depicting such scenes, and observe the comparative failure of Sapphics, by comparing Odes III, 11, 15–24 with this passage.

The feeling which Horace expressed with simple dignity in the Alcaic poems I have quoted is presented with dramatic force in a dactylo-iambic ode, 1, 4. Twelve lines of innocent description of spring lull us into security when suddenly death knocks at the door:

Pallida Mors aequo pulsat pede pauperum tabernas
    regumque turres. o beate Sesti,
Vitae summa breuis spem nos uetat incohare longam:
    iam te premet nox fabulaeque Manes
Et domus exilis Plutonia; quo simul mearis
    nec regna uini sortiere talis
Nec tenerum Lycidan mirabere, quo calet iuuentus
    nunc omnis et mox uirgines tepebunt.[2]

1 'How near I came to seeing the kingdom of dark Proserpina, and Aeacus sitting in judgment, and the abodes of the righteous set apart, and Sappho grieving on her Aeolian lyre over the girls of her people, and thee, Alcaeus, sounding more loudly with golden quill the hardships of seafaring, hardships of exile, hardships of war! Both sing themes worthy of reverent silence to the wonder of the shades, but the crowd with jostling shoulders drinks in more eagerly the tales of battles and tyrants driven out. What wonder, since in amazement at those songs the hundred-headed beast lowers his dark ears, and the snakes entwined in the Furies' hair take pleasure in them? Prometheus too, and the father of Pelops, are beguiled of their pain by the sweet sound, and Orion cares no more to pursue the lions or the shy lynxes.' II, 13, 21 ff.

2 'Pale Death knocks impartially at pauper's hut and prince's palace. O prosperous Sestius, the brief span of life forbids us to engage on long hopes: soon night will be upon you and the ghosts that are but a name and the unsubstantial house of Pluto; whither come, you shall no more throw dice for the mastery of the revels nor admire young Lycidas, who already has set all our youth aflame, and soon will kindle our girls.'

The explosive 'p's' and 't's' increase the violence of the sudden interruption; and then the terror passes and the poem

'fades into the light of common day'.

This ending has been criticised, but without much justification. A quiet, homely ending was preferred on aesthetic grounds by classical poets, and by Horace in particular;[1] and here it serves to bring Sestius back to the preoccupations of his daily life of pleasure, making him feel that at any moment, when least expected, the shadow of death might fall. It is effective for the same reason as Homer's

ἔσσεται ἢ ἠὼς ἢ δείλη ἢ μέσον ἦμαρ—[2]

Horace recast this theme some years later in undramatic form and published the result as Odes IV, 7. Wight Duff calls it a welcome to spring[3] and Wilamowitz dismisses it as an 'unimportant spring-song'.[4] Spring is, however, introduced solely as a foil to the main theme, human mortality. To me this is not only the finest of five splendid Horatian poems in dactylic or dactylo-iambic metre, which are all similar in tone;[5] it is, as Housman once said, the most perfect poem in the Latin language, and for translation I cannot do better than give his rendering of it:

---

1 Cf. *Odes*, IV, 2, 53 ff., where the homely details, seemingly irrelevant, have a similar effect. Also Theocritus, I, 146 ff.; Virgil, *Ecl.* I, 79; Horace, *Odes*, I, 9, 17 ff.; II, 1, 37 ff. etc.

2 *Il.* XXI, 111.

3 *Literary History of Rome* (1927), p. 541. Heinze (*ad loc.*) calls it 'poetically poorer' in comparison with *Odes*, I, 4 (*Soluitur acris hiems*).

4 *Sappho und Simonides* (1913), p. 321: 'Die beiden unbedeutenden Frühlingslieder 7 und 12. . . .' I will translate this sentence and the one that follows it in full, not in any way to belittle the great contribution to Horatian studies made by Wilamowitz in this work (pp. 305–23), but because it illustrates most clearly an evaluation of what is important in Horace's work which differs from mine (see p. 2): 'The two unimportant spring-songs 7 and 12 repeat old themes and only warn us, like Goethe in his old age, "And while time goes rushing by, seasons return again". Incomparably finer sounds the reminder of the passage of time in the two poems to girls composed as complementary pieces' (IV, 11, *Est mihi nonum*; 13, *Audiuere Lyce!*).

5 *Epodes*, XIII; *Odes*, I, 4, 7, 28; IV, 7.

Diffugere niues, redeunt iam gramina campis
    arboribusque comae;
Mutat terra uices et decrescentia ripas
    flumina praetereunt;
Gratia cum Nymphis geminisque sororibus audet
    ducere nuda choros.
Immortalia ne speres monet annus et almum
    quae rapit hora diem.
Frigora mitescunt Zephyris, uer proterit aestas
    interitura, simul
Pomifer autumnus fruges effuderit, et mox
    bruma recurrit iners.
Damna tamen celeres reparant caelestia lunae:
    nos ubi decidimus
Quo pius Aeneas, quo Tullus diues et Ancus,
    puluis et umbra sumus.
Quis scit an adiciant hodiernae crastina summae
    tempora di superi?
Cuncta manus auidas fugient heredis, amico
    quae dederis animo.
Cum semel occideris et de te splendida Minos
    fecerit arbitria,
Non, Torquate, genus, non te facundia, non te
    restituet pietas;
Infernis neque enim tenebris Diana pudicum
    liberat Hippolytum,
Nec Lethaea ualet Theseus abrumpere caro
    uincula Pirithoo.

The snows are fled away, leaves on the shaws
    And grasses in the mead renew their birth,
The river to the river-bed withdraws,
    And altered is the fashion of the earth.
The Nymphs and Graces three put off their fear
    And unapparelled in the woodland play.
The swift hour and the brief prime of the year
    Say to the soul, *Thou wast not born for aye.*
Thaw follows frost; hard on the heel of spring
    Treads summer sure to die, for hard on hers

Comes autumn, with his apples scattering;
    Then back to wintertide, when nothing stirs.
But oh, whate'er the sky-led seasons mar,
    Moon upon moon rebuilds it with her beams;
Come we where Tullus and where Ancus are
    And good Aeneas, we are dust and dreams.
Torquatus, if the gods in heaven shall add
    The morrow to the day, what tongue hath told?
Feast then thy heart, for what thy heart has had
    The fingers of no heir will ever hold.
When thou descendest once the shades among,
    The stern assize and equal judgment o'er
Not thy long lineage nor thy golden tongue,
    No, nor thy righteousness, shall friend thee more.
Night holds Hippolytus the pure of stain,
    Diana steads him nothing, he must stay;
And Theseus leaves Pirithous in the chain
    The love of comrades cannot take away.[1]

The felicity of Housman's rendering brings home the not infrequent affinity between his own poetry and that of Horace, whom he so much admired. The phrase 'the love of comrades' is a passing reminder of *A Shropshire Lad*, but the chief resemblance here (and elsewhere) lies in the tendency of both poets to see in 'the beautiful and death-struck year' a reminder of how short a time we have to enjoy things:

> And since to look at things in bloom
> Fifty springs are little room,
> About the woodlands I will go
> To see the cherry hung with snow.[2]

On the formal side too Housman's *felicitas* was sometimes no less *curiosa* than Horace's. But Horace moralises more conventionally than Housman, and in this he comes nearer again to Gray:

> The boast of heraldry, the pomp of power,
>   And all that beauty, all that wealth e'er gave,
> Awaits alike th' inevitable hour:
>   The paths of glory lead but to the grave.....

1 *More Poems*, v.   2 *A Shropshire Lad*, ii.

Can storied urn or animated bust
    Back to its mansion call the fleeting breath?
Can Honour's voice provoke the silent dust,
    Or Flatt'ry soothe the dull cold ear of death?

The wine that Horace recommends as a cure for trouble is merely
a symbol for enjoyment of the present:

> Sapias, uina liques et spatio breui
> spem longam reseces. Dum loquimur, fugerit inuida
> aetas: carpe diem quam minimum credula postero.[1]

Ah, my Beloved, fill the cup that clears
To-day of past regrets and future fears—
    'To-morrow?'—why, to-morrow I may be
Myself with yesterday's seven thousand years.

Here too, in FitzGerald's *Omar*, we find a spirit akin to Horace's,
the spirit of paganism that lives on in every age and land.

I have dwelt on these odes, and quoted them at length, because
I believe that in them we find the best of Horace's more serious
poetry, prompted by sincere feeling beyond the reach of outside
influences.

MORALITY

As I have said, we need not necessarily see anything more than
convention, poetic appreciation and expediency in the religious
utterances of Horace. What he did share with religion in its modern
significance was a strong moral sense. He was always interested
in human conduct, influenced on the practical side by his father,
on the theoretical by the Hellenistic systems of philosophy. The
discussion whether virtue was natural or conventional, begun by
the Greek Sophists, was one of the stock debates in the schools of
Rome.[2] Horace was inclined to the Stoic view of it, and yet his

---

1 *Odes*, I, 11, 6: 'Be wise, draw wine and cut down hope to match
the shortness of your life. Even as we speak, envious time will have
flown. Cull the passing day, nor believe in the morrow more than
you need.'

2 Cicero, *Topica*, 82.

preference for reasonableness as against reason led him to reject their remorseless conclusions:

> Sensus moresque repugnant
> atque ipsa utilitas, iusti prope mater et aequi.[1]

The denial of absolute justice is Epicurean,[2] but the word 'prope' shows that he is undecided. And undecided he remained. The Stoic arguments were so cogent, their conclusions so absurd. In the long Satire II, 3 the first three hundred lines develop the Stoic Paradox that all save the philosopher are mad; but the conclusion implies that while this theory may be sound as applied to others, it is annoying when applied to oneself.

In middle age, when he came to write the Epistles, Horace was increasingly absorbed in this problem. For a while he could be carried away by idealism, but realistic thoughts were always at hand to bring him to earth again. In Epistles I, I he seems to acknowledge that in theory, as the Stoics said, the virtuous man is always supremely happy; but when it comes to the test, happiness is not proof against catarrh (l. 108). In the Sixth Epistle (31) he protests that the view that virtue is a mere word leads to sordid materialism, but a few lines above (15) he was clinging to a utilitarian standard, 'may the wise be called fool, the just unjust, if he pursue even virtue *more than is enough*', which would be heresy to an orthodox Stoic. The fact is that he wanted a sanction for morality, but could not bear one which involved rigidity. In everything he claimed the right to be free and eclectic, as Cicero had done. To be philosophic it was not necessary to grow a beard and become a professional; as if to emphasise this, he puts philosophic utterances into the mouth of the rustic Ofellus, an 'independent (*abnormis sapiens*). Both Epicureanism and Stoicism provided a way of life rather than a rule of thought; for in both the ethical and metaphysical theories were only in part interdependent. Horace preferred to try to mould his own individual philosophy of life:

> Nullius addictus iurare in uerba magistri.

---

1 *Sat.* I, 3, 97. 'Instinct and custom rebel and expediency itself, which is almost the mother of justice and right.'
2 *Golden Maxim*, XXXIII.

His own standards were high in an age when many people's were
far too low. I am not thinking of his rather priggish emphasis on
virtue—*mea uirtute me inuoluo*—but of his sensitive humanity, which
sometimes takes one by surprise. One is struck by the genuine pity
in his vivid picture of an evicted peasant family:

> Pellitur paternos
> in sinu ferens deos
> Et uxor et uir sordidosque natos,[1]

and of the captured Arab girl and boy, the imagined victims of
Roman imperialism:

> Quae tibi uirginum
> sponso necato barbara seruiet?
> puer quis ex aula capillis
> ad cyathum statuetur unctis
>
> Doctus sagittas tendere Sericas
> arcu paterno?[2]

Such sympathy was probably no more common in his day than
the generosity that prompted his famous tribute to Cleopatra after
her death:[3]

> Quae, generosius
> perire quaerens, nec muliebriter
> expauit ensem nec latentes
> classe cita reparauit oras.
>
> Ausa et iacentem uisere regiam
> uoltu sereno, fortis et asperas
> tractare serpentes, ut atrum
> corpore combiberet uenenum,

1 *Odes*, II, 18, 26–8: 'Forth they are driven, husband and wife, carrying
in their arms their ancestral gods and their ragged children.' It is the
realistic epithet *sordidos* that makes the picture so vivid. Horace was not
wholly complacent about poverty; 'Cur eget indignus quisquam te divite?'
he asks the rich man in *Sat.* II, 2, 103.

2 *Odes*, I, 29, 5–10: 'What foreign girl, her lover killed, shall be your
servant, what boy taken from his palace-home shall stand with scented
locks as your cupbearer, trained formerly to draw back Seric arrows on
his father's bow?' The tone of this ode may be bantering, but the sincerity
of the pathos is surely put beyond doubt by 'sponso necato'.

3 A like generosity is attributed to Octavian by Plutarch, *Ant.* 86.

Deliberata morte ferocior,
saeuis Liburnis scilicet inuidens
privata deduci superbo,
    non humilis mulier, triumpho.[1]

*   *   *

LOVE AND FRIENDSHIP

Among the pleasures of life Horace would probably have put
personal relationships first:

Nil ego contulerim iucundo sanus amico.[2]

That he never married may have been partly due to the extent to
which his emotions were absorbed by his friends, partly to his
unusual position as a man of humble origin moving habitually
among people of higher rank; certainly he was not indifferent to
women. In the Second Satire of Book 1, following Lucilius, he
treats of them academically on the calculating, utilitarian principle
of the Epicureans, who held that sexual instincts should be satisfied
in the easiest way, by 'parabilis Venus', with the avoidance, as
far as possible, of any emotional or social risk. But the more or
less contemporary Epodes show an interest in the object of passion
which is hardly in keeping with this; they are, in fact, not in the
least calculating, and display a frank, animal passion as well as a
strong invective element inherited with the form from Archilochus.
The Eleventh is full of feeling that sounds genuine, a vivid picture
of the misery, helplessness and loss of self-respect that may torment
the lover. The Eighth and Twelfth are invectives crude in the
extreme and yet so forceful that they carry conviction. One feels
that the writer found relief in the sheer brutality of the obscene
words. The Fifteenth is much the best of these poems; it has an
almost Catullian intensity and a touch of imagination:

---

1 *Odes*, 1, 37, 21–32: 'She, seeking to die more honourably, had no
woman's fear of the sword, nor gained sequestered shores with her swift
fleet. She had the courage too to visit her stricken palace with face serene
and the nerve to handle deadly snakes that her body might drink in their
black poison. More fiercely brave when resolved upon death, methinks
she grudged the cruel Liburnian galleys that she, no humble woman, should
be led unqueened in a proud triumph.'

2 *Sat.* 1, 5, 44.

Nox erat et caelo fulgebat luna sereno
    inter minora sidera

Cum tu, magnorum numen laesura deorum
    in uerba iurabas mea,

Artius atque hedera procera adstringitur ilex
    lentis adhaerens bracchiis,

Dum pecori lupus et nautis infestus Orion
    turbaret hibernum mare

Intonsosque agitaret Apollinis aura capillos,
    fore hunc amorem mutuum.

O dolitura mea multum uirtute Neaera!
    nam siquid in Flacco uirist,

Non feret adsiduas potiori te dare noctes
    et quaeret iratus parem,

Nec semel offensi cedet constantia formae
    si certus intrarit dolor.

Et tu, quicumque es felicior atque meo nunc
    superbus incedis malo,

Sis pecore et multa diues tellure licebit
    tibique Pactolus fluat

Nec te Pythagorae fallant arcana renati
    formaque uincas Nirea,

Eheu translatos alio maerebis amores
    ast ego uicissim risero.[1]

---

[1] 'It was night and the moon was shining in a clear sky amid the lesser stars when you, soon to violate the deity of the great gods, swore the oath I prescribed, clinging to me with twining arms more tightly than the tall ilex is embraced by the ivy, that while wolf should be foe to flocks and to sailors Orion that troubles the wintry sea, and while the breeze should fan the unshorn locks of Apollo, my love should be requited. O, you shall suffer much through my manhood, Neaera; for if there is in Flaccus one spark of a man he will not bear that you give nights continuously to a more-favoured rival, and in anger will seek a true match; nor, once he has been injured, will his resolution give way before beauty, if the pain has surely struck home. And you, whoever you are that are luckier and now go about puffed up with my discomfiture, though you be rich in flocks and land and Pactolus flow for you, and though you understand the mysteries of Pythagoras the reborn and surpass Nireus in beauty, alas! you shall weep for love transferred elsewhere; and it will be my turn to laugh.'

Are these poems at all autobiographical? It is hard to say. The condition described at the end of Epode XI,

> Sed alius ardor aut puellae candidae
> aut teretis pueri longam renodantis comam,

corresponds to that which he allows Damasippus to ascribe to himself in Satires II, 3, 325:

> Mille puellarum, puerorum mille furores.

And in Odes I, 16 he confesses, not too seriously,

> Me quoque pectoris
> temptauit in dulci iuuenta
> feruor.[1]

Yet, while it would be a mistake to suppose that the poet did not speak with the knowledge of experience, what he actually says is so traditional, as Leo has shown, that we must be content with the poems in themselves and not seek for stories behind them. All one can say with safety is that he may indeed have been *calidus iuuenta consule Planco*,[2] and that his loves were neither constant nor very romantic. Those who compare him with Catullus should remember that he matured more slowly; he began to write his best poetry at the age of thirty-five, an age at which Catullus, having already left passion for artistry, had now left everything for the grave.

Where he speaks of himself in the Odes as a lover he appears much less passionate then in the Epodes. In this, as in other things, he is a realist. When he sets out in I, 33 to console one Albius (probably the poet Tibullus) for Glycera's unkindness, he will only remind him that that is the way life is arranged.[3] 'Such is the will of Venus, who in cruel sport delights to join under a brazen yoke hearts and forms that are ill-matched.' His 'sic uisum Veneri' here is the counterpart of his

> Durum. sed leuius fit patientia
> quicquid corrigere est nefas

1 'I too in my sweet youth was assailed by frenzy of the heart.'
2 *Odes*, III, 14, 27.
3 The idea of a chain of unrequited lovers had occurred in Moschus (fr. 2); but he drew the cheap moral, 'Love those that love you'.

in the ode on Quintilius' death. Experience seems to have taught him not to expect love to be either perfect or lasting. Wistfully he warns Lydia in I, 13:

> Felices ter et amplius
>   quos inrupta tenet copula, nec malis
> Diuolsus querimoniis
>   suprema citius soluet amor die.[1]

But his attitude to women, though neither romantic nor idealistic, is saved from inhumanity by real affection. There is no trace in him of the contempt that embitters the warnings of Lucretius. He took a genuine delight in feminine charms and companionship. If he represents himself as a seducer, it is not (except in the early Lucilian Satire I, 2) of slaves whom he could compel; Cinara could flee when she would. Love in the Odes is like love in Tibullus or Meleager; and it is treated with the delicacy of language introduced into Roman manners by Panaetian Stoicism, which had revolted against the frankness of the Cynics and the other Stoics.[2] While as for delicacy of feeling, even the *Acmen Septumius* of Catullus cannot rival the dialogue *Donec gratus eram tibi* (III, 9). Horace did not admire women simply for their looks; he liked them to play and sing to him. Her singing is the first attraction of Licymnia that he mentions (II, 12); music is the distinctive charm of Chloe (III, 9),

> dulces docta modos et citharae sciens,

as it is of Phyllis (IV, 11):

>   Age iam, meorum
>   finis amorum
> (Non enim posthac alia calebo
> femina) condisce modos amanda
> uoce quos reddas: minuentur atrae
>   carmine curae.[3]

1 'Thrice happy and more are they who are bound by an unbroken tie, whose love unsundered by wretched complaints will not divide them until life's last day.'

2 See Cic. *De Off.* I, 127–9; *De Or.* III, 164; *Ad Fam.* IX, 22.

3 'Come now, last of my loves (for no other woman shall now inflame me), learn songs to sing with your lovely voice: dark cares will be lessened by singing.'

An amused interest in the psychology and situations of love was inherited by Horace from the Graeco-Roman writers of Comedy and the Alexandrians. In Odes I, 8 he accuses Lydia of 'doing her best' (*properes*) to spoil young Sybaris. That is the way the jealous always talk, and he underlines the point by setting five poems later another ode to Lydia in which he openly confesses to jealousy and tries a subtler way of loosening a passionate young rival's hold on her:

> Non, si me satis audias,
> > speres perpetuum dulcia barbare
> Laedentem oscula, quae Venus
> > quinta parte sui nectaris imbuit.[1]

But youth has such an advantage!

III, 20 is a masterpiece in miniature, sketching with mock-heroic humour a scene that may well have been taken from life. Pyrrhus, pursuing the young Nearchus, is heedless of the danger of touching a lioness' cub; but the boy is jealously watched by a protective woman, who is even now scattering the attendant crowd of young admirers at her approach. Weapons and claws are ready for the fray, but all the while Nearchus himself, the perfect narcissist in all his beauty, is supremely indifferent to the contest, trampling the prize under his naked foot. Asterie in III, 7 is anxious about the fidelity of her absent lover, who as a matter of fact is faithfulness itself; but Horace, the detached observer, can see what is in the wind: it is she who is in danger of temptation by a new lover. The poet himself in III, 26 is ostentatiously proclaiming his hard-won indifference to love by dedicating his siege-train to Venus, only to betray in the last line *ueteris uestigia flammae* by asking her, not to receive his gift, but to give Chloe the lash, just once, for her pride. These are the poems of a satirist, but the satire is so delicate and sympathetic that they have, like their counterparts in Burns, more in common with lyric.

We may leave it to the French to unravel 'La Vie Amoureuse d'Horace'. The girls he mentions all have Greek names and typify

---

[1] I, 13, 13 ff. 'You would not, if you took my advice, hope that he will always be yours who wounds so barbarously those sweet lips which Venus has imbued with the best part of her nectar.' *Quinta* probably refers to the Pythagorean πεμπτὴ οὐσία, the higher element or *quintessence*.

he accomplished courtesans of the day. Some, notably Cinara,
aave the shadow of reality, but it is lost labour to attempt to discover
more about them. There is, however, one poem in this category
which gives more impression than the rest of first-hand experience—
Odes IV, I. Its form is deceptive, and the deception contributes to
he desired effect. The opening, with its reminiscence of I, 19
(*Mater saeua Cupidinum*), suggests the assumption that it is simply
an announcement of the poet's return to lyric (love and lyric being
for him inseparable ideas) after six years and more of silence:

> Intermissa, Venus, diu
>   rursus bella moues? Parce, precor, precor.
> Non sum qualis eram bonae
>   sub regno Cinarae. Desine, dulcium
> Mater saeua Cupidinum,
>   circa lustra decem flectere mollibus
> iam durum imperiis: abi
>   quo blandae iuuenum te reuocant preces.[1]

The tone is light and the imagery conventional. But the mention
of the young suggests a real example, one Paullus Fabius Maximus,
and the poem too becomes real with the Lakes of Albano and Nemi
is setting:

> Tempestiuius in domum
>   Paulli purpureis ales oloribus
> Comissabere Maximi
>   si torrere iecur quaeris idoneum;
> Namque et nobilis et decens
>   et pro sollicitis non tacitus reis
> Et centum puer artium
>   late signa feret militiae tuae;
> Et, quandoque potentior
>   largi muneribus riserit aemuli,
> Albanos prope te lacus
>   ponet marmoream sub trabe citrea.

[1] 'Wars long-suspended, Venus, dost thou stir up again? Mercy, mercy,
pray. I am not what I was in the reign of kindly Cinara. Cease, cruel
mother of the sweet Loves, to bend with thy soft commands one grown
hard in wellnigh fifty years: begone to where the pleasing prayers of the
young summon thee.'

Illic plurima naribus
    duces tura, lyraeque et Berecyntiae
Delectabere tibiae
    mixtis carminibus non sine fistula;
Illic bis pueri die
    numen cum teneris uirginibus tuum
Laudantes pede candido
    in morem Salium ter quatient humum.[1]

The picture so vividly imagined now brings to the surface the half-conscious envy that the middle-aged will sometimes feel for the young, till finally the poet blurts out his secret:

Me nec femina nec puer
    iam nec spes animi credula mutui
Nec certare iuuat mero
    nec uincire nouis tempora floribus.
Sed cur, heu, Ligurine, cur
    manat rara meas lacrima per genas?
Cur facunda parum decoro
    inter uerba cadit lingua silentio?
Nocturnis ego somniis
    iam captum teneo, iam uolucrem sequor
Te per gramina Martii
    Campi, te per aquas, dure, uolubiles.[2]

1 'More timely wilt thou go revelling to the house of Paullus Fabius in thy car drawn by dazzling swans, if thou seekest to inflame a heart that is suited to thee; for he is well-born and comely and not silent in defence of anxious prisoners; and, a youth of a hundred talents, he will bear the standards of thy warfare far and wide. And whenever he has laughed in triumph over the gifts of a lavish rival, beside the Alban Lakes he will set thee up in marble under a citrus roof. There shalt thou breathe much incense, and delight in the mingled strains of lyre and Berecyntian flute and pipe. There twice a day shall boys with tender maidens, praising thy deity, beat the earth thrice in Salian fashion with their white feet.'

2 'Me nor woman nor boy delights any more, nor the credulous hope of love returned, nor contests with the wine-cup, nor binding the brow with fresh flowers.

But why, ah, why, Ligurinus, do the tears steal one by one down my cheeks? why does my once ready tongue falter, as I speak, into unseemly silence: at night in my dreams now I hold you caught, now I pursue you as you fly over the grass of the Campus Martius, or through the rolling waters, hard-hearted one.'

These last lines are as genuine in feeling as they are perfect in art. What a world of experience is summed up in the four words *spes animi credula mutui*! How vividly the metrical overflow of the elided last syllable of *decoro* suggests the dying away of the faltering voice! And what a strangely moving close, defying translation, is provided by the purely artificial contrast of the words *dure, uolubiles*! It is only a few moments since Horace was protesting that he himself was now *durus*.

So those opening lines were after all an integral part of the poem, not merely a prologue to the new book. They showed the poet trying manfully to pretend to himself that 'one can't take such things seriously at fifty'. His attempt to divert his thoughts to his young friend Paullus only made matters worse, until finally he could keep up the pretence no longer. The general idea of the poem is a development of that already used in III, 26 (*Vixi puellis*). The Horace we see here is once more the susceptible Horace of the Epodes, grown subtler and less harsh with the years, not the detached observer that we found in Odes I–III. The closing lines come nearer to being sentimental than any other passage in his works.

Benevolence is perhaps the best word to describe Horace's usual attitude to people; his genius was for friendship rather than love, and on friendship he set as high a value as any Epicurean. In particular he enjoyed feeling that it was in his power to immortalise the names of his friends as he immortalised that of the humble spring on his land. In one of his earliest odes (I, 26) he had referred to this gift as 'mei honores'. In the eighth and ninth odes of his last book he proudly enlarged upon it:

> Carmina possumus
> donare, et pretium dicere muneri.[1]

More than thirty men received odes or epistles from him. Nearly all would have been known to us from other sources. They include all the greatest names of the Augustan Age, but we need not suppose that he was on terms of close friendship with every one. His epistle to the future emperor Tiberius (I, 9) is respectful and shows signs of embarrassment; to Agrippa he sent only a tactful excuse for unwillingness to sing his praises (Odes I, 6). Not all the recipients

[1] IV, 8, 11 f.

deserved their 'honour'; Dellius was a notorious turncoat, Plancu
and Lollius are not attractive figures. But the real friends, beside
Maecenas, were the men nearer to him in station, his fellow-poet
Virgil, Varius and Quintilius Varus, and men like Fuscus and Lamia
To Virgil, 'the half of his soul', he was indebted for his introductio
to Maecenas—for everything, in fact,—and he shared his tastes an
ideals in poetry. But one is struck with the contrast between thei
characters: Virgil, to judge from his poetry and from all we hea
of him, was an 'introvert', sad, other-worldly, shy, perhaps a littl
lacking in humour. Horace was an 'extrovert', gay, worldly, fon
of company and overflowing with humour. He had far more i
common with Maecenas, and of this I shall have occasion to spea
later.

THE COUNTRY

The opinion that the Greeks had no appreciation of nature is sti
sometimes heard, but it is a misconception. Until the fourth centur
B.C. the country is rarely praised in their literature simply becaus
the country was everywhere. One does not praise air for being s
good to breathe. Yet one has only to think of Alcman's wel
known fragment, of the sites of the shrines of Delphi and Bassac
or of the cults of Dionysus and Artemis revealed to us in the *Baccha*
and *Hippolytus*, to realise how powerfully the Greeks were move
by beautiful scenery. As soon as they were deprived of it the praise
begin. The rustics in Aristophanes, cooped up within the walls o
Athens by the Peloponnesian War, become conscious of the loveli
ness of what they have left behind. Socrates is clearly made ou
to be odd in not preferring the shady bank of the Ilissus to the dust
Agora. And with the rebirth of poetry in the Hellenistic Ag
Nature came into her own in literature. Great commercial citie
had arisen, and Theocritus, the poet of Syracuse, might well idealis
the narrow pastoral strip of country between Etna and the sea, a
his friends of Alexandria idealised the island of Cos. The enthusiasr
spread to those who did not live in big towns, and the lonely beaut
of Arcadia was perfectly caught by the epigrams of Anyte of Tege
before it became a poetical convention.

Rome inherited the culture of the great Hellenistic cities. H
houses, like theirs, had landscapes painted on the room-walls if the

were not so fortunate as to have windows with a view of the country. Her courtyards had trees planted in them, a fact which occasioned Horace's famous remark:

Naturam expellas furca, tamen usque recurret.[1]

The Roman noble's villa was no less superbly situated than the Greek god's temple, as anyone can see to-day who walks along the ridge of Tusculum or round the hillside at Tivoli. The merits of country life were among the subjects of debate in schools of rhetoric, and extolled in set compositions in which reality became suffused with the roseate light of the Golden Age legend. Virgil was to rescue Nature from that false lighting by his *Georgics*, but Horace in his early days was attracted by it. The fanciful picture of rural life in the Islands of the Blest in Epode XVI recurs with some realistic colouring in Epode II. I cannot believe that Horace dwelt on this life for as many as sixty-six lines in the latter poem *merely* to swell the bubble which is to be pricked by the concluding word *ponere*.[2] No doubt, in elaborating the commonplace theme, he was quietly poking fun at conventional enthusiasms; it was time a few china shepherdesses were broken. But he treats the subject with a fullness and gusto which betrays his own enthusiasm, and Tyrrell's indignant outburst, 'he is laughing at what we should now call the Lake School of poets',[3] is quite inept; at most he is only satirising the insincerity of the usurer Alfius and his like. But as so often his irony lies in wait for his seriousness; and those who would tie him down to one or the other misunderstand his nature.

But it was not long before Maecenas' generosity gave him the chance of enjoying something very near to the Arcadian life of pastoral convention. It is well worth while to visit the Sabine farm, not only for the charm of the scenery, but also because one realises at once that what Horace wrote about it fits perfectly: he was writing from experience, not from literary suggestion. The train from Rome winds up to Tivoli, past the great gorge—*domus Albuneae resonantis*—and the waterfall—*praeceps Anio*—and on into the Sabine Hills. At Vicovaro, the Varia to which Horace's tenant farmers,

1 *Ep.* I, 10, 24.
2 Here I agree with Campbell, *op. cit.* pp. 140–1.
3 *Latin Poetry*, p. 192.

the *quinque boni patres* of Epistle 14, used to go, the valley of the
Digentia (now Licenza) diverges to the left. One may leave the
train here, or one may go on to Mandela, *rugosus frigore pagus*, and
take the rough path over the hillside. The scenery is not unlike
that of the Yorkshire dales. At the fork of the valley, just before
the road turns to wind up to the high-perched village of Licenza
scarcely noticeable against the stony background, a track to the left
leads in a minute to Horace's farm. There it stands as on an isthmus,
with a view up both arms of the valley, yet sheltered to a surprising
extent by the hill—we will call it Lucretilis—which rises im-
mediately behind. Across the hillside run occasional terraces of
olives watered by a clear runnel, which we will call Bandusia, and
traversed by straggling goats:

> Velox amoenum saepe Lucretilem
> mutat Lycaeo Faunus et igneam
> defendit aestatem capellis
> usque meis pluuiosque uentos.[2]

One can well believe it.

The walls of the house still stand to the height of about two feet
It was a fair-sized farm-house with a sunk garden in front.[3] One
can trace the quarters of the *uernae procaces* and see where Horace
made extensions (Sat. II, 3, 308) shortly after acquiring the place
The rather more elaborate additions made under Vespasian are
easily thought away. *Temperiem laudes:* the climate is delightful
and the Sabine peasants one meets in the valley have a dignity and
openness of manner, and a softness of speech, rare even in those parts
Sitting idly on a warm day, with no reminder of the modern world
one can recapture completely the atmosphere of the Odes and
Epistles and understand not only how Horace fell in love with the
place, but how it may have helped to inspire the slow and tranquil
movement of his poetry.

Such ideas may sound too 'romantic' to apply to one who is
proverbially 'classical'. But those labels only hinder our under-

---

1 See *Ep.* I, 16, 5 ff.

2 'Swift Faunus often deserts Lycaeus for beautiful Lucretilis and fends
off continually the fiery summer and the rainy winds from my goats' (*Odes*
I, 17, 1–4).

3 For a full description see G. Lugli, *Horace's Sabine Farm* (1930).

anding of people if they are made exclusive. Horace did believe
hat Nature can have an effect on poetic sensibility; he says of himself
1 a notable passage:

> Sed quae Tibur aquae fertile praefluunt
> et spissae nemorum comae
> Fingent Aeolio carmine nobilem.[1]

Fingent! 'Beauty born of murmuring sound.' One is reminded of
Wordsworth, who describes in the *Prelude* the calm instilled into
his character in childhood by the sound of the river Derwent which
flowed past his father's house at Cockermouth.[2] And while the
Augustans in general confined their admiration to 'beauty spots',
such as Tibur, and to that 'ubertas' of cultivation which their
practical minds approved, Horace comes near to modern romantic
feeling in his appreciation of fells and lonely places. He protests
to his bailiff, 'what you think desolate and unfriendly wildernesses
are beautiful to him who feels with me', and writes of his Sabine
retreat in terms which suggest that his feeling was by no means
common,

> Hae latebrae dulces, etiam, si credis, amoenae

(*dulcis* meaning dear to the individual, *amoenus* beautiful to all).[3]
'The wise man will love the country' was one of the maxims of
Epicurus.

We saw in Odes IV, 1 a good example of how Horace may slip
almost unawares into a passage suggesting vivid personal experience.
There the subject of the poem is love; in III, 25 it is the enthusiasm
inspired by Caesar. In the opening lines he imagines himself smitten

1 'But the waters that flow past fertile Tiber and the thick leaves
of the woods shall mould him into a poet famed for Aeolian song.'
Odes, IV, 3, 10.

2 I, 271–85 (1805 edn.). Quintilian (X, 3, 22) says that some writers
prefer to compose in the country 'quod illa caeli libertas locorum amoenitas
sublimem animum et beatiorem spiritum parent'. See Peterson, *ad loc.*
Cf. Pliny, *Ep.* IX, 10, 2.

3 *Ep.* I, 14, 19–20; 16, 15. Two lines of Lucretius, V, 1386–7, show a
similar feeling for pastoral solitude:

> 'Auia per nemora ac siluas saltusque reperta,
> Per loca pastorum deserta atque otia dia.'

with Dionysiac frenzy, roaming through the groves and grottoes o
convention; and then suddenly we come upon this:

> Non secus in iugis
> Exsomnis stupet Euhias
>   Hebrum prospiciens et niue candidam
> Thracen ac pede barbaro
>   lustratam Rhodopen, ut mihi deuio
> Ripas et uacuum nemus
>   mirari libet. . . .[1]

It would be hard to find in all Latin literature so romantic a picture—
the Bacchant on the mountain-side gazing out over the landscape
the river in the plain below and the snowy peaks in the distance
*Mirari—wonder—*how often that word was on Wordsworth's lips
And what a fine touch of romantic imagination there is in *ped
barbaro*! Where else in Classical literature do we find the exaltatio
of simply being alone in the remote country compared with Bacchi
ecstasy and connected with poetic inspiration? Only, perhaps, b
implication, in Virgil's outburst in his eulogy of country life, whe
he is thinking also of his own poetry:

> O ubi campi
> Spercheiusque et uirginibus bacchata Lacaenis
> Taygeta, O qui me gelidis conuallibus Haemi
> sistat, et ingenti ramorum protegat umbra?[2]

There are those who say that Horace's love of the country is onl
that of a townsman:

> Romae Tibur amo, uentosus Tibure Romam.

That is true; but most of his modern readers are townsmen no les
than he, however fond they may be of escaping to the country
I would not suggest that he had any mystical feeling about Natur
such as Virgil and Wordsworth had. But then, how many o
us have?

1 'Even as on the mountains the wakeful Bacchant is amazed as she
gazes out over the Hebrus and Thrace white with snow and Rhodope
traversed by barbarian feet, so I in the remote country love to wonder a
the banks and deserted woods.'
2 *G.* II, 486 ff. Here *Virginibus bacchata Lacaenis Taygeta* has the sam
effect as *pede barbaro lustratam Rhodopen.*

HUMOUR

To embark on a lengthy analysis of Horace's humour would not be appropriate here (or anywhere); in the Satires it varies from the laboured (dare I say, Plautine?) crudities of I, 7 (Rex v. Persius) to the delightful Terentian wit of I, 9 (The Bore); high spirits, surprises and pleasant malice are the chief ingredients. But it may be worth while to say something of the subtler humour of the Odes, that pervading spirit which the Romans called *facetiae*.[1] It consists chiefly in mock-solemnity (which is too often taken at its face value) and in irony.

Horace loved burlesque. The charming ode to a wine-jar (III, 21, O nata mecum...) is a complete parody of the Roman invocatory prayer.[2] The solemn 'pia testa' and 'descende' set the religious tone, and there are amusing *double-entendres*. The form was as regular as that of the English collects (O..., Seu...seu..., quo-umque nomine..., tu..., tu...tu), and Horace keeps to it throughout.

He also loved to set his own familiar person in a mythological or heroic setting. He represents himself as spirited from the field of Philippi by Mercury, just as Paris was snatched from the contest by Aphrodite:

> Sed me per hostes Mercurius celer
> denso pauentem sustulit aere.[3]

Pauentem is a characteristic touch: how nervous he would feel, rapt into mid-air like that!) When he is in love, it is

> In me tota ruens Venus
> Cyprum deseruit—;[4]

when he is courting a timid girl,

> Atqui non ego te tigris ut aspera
> Gaetulusue leo frangere persequor.[5]

---

1 'Facetiousness' is the last idea to connect with it. The Greek word was χάρις. See G. C. Fiske, *Lucilius and Horace*, p. 119 f.

2 E.g. the prayer in Apuleius, *Met.* XI, 2. E. Norden, *Agnostos Theos*, p. 143. This is the only ode that Horace wrote for the great Messalla Corvinus. Messalla was noted for his addiction to wine; at any rate he was chosen to sing its praises in a Symposium written by Maecenas in which Virgil and Horace also were given parts. (Servius on *Aen.* VIII, 310.)

3 *Odes*, II, 7, 13 f.   4 *Odes*, I, 19, 9 f.   5 *Odes*, I, 23, 9 f.

In the same spirit of amusement at the transfiguration of his homely
bourgeois self he liked to 'write up' incidents in his life in such a
way as to make them approximate to stories told of famous poets.
The shield that he admits with scarcely a blush (how this has worried
some of his admirers!) to have left on the field of Philippi, had been left
in a bush by Archilochus, and before the walls of Sigeum by Alcaeus.
(As a matter of fact, being a tribune, he may not even have had a shield
to lose.) The birds that covered his infant body with leaves recalled
the nightingale that sang on the lips of the infant Stesichorus[2] and
the bees that laid honey on the lips of the infant Pindar.[3]

Sometimes the mock-solemnity is used with ulterior purpose. In
I, 16 (*O matre pulchra*) Horace wants to appease a girl whom he had
once attacked in scurrilous lampoons. He adopts the same device
as Pope used in the *Rape of the Lock*—a mock-heroic treatment
which makes the offence seem absurdly trivial. Nothing, he says,
is so violent as anger; not even the frenzy of those possessed by
Cybele or Delphian Apollo or Dionysus or the Corybants: it is
turned aside by no threat of barbarian sword or raging sea or fire
or the Thunderer himself; Prometheus in creating man laid next
his vitals a portion of the lion's violence; anger brought ruin on
Thyestes and overthrew mighty cities to utter destruction:

> Compesce mentem: me quoque pectoris
>   temptauit in dulci iuuenta
>   feruor et in celeres iambos
> Misit furentem.[4]

Who can doubt that she was appeased?

The bathos used here for ulterior ends is used in III, 17, I take it
simply for fun. (This is not usually considered sufficient excuse for
any but a modern poem,[5] so subtle interpretations have had to be

1 *Odes*, II, 7, 10. Archilochus fr. 6 D; Alcaeus, fr. 49 D. (Refs. to Greek
Lyric poets are from Diehl's *Anthologia Lyrica Graeca*.)

2 Pliny, *N.H.* X, 82.   3 Pausanias, IX, 23, 2; cf. VIII, 25, 11.

4 'Keep calm: I too in my sweet youth was assailed by rage and driven
in fury to swift iambics.'

5 'What is the point? And where is the poetry?' asks Campbell, *op. cit.*
p. 5. Müller bracketed lines 2–5 as an interpolation. Byron had the same
delight as Horace in bathos for its own sake. There are countless instances
in *Don Juan* and *Beppo*. But Byron was a romantic half-ashamed of his
emotions, Horace a realist with no romantic illusions.

:volved to explain the poem.) Horace is staying in the country with
Aelius Lamia, and he thinks the weather is going to take a turn for
he worse. So he amuses himself by saying so in the following way:

> Aeli uetusto nobilis ab Lamo—
> quando et priores hinc Lamias ferunt
>   denominatos et nepotum
>   per memores genus omne fastos,
>
> Auctore ab illo ducis originem
> qui Formiarum moenia dicitur
>   princeps et innantem Maricae
>   litoribus tenuisse Lirim,
>
> Late tyrannus:— cras foliis nemus
> multis et alga litus inutili
>   demissa tempestas ab Euro
>   sternet, aquae nisi fallit augur
>
> Annosa cornix. Dum potes, aridum
> compone lignum: cras genium mero
>   curabis et porco bimestri
>   cum famulis operum solutis.[1]

The solemn, Pindaric opening will not have deceived his friend;[2]
Horace was not the man to view with an unsatirical eye the fashion
or deriving Roman family names from Homeric heroes by etymo-
ogical fudge. ('Burke's Romano-British Families' would scarcely
e a more fantastic production than Varro's *De Familiis Troianis*.)
And who was this Lamus? A cannibal-king in a fairy story, the
enth Book of the *Odyssey*. And even if he was a respectable

---

1 'Aelius, ennobled by descent from ancient Lamus—since they say that
om him the Lamiae of old received their name and all the stock of their
escendants throughout time's mindful records, you derive your origin
om that founder who is said to have first possessed the walls of Formiae
nd the Liris that floods the shores of Marica, a ruler of wide acres—:
)-morrow a storm let loose from the East will strew the wood with many
aves and the shore with useless seaweed, unless that prophet of rain deceives
ne, the aged raven. While you can, lay in dry firewood: to-morrow you
hall indulge your heart with wine and a sucking pig amid your work-free
ervants.'

2 Syme, *op. cit.* p. 83, is surely not justified in assuming that the Lamiae
ad actually made such a claim.

ancestor, 'Lamia' was a *cognomen*, not a family name. And as fo
the 'records'...!¹ The point of the poem lies simply in the descen
from this burlesque pomposity to the reality of seaweed and a raven
logs and a sucking pig.

The equally solemn and pompous opening of Odes I, 22 (*Intege
uitae*) has led many into taking it for a serious poem. There ar
institutions in which it is regularly sung as though it were a hymn
But on Horace's lips, complacent though he was, the propositio
'I am so good I can come to no harm: only lately a monster of a
wolf ran away when it saw me' is hardly serious, especially whe
it is dressed up in high-flown rhetoric. By all the laws of compositio
he should have ended as he began: 'I will keep myself "Intege
uitae scelerisque purus"'; but he has forgotten all that:

> Dulce ridentem Lalagen amabo,
> dulce loquentem.

Half the point, as in *Aeli uetusto*, lies simply in the sudden descen
from high rhetoric to the homely affairs of the moment.

In II, 20 (*Non usitata*) Horace imagines himself, seriously enough
as flying to all lands, like Theognis' Cyrnus, on the wings of hi
poetry. But the idea was too much for his sense of humour, i
seems, and he describes his metamorphosis into a bird with grisly
exactitude:

> Iam iam residunt cruribus asperae
> pelles, et album mutor in alitem
> superne, nascunturque leues
> per digitos umerosque plumae.²

So far so good: Horatian irony and Horatian bathos. But in the
succeeding stanzas he makes the fatal mistake of trying to be seriou
again with the same fancy. You cannot smash an illusion and hope
to put it together again.

But there are many passages in which there is a touch of humour
or fancy or whimsicality which does not prevent the rest of the
poem from being serious, like the mention of the Chimaera and

---

1 See Heinze, *ad loc.*
2 ll. 9–12. 'Already the rough skin is forming on my legs and abov
I am changing into a white bird and smooth feathers sprout all over my
fingers and shoulders.'

he astrological excesses in II. 17 (*Cur me querellis*), the amusing
close of III, 14 (*Herculis ritu*), or the comic exaggerations at the
beginning of II, 13 (*Ille et nefasto*). The strict segregation of humour
and seriousness is imposed by the taste of some societies far more than
others.[1] The Romans, with their Stoic doctrine of 'propriety'
(τὸ πρέπον), were inclined to be rather rigid,[2] and Horace is a
refreshing exception.[3] Occasionally, indeed, the effect is incongruous.
In the highly serious Ode I, 2 (*Iam satis terris*) he speaks of floods in
Rome as one of the omens of the times: men have feared that the
great flood of mythology might be repeated:

> Omne cum Proteus pecus egit altos
> uisere montes
> Piscium et summa genus haesit ulmo
> nota quae sedes fuerat palumbis....[4]

'Leuiter in re tam atroci et piscium et palumbarum meminit',[5]
says the scholiast, and one must admit that he is right. Horace has
got on to a well-known *locus* and let his fancy lead him astray.

His amusement at the incongruity of his own person and the
sublime sprang from the same source as his self-depreciatory,
Socratic irony. Like Maecenas,[6] he did not care to conceal his
faults', and showed a true sense of values in not being too ashamed
of things which are not, after all, very shameful, and which are the
less so for his consciousness of them. Stertinius the Stoic and Davus
the slave are in turn allowed to expose him.[7] He introduces himself
without compunction in scenes in which he gets the worst of it,
including the rout at Philippi. It was a rare thing to find a Roman
who could laugh at himself. Mark Antony was noted and appreciated by the Alexandrians as an exception to this well-known rule:

1 φημὶ χρῆναι τὸ μὲν σπουδαῖον σπουδάӡειν, τὸ δὲ μὴ σπουδαῖον μή.
Plato, *Laws*, VII, 803 c. Homer, Socrates and Aristophanes had been freer,
and Plato himself in his younger days.
2 See the remarks in Cicero, *De Off.* I, 144 on εὐκαιρία.
3 See his recommendations at *Sat.* I, 10, 11–15.
4 'When Proteus drove his whole herd to visit the high mountains and
the race of fishes stuck in the elm-tree tops which had been the haunt of
wood-pigeons.'
5 Porphyrio. 'It is frivolous of him to mention fishes and wood-pigeons
in such a serious context.'
6 Attacked on this account by Seneca, *Ep.* 114, 4. 7 *Sat.* II, 3 and 7.

he liked being laughed at as much as laughing at others.[1] But while Antony may have erred from the golden mean in the direction of buffoonery (βωμολοχία, in Aristotle's terminology[2]), Horace did not. He dispensed with the eternal Roman *grauitas* and yet succeeded in making himself familiar without being contemptible. The test is that whenever he claims to be taken seriously, we never question his right. In so trusting his readers he risked his reputation. As Desmond MacCarthy has well observed: 'It is always dangerous to make jokes about yourself, for the humourless are sure to repeat them as examples of your astonishing lack of self-awareness, while the malicious fling them back at you as stones. Still, no generous minded man can resist the temptation. . . .'[3] Horace had that generosity, and by it has won the affection of those whom he would have wished to please.

THE STATE

Harold Nicolson, in his book on Tennyson, showed how that poet had a spurious self imposed upon his real self by circumstances. Born and bred in a desolate part of Lincolnshire, Tennyson grew up with a deep strain of melancholy which found expression later in his finest poetry; in his Classical poems such as *Ulysses* and *The Lotus-eaters*, he shows how sympathetic he found the fundamental sadness of Greek paganism; and the best of his shorter poems, such as 'Break, Break, Break' and 'The Two Voices', were written in moods of black despair. But he was lionised by his friends, who persuaded him that he had a mission to be a public bard, the prophet of Victorian optimism and imperialism. Such a master of word could hardly fail to write fine rhetoric sometimes in this spurious role, half-persuaded for the moment that it expressed his sincerest feelings.[4] But the real Tennyson was not in it.

1 Plut. *Ant.* 24, 7. Cicero censures him for having in his company a schoolmaster, one Sextus Clodius, prototype of the medieval Fool, who was allowed to make what jokes he liked about him: *Phil.* II, 42–3; cf. Suet. *Rhet.* v. Quintilian considered telling stories against oneself to be worthy only of the professional buffoon: VI, 3, 82.

2 Aristotle's discussion of this topic in the *Ethics* (IV, 8) is most interesting

3 On Oscar Browning, *Portraits*, p. 35.

4 In moments of confidence, however, he would betray the truth, as when he confessed that the close of *In Memoriam* was more hopeful about the universe than he really felt.

The case of Horace is to some extent analogous. Son of a freedman, bred in distant Apulia, and educated on Greek poetry and Hellenistic philosophy, he found himself not only admitted to the inmost circle of a reforming political party, but bound to its leaders and prophets by all the ties of gratitude and friendship. He too was a master of words and wrote patriotic poetry which is often fine rhetoric, and sometimes more than rhetoric. But his heart was not really in it—so I have always felt. A story like that of Regulus might fire his imagination, or the recollection of the Civil Wars arouse genuine emotion, but in general the state poems are uninspired compared with the personal and individualistic.

'Public affairs vex no man', said Dr Johnson, and there have been few societies in which this has not been true. Cicero soon found, when he put political questions to farmers and burghers in Southern Italy, that they cared for nothing but their lands and farm houses and cash.[1] Horace had abandoned his native locality, and at Rome he could have no hope of making his mark in politics. To have been a military tribune for a short space must have astonished him enough. There was no reason for him to be a Republican beyond his association with young Republican nobles at Athens, and his appearance at Philippi was but an aberration on the part of *anima naturaliter Epicurea*. After the rout he did not join Sextus Pompeius with the die-hards, but returned to Rome, as he wryly recalled, 'with wings clipped'.[2]

It is a great pity that we cannot say with certainty which was Horace's first political poem. The question turns on the dating of Epode XVI. Was this escape-poem prompted by the outbreak of the Perusine War in 41 B.C., when the victors of Philippi fell out among themselves? If so, then Virgil's famous 'Messianic' Eclogue IV, inspired by the Treaty of Brundisium in 40, was a reply to this new poet: 'Do not seek the Golden Age elsewhere; it is dawning here in Italy.' It must be admitted that strong, if not conclusive, arguments against the priority of the Epode have been adduced.[3] But even supposing it was written a few years later, it would still be remarkable that a Roman lyric poet, especially one of humble birth,

---

1 *Ad Att.* VIII, 13, 2; cf. VII, 7, 5.   2 *Ep.* II, 2, 50.
3 See B. Snell, *Hermes*, LXXIII (1938), pp. 237–42; but against his view, K. Büchner, *Horaz* (*Bursian*, 1939), pp. 164–5.

should have ventured to address his countrymen at large. Horace may have been influenced to do so by the example of his model Archilochus; but it would be a mistake to minimise the significance of his attitude. He felt already that a true poet has a claim to the ear of the public, and that he himself was such.

The first fourteen lines bewail the plight of Rome, and introduce an idea which occurs in Horace's early work, that the city is under a curse.

> Impia perdemus deuoti sanguinis aetas
> ferisque rursus occupabitur solum.

And the cure is to migrate to some distant land and begin a new life in the innocent surroundings of the Isles of the Blest, the life of the Golden Age. The idea was not entirely a metaphor or dream-fantasy. Though the desire to escape anywhere from Rome is uppermost,

> Ire pedes quocumque ferent, quocumque per undas
> Notus uocabit aut proteruus Africus,

there was always at the back of people's minds in those troubled generations the possibility of finding such a life in remote lands. Sertorius had been eager to sail west from Spain for the Isles of the Blest, of which sailors newly returned from the Atlantic told him tales,[1] and at one moment after Actium Cleopatra set about dragging her ships across the Isthmus of Suez in quest of some Lotus-land of forgetfulness in the East.[2]

The Seventh Epode, another protest against Civil War, might have been written any time between 42 and 32 B.C. Again the idea that Rome is under a curse appears, but this time there is a suggestion of original sin—the primeval blood-guilt of Romulus himself, who killed his brother:

> Sic est: acerba fata Romanos agunt
> scelusque fraternae necis
> Ut immerentis fluxit in terram Remi
> sacer nepotibus cruor.[3]

1 Plut. *Sertorius*, 8–9. Sallust, quoted by Ps.-Acro on this Epode.
2 Plut. *Antony*, LXIX.
3 'Thus it is: a cruel destiny pursues the Romans and the crime of a brother's murder, ever since the blood of innocent Remus flowed to the ground to curse generations to come.'

The Satires, contemporary with the Epodes, offered little scope
or mention of public affairs; where we might expect it, in the
escription of Maecenas' vitally important journey to Brundisium
(ı, 5), there are indeed two tactful lines referring to his role of
econciler;[1] but before ıı, ı, which probably dates from after the
battle of Actium, Octavian is only mentioned twice,[2] and then
without any special mark of favour. Five or six years passed after
Horace joined the circle of Maecenas before he became an active
partisan. The Triumvirs, who were responsible for the proscriptions,
had done nothing to inspire enthusiasm.

The change came in 32 B.C., when the breach between Octavian
and Antony became open. The triumviral powers had served their
purpose by now, and both Octavian and Antony had to seek some
other basis for continued domination. A war of propaganda began
on lines with which we are now only too familiar. Octavian fixed
on Antony's connection with Cleopatra and his donations to her
children. Expanding this theme he developed the struggle into a
symbolic conflict between the manly West and the corrupt de-
generate East. The echoes of this campaign resound in the Augustan
poets' descriptions of Actium:

> Hinc Augustus agens Italos in proelia Caesar
> cum patribus populoque, penatibus et magnis dis...
> Hinc ope barbarica uariisque Antonius armis
> uictor ab Aurorae populis et litore rubro.[3]

It was the *Itali* whom Octavian led, for the campaign succeeded
at last in giving reality to the union of Rome and Italy that had
officially followed the Social War. A sort of 'spontaneous' plebiscite
was organised: 'All Italy of its own accord swore an oath of allegiance to me and chose me as its leader'[4]—all Italy, that is, which
was not with Antony, as the consuls and over three hundred senators
were. The 'National Government' slogan has never been more successfully exploited. Men like Messalla wrote bitter pamphlets against

---

1 28–9.   2 ı, 3, 4; ıı, 6, 56.
3 *Aen.* vııı, 678 ff. Cf. Propertius, ııı, ıı, 29 ff.; ıv, 6, 13 ff.
4 *Res Gestae*, 25. For the history of this propaganda campaign see
.. Syme, *op. cit.* ch. xx.

Antony. Rumour had it that Cleopatra's favourite oath had become 'As surely as I shall dispense justice on the Capitol',[1] just as the Kaiser in 1914 was said to have sworn to eat his Christmas dinner in Buckingham Palace.

Horace was swept off his feet. The ninth Epode records his feeling at the time. Artistically it is not a satisfactory poem because the *mise en scène* is not made clear. I suspect that it is intended to represent the successive emotions of a Caesarian aboard a galley at Actium in the days before and during the battle, telescoped as they must be for the purpose of the poem if not also in the imagination or recollection of the poet.[2] Maecenas was probably not present at the battle, and even if he was, he probably left Horace behind, though this point too is disputed.

The relief which the victory brought is expressed in Odes I, 37, but Cleopatra steals that poem. For the rest Horace referred to the clash more covertly in parables. One such parable, in all probability, is Odes I, 15. The scholiast tells us that this is an imitation of Bacchylides, which means presumably that the idea of the situation and the ballad-form come from him. It may be so. But the amorous and adulterous Paris might well remind contemporary Romans of Antony:[3]

> Nequiquam Veneris praesidio ferox
> pectes caesariem grataque feminis
> inbelli cithara carmina diuides;
>   nequiquam thalamo graues
>
> hastas et calami spicula Cnosii
> uitabis—[4]

There are many who, driven into utter scepticism by the fantastic allegorisations of ancient and modern commentators, will see no symbolism in Augustan poetry unless it is too obvious to be denied.

---

1 Dio, L, 5, *fin.* Compare the indignant juxtaposition *Capitolio regina* at *Odes*, I, 37, 6.

2 See *C.R.* XLVII (1933), pp. 2–6.

3 See Heinze on this ode. Plut. *Comparison of Demetrius and Antony*, III

4 *Odes*, I, 15, 13 ff.: 'In vain, emboldened by Venus' guardianship, you will comb your locks and give out on the unwarlike lyre songs such as women love; in vain in her chamber you will shun the heavy spears and the shafts of the Cretan bow—.'

But such an approach, not only to the *Aeneid*, but also to the *Eclogues* and to Horace's Odes, will not do. We must keep our sense of proportion and probability without sacrificing the rich under-current of topical application. The Augustans rarely wrote that kind of allegory in which every detail is a symbol. But they also rarely wrote without consciousness of the present. We shall meet with other examples of this half-allegorical technique.

When Octavian returned to Rome in 29 B.C. laden with the spoils of Alexandria, the general opinion was that he alone could secure peace at home. The peroration to the First Book of the *Georgics*, which were published about this time, expresses the weariness of civil war in a passionate outburst:

> Di patrii indigetes et Romule Vestaque mater,
> quae Tuscum Tiberim et Romana Palatia seruas,
> hunc saltem euerso iuuenem succurrere saeclo
> ne prohibete; satis iam pridem sanguine nostro
> Laomedonteae luimus periuria Troiae.[1]

Here again is the idea of original sin, the treachery of Laomedon corresponding to the murder of Remus in Epode VII. And the *Iam satis* with which Horace began his second ode of Book I, probably written at this time, is perhaps an echo of Virgil. A Messiah was needed, he felt:

> Cui dabit partes scelus expiandi
> Iuppiter?

The illness of Octavian in this year may have increased the intense anxiety which both poets here betray: *Serus in caelum redeas.*

But there was another anxiety, even more pressing. Would this Triumvir who had put his name to the proscriptions of 42, take vengeance on the remnant of the Antonians? The fact that he did not do so in the event must not lead us to belittle in imagination the keenness of this anxiety in the months between the battle of Actium and the return from Alexandria. I believe that it lies behind that enigmatic but important ode, III, 4.[2]

1 498 ff. 'Gods of our fatherland, Romulus, and thou, our mother Vesta, who guardest the Tuscan Tiber and the Roman Palatine, do not forbid this young leader at least to succour a world in ruins; enough long since we have paid with our blood for the treachery of Laomedon's Troy.'
2 See L. A. Mackay, *C.R.* XLVI (1932), pp. 243–5.

The first nine stanzas deal with the poet himself. He is inspire
by Calliope. He has been under a special providence from infancy
when he lost himself in the Apulian forests and was protected b
wood-pigeons with a covering of leaves,

> Non sine dis animosus infans;

and on several subsequent occasions, at the battle of Philippi, o
his farm when a tree once fell beside him, and in a shipwreck, hi
escape has seemed almost miraculous; it must be the Muses tha
watch over him. What is the point of all this? We shall see. B
a clever use of anaphora he passes from himself to Caesar as th
Muses' friend:

> Vos Caesarem altum, militia simul
> fessas cohortes abdidit oppidis,
> > finire quaerentem labores
> > Pierio recreatis antro.
>
> Vos lene consilium et datis et dato
> gaudetis, almae.[1]

This last line and a half are the kernel of the poem. In the firs
nine stanzas Horace gave his credentials, and asserted his right to
speak in the name of the Muses, of the λόγος, of civilisation, to
ruler who was himself not insensitive to them. The Muses counse
mildness, and approve when men give such counsel. But from the
freedman's son it must be no more than a hint, or it may misfire
So Horace hastens on to a fine description of the battle of the God
and Giants, civilisation and barbarism,[2] culminating in the radian
figure of that Olympian

> Qui rore puro Castaliae lauit
> crines solutos, qui Lyciae tenet
> > dumeta natalemque siluam,
> > Delius et Patareus Apollo.[3]

1 Ll. 37–42. 'You refresh in the Pierian cave exalted Caesar, when he
has hidden away his tired cohorts in the towns and seeks to end his labours.
You give mild counsel, and rejoice in its giving, kindly ones.'

2 The meaning of the symbolism was well known from Greek art. See
W. Theiler, *Das Musengedicht des Horaz* in *Schrif. der Königsb. Gel. Ges.* (1935)

3 Ll. 61–4: 'He who laves his flowing locks in the pure water of Castalia,
who haunts the woodlands of Lycia and his native grove, the God of Delos
and Patara, even Apollo.'

Apollo was the god who, from his temple on the shore, had upheld
Octavian at Actium; he was now the adopted favourite of the
victor's house. His famous shrine on the Palatine was soon to be
begun. There can be little doubt that Horace meant it to cross the
mind of his hearers that in that battle civilisation had overcome
barbarism; the Caesarians are Olympian, the Antonians Titanic.
Then comes another hint:

> Vis consili expers mole ruit sua:
> uim temperatam di quoque prouehunt
> in maius, idem odere uires
> omne nefas animo mouentes.[1]

Ostensibly this refers to the Giants, but the victors too are in their
turn powerful and in danger of hybris. The Muse's mouthpiece is
appealing for *uim temperatam*. But once again he must press swiftly
on; he returns to the fate of those who stood up against the Olympian
gods, ending significantly with the great lover, Pirithous, a figure
who even evokes our sympathy. There is no note of triumph:

> Iniecta monstris terra dolet suis
> maeretque partus—.[2]

It is not only the mythical Earth-mother, but the world of Horace's
day that mourns for her punished sons, *monstra* though they had been.
The tone is rather that of Shelley's poem:

> O cease! must hate and death return?
> Cease! must men kill and die?

The plan of the poem is thus discerned. Horace wants to plead
for a real amnesty. He dare not do more than hint. He must give
his credentials first, to justify his claim to a hearing. He must
make it quite clear that he is on the victor's side. He must not
appear to be giving advice directly. And yet, if he manages things
skilfully, the real intention cannot escape the person who is to
profit by it. So the poem must be an enigma, working by suggestion
rather than by ostensible meaning. All this Horace contrives with
consummate skill and tact; and artistically the crescendo from the

1 'Force without wisdom crashes by its own weight; force tempered
the gods themselves lead on from strength to strength, but they hate the
power that abstains from no device of evil.'

2 'Cast upon her own monsters Earth groans, and bewails her brood—.'

half-humorous tone of the second stanza and the homely scene near
the cottage of his nurse Pullia[1] to the thunderous music of the Titanic
battle, dying away again into the grim lament for the damned, is
an effect which few others could have achieved. The poem is strongly
influenced by Pindar, with its personal passage, its mythical 'para-
deigma', its sudden switch at 'scimus', its gnomic utterances (ll. 65-
8), and the fine description of Apollo (ll. 61-4), inspired by the
First Pythian (l. 39).[2] It is an epinicion for Octavian, but as in
that other song of victory, the Cleopatra ode, partisanship loses
itself in a deeper feeling for humanity.

Horace's enthusiasm for Octavian is strikingly expressed in
Odes III, 25:

dulce periculum est,

O Lenaee, sequi deum.

It was the complement of his horror of civil war. To the fear of
proscriptions past, there succeeded the fear that the Republic might
really be restored and the whole fatal process begun again. There is
one ode at least which was prompted, I believe, by this anxiety—I, 14.
It is a true allegory, following with unusual fidelity an original by
Alcaeus.[3] Since Alcaeus' poem was probably a political allegory,
indeed the prototype of political allegory,[4] it is hard to believe that
Horace's was not. His audience knew their Alcaeus and were bound
to make the application. The ship here can only be the ship of state, in
danger of being swept out again into tempestuous and rocky seas; and
the lines

Nuper sollicitum quae mihi taedium,

nunc desiderium curaque non leuis,

can only refer to the poet's distaste for politics in the Triumviral period,
and his awakening in the period of the war of Actium to a realisation
that no individual can be indifferent to what is happening in the state.

1 This is the best reading. She was probably a freed-woman of some
Pullius. See Heinze, *ad loc.*

2 See R. Reitzenstein, *Neue Jahrb.* 1922, p. 34; R. Heinze, *Neue Jahrb.*
1929, pp. 681–2; E. Fraenkel has shown that the myth also was inspired by
the First Pythian; *Horace* (1957), pp. 293 ff.

3 Fr. 30 D; Ps.-Heraclitus, *Homeric Allegories*, c. 5.

4 See Quintilian, VIII, 6, 44. Those who think that the ship is a real one
bearing Octavian himself must suppose that the ruler of the world set sail
in a leaky ship, to which the poet oddly refers as *nuper sollicitum mihi taedium*!
Some would date this ode in the months before Actium.

Character and Views

In January, 27 B.C., Octavian entered the Senate and proposed, with what sincerity we shall never know, to restore the Republic. Though Dio represents opinion in that assembly as being divided, an overwhelming majority urged him to retain the leadership of the state.[1] Among the many honours heaped upon him was the title Augustus, by which we must call him from now onwards. But there must have been many whose republican consciences were uneasy, if not shocked; and it was these, as well as Augustus, for whom I believe Horace to have written Odes III, 3, a poem as long and as obscurely suggestive as that which he placed next after it in his collection.

This ode has been endlessly discussed. Does it oppose the rebuilding of a real or a symbolic Troy? Surely a symbolic. Any proposals there may have been in Julius Caesar's day to transfer the Capital to the East were now unthinkable.[2] A war had just been fought and won in which the whole burden of the victor's propaganda had been directed against a supposed attempt to raise Alexandria to the level of Rome and against orientalism in general. This poem was not written before Actium; it was not even written before 27, since Octavian is referred to as *Augustus* in line 11. We can only conclude that it refers to something else.

What, then, is symbolised by Troy whose rebuilding is so solemnly forbidden? Wealth and luxury, say some, pointing especially to the parenthetical lines 49–52.[3] But these lines, and the general reputation of Troy, are not sufficient to be the key to the poem. One returns inevitably to the theory of Kiessling, that Troy symbolises the 'Optimatenzeit', the decadent Republic, and that the ode was designed to reconcile the reluctant to the rule of Augustus.

The first four stanzas praise the man who is *iustus et tenax propositi*. It is a mistake, I think, to scan the wording too closely; the instances of what he has to face are conventional, not topical. The just and steadfast man will not be diverted from his purpose by any fear; such were the demi-gods, and such is Augustus, who is destined to drink nectar as their peer. The mention of Romulus-Quirinus among these provides the transition to a speech of Juno. The full undertones of this speech are inaudible to us because we

---

1 Dio, LIII, 11, 1.
2 Suet. *Caes.* LXXIX; Nicol. Dam. *Caes.* 20; Heinze, Introduction.
3 Campbell, *op. cit.* pp. 110–11.

do not possess its literary predecessor, the conciliatory speech c
Juno in the First Book of Ennius' *Annals*, which Virgil also seem
to have used at the end of the *Aeneid*.[1] But it had topical undertone
which can have escaped no one then and should not escape us now

> Ilion, Ilion,
> fatalis incestusque iudex
> et mulier peregrina uertit
>
> In puluerem, ex quo destituit deos
> mercede pacta Laomedon mihi
> castaeque damnatum Mineruae
> cum populo et duce fraudulento.[2]

The phrase *mulier peregrina* had an all too familiar ring. There wa
only one such who had threatened Rome, and Antony was he
Paris. The symbolism of Odes 1, 15 is thus reiterated here; so i
the symbolism of Virgil's peroration to *Georgics* 1, published no
long before:

> Satis iam pridem sanguine nostro
> Laomedonteae luimus periuria Troiae.

This last allusion supports the view that Troy stands for the Rome
of the decadent Republic, the Rome of luxury and civil war, since
in Virgil's passage it had that connotation; there Laomedon's
treachery was the original sin with which the city was cursed, and
Octavian was to be the redeemer:

> hunc saltem euerso iuuenem succurrere saeclo
> ne prohibete—

Clearer and clearer become the topical allusions in Juno's words:

> Iam nec Lacaenae splendet adulterae
> famosus hospes—
>
> Nostrisque ductum seditionibus
> bellum resedit.

---

1 XII, 818 ff., esp. 828:
> 'Occidit occideritque sinas cum nomine Troia.'

2 Ll. 18–24. 'Ilium, Ilium a fatal and adulterous arbiter and a foreign
woman have turned to dust, a city condemned by me and by chaste Minerva
with its people and treacherous leader from the time when Laomedon
cheated the gods of their promised reward.'

The founder of the new city, Romulus, is to be allowed a place in heaven in token of reconciliation: he is to drink nectar with the gods, a touch that can only be meant to point the parallel with Augustus, for whom the same destiny was foretold in line 12. Romulus was to be the founder of the city which would rule the world so long as Troy was not rebuilt; Augustus was the second founder,[1] whose regenerated city would rule the world so long as it turned its back resolutely on the past, on luxury as well as civil war. The curse of original sin, which we heard of in Epodes VII and XVI and in Odes I, 2 and III, 6, can now be expelled. With the advent of Augustus the gods are reconciled.

Fear of a fresh outbreak of civil war was always at the back of Horace's mind. When Augustus returned from Spain in 24, he welcomed him with significant words:

> Hic dies uere mihi festus atras
> eximet curas: *ego nec tumultum*
> *nec mori per uim metuam* tenente
> Caesare terras,[2]

and turned with relief to the pleasures of peace. 'The Ode', says Page, 'has been severely criticised, and certainly not only are the first three stanzas commonplace, but the contrast between their formal and official frigidity and the licentious vigour of the rest of the ode is very harsh.' If 'licentious' is a severe word to apply to the harmless celebrations Horace proposes—unguents, wine, garlands and, if she will come of her own accord, a girl with brown hair and a pretty voice—yet it is true enough that the public part of the victor's welcome leaves Horace cold, its significance for him lies in the assurance of personal safety, and his enthusiasm is reserved for the 'licentiousness'.

1 There was actually talk of giving him the title of Romulus *quasi et ipsum conditorem urbis* (Suet. *Aug.* VII); Dio, LIII, 16; Florus, II, 34. But the legend of Romulus' fratricide, recalled by Horace in *Epode* VII, was a fatal obstacle; the idea of a second founding, however, was retained, if it is true that we are to see in the name *Augustus* an echo of Ennius' line (*Annals*, 496):

'*Augusto* augurio postquam incluta condita Roma est....'
(The reference to Ennius in Suetonius is considered by some to be an interpolation.)

2 III, 14, 13. 'This day, truly a holiday for me, will remove my dark anxieties: I shall not fear riot and death by violence while Caesar rules the world.'

The attitude of Horace to foreign campaigns was also coloured by his fear of civil war. Although he occasionally refers to the positive and professed aim of Augustan imperialism, to spread civilisation by arms—*dare iura Medis*—yet he has at the back of his mind the idea that foreign war was a cure for civil strife:

> O utinam noua
> Incude diffingas retusum in
> Massagetas Arabasque ferrum.

and again:

> Audiet ciues acuisse ferrum
> quo graues Persae melius perirent.[1]

It is clear from the state poems which we have considered that Horace was a man of peace who had despaired of its attainment in the Triumviral decade, and was only too glad to accept the rule of one man, if that was the only solution. But we must distinguish in our minds between Augustanism as the rule of a single man and Augustanism as an ideology of national regeneration: a man might be enthusiastic for the one while caring little for the other. This regeneration was to be encouraged by every conceivable means. I have already discussed the attempt to revive the national religion. The chief task was to infuse public spirit into a ruling class which had become too individualistic. The end was excellent, but the means were not always so creditable.

We may be inclined to criticise too harshly these sanguine attempts to reform a nation, sickened as we are by the absurdities and excesses of those who have avowedly imitated them in modern times. There was a little more excuse for Augustus' restriction of inter-marriage between Romans and others than there is for the modern doctrine of racial purity; the Romans were at least superior in general to those whose blood they would not mix with their own. The attempts to increase the birth-rate were due to a desire to preserve the governing stock rather than to ambitions for world-domination. The awakening of interest in the past and revival of old institutions was well enough, but the intensely nationalistic propaganda designed

1 *Odes*, I, 35, 38 and I, 2, 21. Similarly Isocrates had seen no cure for strife between Greek cities save a common crusade against the Persians. It is unpleasant to note that Horace has forgotten here the sympathy for the Arabs, victims of a frankly predatory attack, which he showed in I, 29.

specially for the war against Cleopatra left too many ugly traces. The exclusion of delegates of allied and foreign communities from the best seats at the games is one symptom of a general tendency.

The state now undertook to impose a moral code by decree. The idea was not new: it is implied in the powers previously given to the censors. Sumptuary laws were made to check private extravagance. The state began to take cognisance of sexual matters. Augustus was at pains to defend his decrees by appeal to ancient precedent, reading to a long-suffering Senate Metellus 'On Increasing Population' and Rutilius 'On the Limitation of Houses'. But it may well be doubted whether artificial respiration can ever resuscitate primitive qualities. Once men have tasted 'enlightenment' and individualistic freedom, they will not easily concede to public control anything more than they allow to be absolutely necessary. The state was made for man, not man for the state. In the small city-states communal feeling had flourished; but the Graeco-Roman world was not conducive to it; Stoicism admitted participation in public affairs only as a secondary duty; Epicureanism did not recognise it as a duty at all. Livy well summed up the state of affairs in his day when he said in his Preface (9) · 'We have got to such a pitch that we can tolerate neither our faults nor their remedies.' In the old days of Rome the state and family had been everything, the individual nothing; in the ruling class son after son had been content to bear the same name, and follow the same career, as his father. But all that changed with the increasing influx of Greek culture in the second century. The era of individuals began. Lucilius, a man of minor importance, could now be confident of finding a large audience when he committed to paper his every thought and experience. In the era of the Optimates Rome was unsuited to rule her Empire, yet the Empire had to be ruled. Our regrets for the loss of liberty under Augustus, sharpened by analogies with the modern world, must not blind us to the fact that his despotism replaced, not democracy, but a narrow oligarchy composed largely of selfish men.

The religious revival failed. The sumptuary laws failed. The attempts to regulate marriage and increase the birth-rate were stubbornly resisted. Tibullus' liaison with Delia is casually represented as adulterous,[1] while Propertius openly rejoiced at the success

1 I, 2, 41 and 6, 15–42.

of the public outcry against the marriage regulations mooted
in 28:

> 'At magnus Caesar.' Sed magnus Caesar in armis:
>   deuictae gentes nil in amore ualent.[1]

Virgil, Horace, even the consuls who gave their names to the final
legislation, were bachelors to the end.[2]

The most striking case of a man who supported the monarchy
without caring so much about the party policy of regeneration is
that of Maecenas himself. Apart from the eulogies of his protégés,
the *locus classicus* for his character is the 114th letter of Seneca.
Seneca has an axe to grind, for he is trying to illustrate the maxim
'Le style c'est l'homme même' by showing that Maecenas' character
is as flamboyant as his oratorical style; but there are other indications,
including the title of a lost work by him, 'De Cultu Suo', which
point the same way.[3] 'How Maecenas lived', writes Seneca, 'is too
notorious to require comment, his manner of walking, his softness,
his love of displaying himself, his unwillingness to conceal his
faults....He would have been a man of great powers if he had gone
about his business with more simplicity, if he had not avoided being
intelligible, if he had not been so loose in his style of speech also.'
And again: 'Can you not at once imagine, on reading through these
words, that this was the man who always paraded the City in a
loose tunic (for even when he was performing the functions of the
absent Emperor, he was always in undress when they asked him
for the password)? Or that this was the man who, as judge on the
bench, on the rostra, or at any public function appeared with a cloak
wrapped round his head with his ears protruding, like the mil-
lionaire's runaway slaves in the mime? Or that this was the man
who, at the very time when the state was embroiled in civil strife,
when the city was in trouble and under martial law, was attended
in public by two eunuchs—both more man than himself.' After
his death two elegies, to be found in the *Appendix Vergiliana*, were

1 II, 7, 5–6.
2 Papius and Poppaeus. Dio, LVI, 10, 3. See also Tac. *Ann.* III, 25.
3 Juvenal refers to him as 'supinus' (I, 66) and 'tener' (XII, 39), and
Velleius noted that he was, for all his political efficiency, 'otio ac mollitiis
paene ultra feminam fluens' (II, 88, 2). Pliny speaks of his instituting a
fashion of eating young asses' flesh (*N.H.* VIII, 170), and Martial mentions
his fine clothes (X, 73, 4).

written upon him; although he died at least sixty years old, it is as a voluptuary that he is here chiefly remembered, with the apology,

> Omnia uictores Marte sedente decent.

What more engaging tribute has ever been paid to an energetic organiser of police than line 29:

> Nocte sub obscura quis te spoliauit amantem?

Augustus might exclaim bitterly when he saw youths wearing cloaks in the Forum, 'En "Romanos rerum dominos gentemque togatam"', but his right-hand man regularly deputised for him in a cloak.[1] He might read to the Senate Rutilius 'On the Limitation of Houses', but the senators had only to look up to the Esquiline to see the great palace of the knight and his tower, *molem propinquam nubibus arduis*, from which Nero was one day to watch the burning of Rome. No doubt he resigned himself to letting Maecenas be Maecenas. After all the man was an Etruscan by origin, not a Roman, and his ancestors were kings.

We need not be surprised that such a character should have been an energetic administrator. Recent history provides parallels enough. For months, and even years, on end Maecenas governed Rome in Augustus' absence. His organisation of a police force was a great blessing to the city. But he was not only loyal and competent; he had other attractive qualities. Even Seneca concedes him clemency:[2] 'he spared the sword, and showed his power only in his licence'. There is a story that once when Augustus was dealing out sentences of death in the law-courts, Maecenas came in and whispered in his ear, 'Surge, Carnifex', 'Get up, executioner!'[3] Unlike most Romans he did not care for rank and titles, and the Emperor could be confident that his vicegerent had no ambition to supplant him. His reward was his popularity, which moved the whole theatre to rise spontaneously to cheer him on his first entry after an illness.[4]

---

1 Suet. *Aug.* XL; Seneca, *Ep.* 114, 6.   2 *Ep.* 114, 7.

3 This was a particularly strong word to use at Rome, where the public executioner was traditionally taboo.

4 If he had been the kind of man that Syme depicts (*op. cit.* pp. 341–2) he would surely not have been the beloved and intimate friend of men like Virgil and Horace. I do not know what authority Syme has for his account of Agrippa's alleged loathing for Maecenas. The attack on p. 409 is based simply on Seneca's humourless horror at some light-hearted verses on the subject 'while there is life there is hope' (*Ep.* 101, 10 ff.).

Horace differed from his patron in his preference for *simplices munditiae* to *Persici apparatus* both in life and in literary style. That was only a matter of taste. For the rest there was a real understanding and sympathy between the two. Both were realists in outlook, both enjoyed the good things of life, both thought conciliation better than force. Maecenas was not a snob. Contented with equestrian rank for himself, he chose his friends for merit rather than rank. (One of them, Gaius Melissus, was a slave, and remained so from choice.) Horace greatly appreciated this, and said so at length in Satires I, 6.[1]

Everything that we know of Maecenas reveals him as an individualist; and Horace too was an individualist. As a self-made man he was likely to be so, but the tendency was greatly increased by his education. Philosophy to him meant Hellenistic philosophy, which had attempted to solve the problem of the individual soul newly isolated from the warm collectivism of city-state life. His lyric models were the early Greeks, intensely preoccupied with their own personal feelings; and he was no less influenced by the Alexandrians, who were interested in psychology, not at all in politics or even in morality. The acknowledged forerunners of his Satire Bion the Borysthenite and Lucilius, had both been intensely individualistic. He may have remembered Bion, the salt-fish seller's son who became the friend of King Antigonus Gonatas, when he described his own first meeting with Maecenas;[2] he admired Lucilius, the Campanian knight, for the egoistic and minute self-revelation of his *Saturae*.[3]

How far did Horace, in the Odes of the first collection, consciously

1 Varro's *De Familiis Troianis* and the similar researches of Atticus (Nepos, *Att.* 18, 2), and Virgil's introduction into the *Aeneid* (v, 116–23) of mythical ancestors for the Iulii, Sergii and Cluentii, attest the prevalent interest in genealogies. Horace laughs at it in his Ode to Lamia (III, 17 see p. 61). Agrippa was jeered at for his humble gentile name, Vipsanius and was sensitive about it. (Sen. *Contr.* 4, 13.)

2 *Sat.* I, 6, esp. ll. 56 ff. See R. Heinze, *De Horatio Bionis Imitatore* G. C. Fiske, *Lucilius and Horace*, p. 316. The similarity between the fortune of the two led to an interesting confusion in Suetonius' *Life of Horace* par. 1. Suetonius says that his father was commonly believed to have been a salt-fish seller on the evidence of a story which really refers to Bion See Diog. Laert. IV, 46; Auct. *ad Herennium*, 54, 67.

3 *Sat.* II, 1, 28 ff.

try to promote the Augustan ideology? Here and there, as in the Ode III, 6 on the repair of the temples, he is obviously supporting contemporary policy. The odes in praise of courage (III, 2 and III, 5) were certainly in the spirit of the new movement; so was the general tenor of III, 24. But we must beware of seeking too far.[1] For every one of the poems which can be interpreted as supporting the party policy there is at least one which could equally be interpreted as hindering it. Some of the odes praise simplicity and might therefore be said to support the sumptuary laws. These are in fact simply the expression of Horace's personal choice, influenced by Stoic-Cynic ideas of the 'life according to nature'.[2] The Stoic hatred of all progress finds a place in Odes I, 3:

> Nequiquam deus abscidit
> prudens Oceano dissociabili
> Terras, si tamen impiae
> non tangenda rates transiliunt uada.

Did Horace really think it was impious to cross the sea? Of course not. But these were the commonplaces of Roman moralistic writing. If we were to take them seriously we should have to include Maecenas' Tower of Babel on the Esquiline among those condemned for impiously aspiring to heaven, his treasured jewels among those which ought to be given to the Capitoline god or thrown into the sea (III, 24, 45). There is an element of reason, of course, in all cries of 'Back to Nature!', and these poems of Horace no doubt reflect a genuine reaction against the commercialism and ostentation of the day. He preferred enlightened to unenlightened hedonism:

> Cur ualle permutem Sabina
> diuitias operosiores?

1 'The wantonness of youth cannot be prevented, and the political purpose, if one may call it so, of Horace's erotic odes is to direct it into a (supposed) socially harmless channel'! Campbell, *op. cit.* p. 294.

2 The influence of the Stoic-Cynic 'diatribe', originated by Bion the Borysthenite, is strong in the *Satires*, and can be traced in odes such as I, 2 (*Nullus argento*), where the simile of dropsy for avarice is borrowed from Bion. Cf. *Odes*, III, 27; Bion in Stobaeus, III, 1, 98.

But it is only on rare occasions that a topical application is given to the commonplace sentiments.[1]

Those who wish to claim all such poems as evidence of a desire to propagate the policy of the régime must admit that many of the odes actually run counter to it. Augustus tried to induce Senators, whose real power he had taken away, to take part in public life, and revived offices that were obsolete in the hope of tempting them. But what was the good when his right-hand man, Maecenas, refused senatorial rank? Horace too consistently poured cold water on such ambitions:

> Non enim gazae neque consularis
> summouet lictor miseros tumultus
> mentis et curas laqueata circum
> tecta uolantes.[2]

Always the tacit assumption that the Epicureans were right: the pomp of office had no more value than wealth for the great object of life, the banishment of care. Horace expostulates with Hirpinus (II, 11) for worrying about the Cantabrians beyond the sea, and with Maecenas for being over-diligent in his care for the city:

> Neglegens ne qua populus laboret
> parce privatus nimium cauere et
> dona praesentis cape laetus horae;
> linque seuera.[3]

When Maecenas suggested that Horace should write of the victories of Augustus, his protégé made the same excuse as he had made to Agrippa: he is a lyric poet, and love is his theme. It was always easy to put Maecenas off with a *tu quoque*; Propertius slyly

1 As at *Odes*, II, 15; III, 24, 25 ff. The reference in the latter passage to the unpopularity which Augustus' reforms might entail in his lifetime is echoed in *Ep.* II, 1, 13–17. These lines are characteristically sandwiched between two completely academic 'loci', the praise of the noble Scythians and the condemnation of seafaring merchants.

2 'For no treasures nor consul's lictor can remove the wretched tumults of the mind and the cares that flit round the coffered ceilings' (*Odes*, II, 16, 9–12).

3 *Odes*, III, 8: 'Holding no office you should be care-free and cease to worry overmuch about the troubles of the people. Gladly seize the gifts of the present hour: leave serious things.' Cf. III, 29, 16–28.

undertook to sing of battles if Maecenas was the victorious general;[1]
Horace no less slyly urged his patron to tell of Caesar's battles himself in prose history—the last thing he would have cared to do—
and added by implication that he was well aware that Maecenas too
thought love more important:

> Num *tu* quae tenuit diues Achaemenes
> aut pinguis Phrygiae Mygdonias opes
> permutare uelis crine Licymniae
>   plenas aut Arabum domos,
>
> Cum flagrantia detorquet ad oscula
> ceruicem, aut facili saeuitia negat
> quae poscente magis gaudeat eripi,
>   interdum rapere occupat?[2]

Even if battles were unsuited to the lyre, Horace might have
furthered Augustus' aims by celebrating the heroes of Roman legend
whose statues the Emperor had set up with appropriate inscriptions
round his new forum. But the Regulus ode had no parallel. He
preferred to retain his freedom to choose his own subjects. And
it is worth noting that, out of eighty-eight odes that form the
first collection, only some twenty can by any stretch of imagination
be counted as political.

The prevailing cult of Romanism was also treated by Horace with
reserve. Rome stood indeed for peace and good government in
the civilised world, which Greece had failed to achieve; but she
also stood for commercialism as against Greek philosophy, poetry
and art. He may fairly be called a Philhellene. Unlike Virgil, he
sprang from a Hellenised part of Italy, and had spent an impressionable
period of his life at Athens. Satires I, 7 describes how a hybrid
Graeculus scored a verbal victory over a coarse and rustic Italian.

---

1 Prop. III, 9, 21 ff.

2 II, 12, 21: 'Would *you* take all that rich Achaemenes owned, or the
Mygdonian wealth of teeming Phrygia, or the well-stored houses of the
Arabs, for one hair of Licymnia, when she bends her head to your burning
kisses, or with mock-cruelty refuses what more than the asker she would
love to be snatched, and sometimes snatches first herself?' The *tu* is emphatic, picking up the *me* of line 13.

In the Epistle to the Pisos he speaks out finely for Greek παιδείο
contrasting it with the utilitarian education of Rome:

> Graiis ingenium, Graiis dedit ore rotundo
> Musa loqui, praeter laudem nullius auaris;
> Romani pueri longis rationibus assem
> discunt in partes centum diducere.[1]

So long as her schoolmasters' enthusiastic praise, 'Eu! Rem poteri
seruare tuam', instils commercial ideals into the boys, how ca
Rome hope for poets whose works would be worth keeping?

Horace was equally unsympathetic to the cult of primitive Roma
literature which was encouraged in some circles. He was bol
enough to deride it in an Epistle written by request for the Empero
himself (II, I), in which he expresses the tenet of the 'fautore
ueterum' in an ironical *non sequitur*:

> Venimus ad summum fortunae: pingimus atque
> psallimus et luctamur Achiuis doctius unctis.[2]

Ennius has become 'a second Homer', Pacuvius is 'learned', Acciu
'sublime', Afranius 'the Roman Menander', Plautus 'the inherito
of the mantle of Epicharmus':

> *Hos* ediscit et *hos* arto stipata theatro
> spectat Roma potens, habet *hos* numeratque poetas.[3]

There is scorn in the 'hos' repeated thrice in an emphatic position
and a sneer in the 'potens' at those who confused power wit
civilisation. It was Greece who had civilised Rome:

> Graecia capta ferum uictorem cepit, et artes
> intulit agresti Latio.[4]

If I have stressed the extent to which Horace was unaffected b
Augustan ideology up to the time of the publication of Odes I–I

---

1 *A.P.* 323 ff.: 'To the Greeks the Muse has given genius, to the Greek
the voice of eloquence: they care for nothing beyond glory. Roman boy
learn by lengthy calculations to divide an *as* into a hundred parts.'

2 L. 32: 'We have come to the height of prosperity: *ergo* we paint an
dance and wrestle more skilfully than the polished Greeks.'

3 L. 60: 'It is these that Rome the mighty learns by heart, these that sh
crowds the theatre to watch, these that she reckons as her poets.'

4 L. 156: 'It was captured Greece that led her rude captor captive an
introduced the arts to rustic Latium.'

23 B.C., it is because one hears it so often assumed that he was merely a willing tool of authority. Virgil was an Augustan through and through; Horace only caught the Augustan spirit as it were by infection. But he did catch it, like Propertius, in the later years of his career. In the six years that followed several things happened which may have helped to change his attitude. It would be uncharitable and unjust to say that he drew away from Maecenas, in so far as he ever did, because of the latter's disgrace. But Augustus was now more often in Rome, and Horace got to know him better. About 18 B.C. the *Aeneid* was published posthumously, and its influence can be traced both in detail and in spirit through Horace's subsequent lyrics.[1] Finally in 17 came the call to break silence and compose the Carmen Saeculare as the recognised laureate of Rome. All these factors must be taken into account.

The fourth book of the Odes shows Horace as wholeheartedly Augustan as he is generally represented to have been throughout. Its dominant motive is the glory of heroes and poets. The sixth and fifteenth poems represent the Golden Age as already restored by this *Empereur Soleil*, peace enthroned at home and abroad, and antique virtue flourishing. One wonders how Ovid got anyone to listen to his poems! There are also the two laureate epinicia for the successes of the Emperor's stepsons in frontier fighting. These contain some fine rhetorical poetry worthy of Virgil:

> Gens quae cremato fortis ab Ilio
> iactata Tuscis aequoribus sacra
>   natosque maturosque patres
>   pertulit Ausonias ad urbes
>
> Duris ut ilex tonsa bipennibus
> nigrae feraci frondis in Algido
>   per damna, per caedes, ab ipso
>   ducit opes animumque ferro.[2]

---

1 *C.S.* 37–44, 49–52; *Odes*, IV, 4, 53 ff.; 6, 21 ff.; 15, 31–2 (his final words).
2 4, 53–60: 'The race which bravely from the ashes of Ilium bore its gods tossed on the Tuscan seas, its children and fathers of ripe age, safe to the cities of Ausonia, like a holm oak shorn by the hard axes on Algidus that bears dark foliage, through loss and slaughter draws prosperity and spirit from the very steel.'

And yet neither piece seems to me wholly successful; for the fourt
wears its Pindaric garments uneasily, while the fourteenth slip
here and there into the Horatian fault of prosaic cataloguing.

Full surrender to Augustus also entailed, to my mind, a certai
blunting of sensibility. The poet who had shown such fine imagina
tive sympathy for the captive barbarian boy and girl in the od
Icci beatis (I, 29) now mentions the courage of the Rhaetians i
defence of their freedom merely as enhancing the prowess of th
young Tiberius:

> Spectandus in certamine Martio
> deuota morti pectora liberae
> quantis fatigaret ruinis.[1]

And the mission of Rome, 'dare iura', is forgotten as he describe
with bloody relish how the young man had 'made a solitude an
called it peace':

> ...ut barbarorum Claudius agmina
> ferrata uasto diruit impetu
> primosque et extremos metendo
> strauit humum sine clade uictor.[2]

But it would be ungracious to end this account of his characte
on a note of criticism. He may have had lapses from good tast
and feeling; he may have been a trifle complacent, a shade to
egotistical. But he had so many qualities on the credit side beside
his incomparable gift of eloquence—wit, humour, intelligence, goo
sense, affection, kindness, loyalty, tact. These are the qualities whic
the best of the Romans admired, summing them up as *urbanit*
when they were of the mind, *humanitas* when they were of the sou
And Horace had them in such perfect balance that he wins admira
tion as well as love.

1 IV, 14, 17 ff.: 'A sight to behold in the martial strife, with such devasta
tion did he bring low breasts sworn to die a free man's death.'
2 Ll. 29 ff.: '...how Claudius with mighty onset laid low the iron-cla
ranks of the barbarians and mowing down first and last strewed the groun
a victory without loss.'

CHAPTER IV

ATTITUDE TO POETRY

A POET'S views on his own art, and on his own merits as a practitioner, can hardly fail to be interesting, even though they may be fallacious guides in forming an estimate of is work. What is the essence of poetry? Why do I write it? What rinciples do I consciously follow? How do I stand in relation to iy contemporaries and predecessors? All these questions were raised y Horace, and not always answered in a manner consonant with is own practice. Wordsworth only half obeyed the Preface to *yrical Ballads*: Horace only half obeyed the Epistle to the Pisos.

THE NATURE OF POETRY

'he eternal question of the nature of poetry was approached by Iorace in a lively but tantalising passage, Satires I, 4, 39 ff. It seems iat his satires had been criticised for being unpoetical as well as nkind, and his answer to the first accusation is, that he never .aimed that they were poetry: the presence of metre cannot entitle ie purveyor of matter which is *sermoni propiora* to be called a poet:

> Ingenium cui sit, cui mens diuinior atque os
> magna sonaturum des nominis huius honorem.[1]

ome, he says, has questioned whether Comedy is poetry because, i spite of the metre, neither words nor subject have *acer spiritus uis*. But in any case such vehemence and intensity do not of iemselves make poetry,[2] for the angry father in the comedy does isplay them, yet his words are not poetry; they are simply the

---

1 'To the man who has genius, who has a mind inspired above others id lips framed for noble utterance—to him you may give the honour f that name.'

2 I take it that Horace disagrees with the *reason* given by those who deny iat Comedy is poetry. *Ardens* (48) is the emphatic word, corresponding acer spiritus et uis. For the meaning of *acer* see Auct. *ad Her.* III, 13, 23; ic. *Or.* 109; for *uis*, Cic. *de Or.* I, 255; *Tusc. Disp.* II, 57. M. A. Grant, *ncient Rhetorical Theories of the Laughable*, pp. 132–3.

words any angry man would use. It is the same with satire: take away the metre and restore the natural word-order and you have plain prose, whereas if you do the same to Ennius' lines

> Postquam Discordia taetra
> belli ferratos postes portasque refregit,

you will detect even then the limbs of a poet torn asunder. And here Horace breaks off and turns to meet the second accusation leaving us with a promise to return to the subject elsewhere which he never fulfilled.

But perhaps it is no great matter, for already his remarks have raised doubts. As Wordsworth would have told him, natural words in their natural order, conjoined with rhythm and metre, *may* form poetry of the highest quality. At Rome the difference between colloquial and literary language was greater than it is with us, and this may help to account for Horace's attitude. But it is interesting to note that twenty years or so later, in the Epistle to the Pisos (240 f.), he expressed a different view. The text chosen from Ennius is also curious; for the words seem all to be good prose words, and the *membra* could not, as a matter of fact, have been recognised as belonging to a poet; what makes the phrase poetical, besides the fine alliteration of *postes portasque*, is something else—the personifica-tion of Discordia breaking open the symbolic gates of Janus' temple that were always closed in time of peace.

Roman critics were inclined not to distinguish between poetry and high oratory, both being characterised by a certain impetuosity-*contentio*. Cicero, after citing the opinion that not only Plato, but also Democritus, is more poetic than the comic poets in virtue of this quality and of 'flashes' (*lumina*) of diction, expresses doubt whether there is any point in such an enquiry;[1] and when Horace (Sat. I, 10, 11) contrasts *rhetoris atque poetae* with *urbani* he is classing the high orator and the poet together and distinguishing them from the plain-style orator (*urbanus*).[2] And indeed high oratory in metre would be a fair definition of much that passed for poetry at Rome.

1 *Orator*, 67.
2 See Fiske, *Lucilius and Horace*, pp. 124–6. *Urbanitas* is the recognised quality of the plain style writer.

Horace clearly regarded this quality, the *os magna sonaturum*, as characteristic of the greatest poets. It goes with *ingenium*, as he suggests elsewhere (A.P. 323),

> Graiis *ingenium*, Graiis dedit *ore rotundo*
> Musa loqui.

If you had asked him what poet possessed it above all others, he would probably have answered, 'Pindar':

> Monte decurrens uelut amnis, imbres
> quem super notas aluere ripas,
> feruet immensusque ruit profundo
>   Pindarus ore.[1]

Horace is the first Roman whom we know to have studied Pindar. He echoes him several times in the first three books; but it is in the fourth that he reveals the extent of his admiration. At the outset, in this second ode, he emphasises the risk—*dulce periculum*—of trying to emulate him, a risk that others may be well advised to take, though not himself.[2] That apparently spontaneous effusion, that soaring poetry, was something that Minerva did not grant to him:

> Multa Dircaeum leuat aura cycnum,
> tendit, Antoni, quotiens in altos
> nubium tractus: ego apis Matinae
>   more modoque
>
> Grata carpentis thyma per laborem
> plurimum, circa nemus uuidique
> Tiburis ripas operosa paruus
>   carmina fingo.[3]

Of course his self-depreciation is ironical, but it is clear that he regards Pindar as moving in a higher sphere of poetry altogether. In effect he subscribes to the 'doctrine of the sublime' held by some

1 IV, 2, 5 ff.: 'Like a torrent rushing down from a mountain, which rains have swollen above its accustomed banks, deep-voiced Pindar surges and sweeps on amain.'

2 For the interpretation of this ode see E. Fraenkel, *Horace*, pp. 432 ff.

3 25–32: 'Many a gale uplifts the swan of Dirce so often as he soars, Antonius, to the lofty regions of the clouds: I, like a Matine bee that gathers sweet thyme with much labour, around the grove and slopes of watery Tibur humbly mould wilful songs.'

Hellenistic critics and best known to us from the famous treatise
whose anonymous author we may as well call by the traditiona
name of Longinus.[1] Yet he was not incapable, when he chose, o
writing at least in the grand manner:

> Iam nunc minaci murmure cornuum
> perstringis aures, iam litui strepunt,
>   iam fulgor armorum fugaces
>   terret equos equitumque uoltus.
>
> Audire magnos iam uideor duces
> non indecoro puluere sordidos,
>   et cuncta terrarum subacta
>   praeter atrocem animum Catonis.
>
> Iuno et deorum quisquis amicior
> Afris inulta cesserat impotens
>   tellure uictorum nepotes
>   rettulit inferias Iugurthae.
>
> Quis non Latino sanguine pinguior
> campus sepulcris impia proelia
>   testatur auditumque Medis
>   Hesperiae sonitum ruinae?
>
> Qui gurges aut quae flumina lugubris
> ignara belli? quod mare Dauniae
>   non decolorauere caedes?
>   quae caret ora cruore nostro?[2]

To obtain a special effect Horace has here, as it were, pulled out a
the stops of his organ, playing especially on the rolling '*or*', '*a*

1 See further Immisch, *op. cit.* pp. 41 ff.
2 *Odes*, II, 1, 17 ff.: 'Even now you pierce our ears with the trumpet
threatening din, now the clarions blare, now the glitter of arms terrifies int
rout the horses and the riders' faces. I seem now to hear of great captai
befouled with not inglorious dust and the whole world subdued except th
grim spirit of Cato. Juno, and every god more friendly to Africa that ha
retired powerless to avenge the land, has offered the descendants of th
victors as a sacrifice to the ghost of Jugurtha. What field is not enriche
with Latin blood, bearing witness by its graves to our unhallowed battl
and the crash of the downfall of Italy heard by the Parthians? What floo
what rivers have not known the sorrow of war? What sea has not been dye
with Daunian slaughter? What shore is without our blood?'

nd '*ur*' sounds. And more than that, he has used his imagination; *quitumque uultus* is a fine touch—we see in a flash the faces of the horsemen white as they turn to fly like the face of Darius pursued by Alexander in the famous mosaic at Naples. The suicide of Cato set suddenly against a background of unheroic submission, the ghost of Jugurtha drinking the blood of his enemies' children, even the Parthians on the farthest frontiers of the Empire hearing the crash of Rome—these are the *lumina ingenii* of high poetry. And yet in the last stanza, with a caution to his Muse, he puts such poetry behind him. It was not this that he was born to write.

Let me set beside this another passage, Epistles II, 1, 250 ff. Here again he shows that he is master of the grand manner, and again he makes the great refusal:

> Nec sermones ego mallem
> repentes per humum *quam res componere gestas*
> *terrarumque situs et flumina dicere et arces*
> *montibus impositas et barbara regna tuisque*
> *auspiciis totum confecta duella per orbem*
> *claustraque custodem pacis cohibentia Ianum*
> *et formidatam Parthis te principe Romam,*
> si quantum cuperem possem quoque . . .

Typically Virgilian is the culminating line of this period with its alliteration and its heavy spondees in the middle,

> Et formidatam Parthis te principe Romam,

the extra line that sums up the sense and completes the movement, which Mackail has called the 'overarching superflux'. But having ironically shown what he can do, Horace professes that he cannot do it.

To some extent this refusal was due, I believe, simply to literary fashion. The most refined sensibilities of the Ciceronian Age, men like Caesar, Calvus, Brutus, and (later) Pollio, had reacted against the pomp and grandiosity of the prevailing style—reacted too far, in Cicero's opinion.[1] They would rely, not on a torrent of magni-

---

[1] *Brutus*, passim. Dion. Hal. *Ancient Orators*, Pref.: 'I believe that this great revolution was caused and originated by Rome, the mistress of the world, who compelled entire nations to look to her; Rome, I say, and her nobles, men of high character, excellent administrators, highly cultivated and of fine critical intelligence' (tr. Frank).

loquence, but on directness, wit, humour and the impression ç
sincerity. (The twentieth century has reacted in the same wa
against the nineteenth.) And Horace may well have grown u
with a healthy suspicion of *ampullae et sesquipedalia uerba*.

But there is a more fundamental cause which we shall perceiv
more clearly, perhaps, if we get away from the idea of oratory an
substitute for *contentio* the word 'passion', its counterpart in moder
discussions of the nature of poetry. The 'fine frenzy' of the tru
poet was a familiar conception ever since Democritus 'excluded san
poets from Helicon' and Plato extolled poetic μανία in the *Phaedrus*
'I would confidently maintain', says Longinus, 'that there is n
tone so lofty as that of genuine passion in its right place, when
bursts out enthusiastically as though through some kind of madne
and inspiration and fills the speaker's words with frenzy.'[2] Its 'rigl
place' *par excellence* is lyric poetry, and Horace knew this to be sc
But though on occasion he could feign Dionysiac frenzy, as in tl
remarkably successful odes II, 19 (*Bacchum in remotis*) and III, 2
(*Quo me, Bacche, rapis?*), it *was* feigning, and he preferred to mak
genuine feeling the life-blood of his poetry.

Neither innate temperament nor 'albescens capillus' was, I thinl
the chief reason for this absence of passion: Horace was a seriou
philosopher in the sense that he led the 'examined life'; and tl
whole burden of the philosophies he pondered, those of the He
lenistic Age, was that passion should be damped. Plato himsel
more cautious and Puritanical in the *Republic* than in the *Phaedru*
had used as an argument against tragedy that 'it increases the emc
tions, which ought to be diminished' (606D).[3] The old advic
μηδὲν ἄγαν σπεύδειν, became exalted into a ruling principle. ἀθαυ
μασία, ἀταραξία, ἀπάθεια, ἀλυπία, *nil admirari*—all impulse w;
checked at birth by the philosophies of a tired age that cared fc
safety first; and in Augustan Rome the Civil Wars had set an extr
premium on tranquillity. No voice proclaimed like Blake's th:
'the road of excess leads to the palace of wisdom'.

To be a great poet of passion, like Catullus, entailed living tl
life of a Catullus. Horace faces this fact in the Epistle to the Pisc

1 Horace, *A.P.* 297; *Phaedrus* 244A–245A. Cf. *Ion*, 533E ff.
2 *On the Sublime*, VIII, 4.
3 Cf. Sextus Empiricus, *Adv. Gram.* I, 298 (P. 282). Kroll, *op. cit.* p. 7·

301 ff.). If sane poets are excluded from Helicon: 'What a fool am to purge my bile to the approach of spring; else no one would write finer poetry. But *nothing is worth such a cost.*' The passage is ironical but conveys a genuine feeling, that if it came to a choice between his happiness and his art, he would plump for happiness every time. The choice was pre-determined, in any case, by his nature.

But the true 'Classics', the Greeks of the fifth century, men like Simonides and Thucydides, achieved their sublimity by the austere restraint of emotion, as did the carvers of the funeral στῆλαι at Athens; and it is this quality that we find in Horace's Odes wherever there strong and genuine feeling beneath, as in the poem on the death of Quintilius (1, 24). It is what we should expect from the very negativity of almost all that he has to say;[1] and it is admirably embodied in the slow movement and strict discipline of the Aeolic stanza-forms. With most good poets there is an abundance of feeling, and they are successful only when they succeed in subjecting it to the stringencies of form. With Horace the order and the faultless economy are always there, and he had at his beck and call every device of style; but it required an intensity of feeling above his normal state to quicken his verse into real poetry. The modern poet usually a person of strong emotions seeking to express them because he must; Horace was a man of leisure writing verse in an age when verse-writing was in vogue, who on occasions and on subjects about which he felt strongly came out as a true poet. *Insurgit aliquando*, as Quintilian justly remarked. Though he may reason fervently, like Lucretius and our Metaphysicals, the control of reason never relaxed. At his best he fulfils the conditions of poetry as formulated by Coleridge, the reconciliation of 'a more than usual state of emotion with more than usual order, judgment ever awake and steady self-possession with feeling profound or vehement'.

In lines which I have already quoted (Sat. 1, 4, 43) Horace gives *genium* and *mens diuinior* as the essential quality of the poet. In the Epistle to the Pisos (409) he sensibly shelves the question whether nature or art is the more important: 'I do not see what is the good

[1] Most of the odes are in some sense poems of refusal, dissuasion or deprecation.

of toil without a rich poetic vein or of genius untutored.' But h makes the mistake, common in antiquity and not unknown to-day of mixing up morality with inspiration (309 ff.). To this I sha return when dealing with the function of poetry.

It would seem, then, that Horace had an admiration, not untinge with a trace of irony, for the grand manner in poetry, for sublim effusions, for swans of Dirce, eagles of Zeus and birds of Maeonia song; but his comparison of himself to a busy bee, made as it in a poem designed to excuse himself from writing a laureate od is also ironical. He was aware of his own immortality as few poe have dared to be. The man who could refer to his poems as 'm honores' and could say to a spring,

> Fies nobilium tu quoque fontium
> me dicente —,

had no false modesty at heart. Indeed desire for an immortal nam was his one irrational trait, and it inspired him, like so many othe poets, to some of his finest poetry, particularly in the epilogue to th first three books and the third, sixth, eighth and ninth odes of th fourth book. He seems to feel that he, a 'dumb fish', has somehov entered the Muse's temple by the back door, but that once insid he can hold his own with the legitimate entrants, even with Pinda the swan; it has all happened somehow without his knowing i as though through some outside helper whom he naturally object fies as the Muse herself:

> O testudinis aureae
> 	dulcem quae strepitum, Pieri, temperas,
> O mutis quoque piscibus
> 	donatura cycni, si libeat, sonum,
> Totum muneris hoc tui est
> 	quod monstror digito praetereuntium
> Romanae fidicen lyrae:
> 	quod spiro et placeo, si placeo, tuum est.[1]

[1] IV, 3, 17 ff.: 'O thou Pierian maid that attunest the sweet sounds the golden lyre, O thou that, if thou wilt, canst give even to dumb fish the voice of the swan, it is all thy gift that I am pointed out by the finge of the passers-by as the bard of the Roman lyre: that I have inspiration an please, if please I do, is all thy gift.'

'ARS POETICA': THE FUNCTION OF POETRY

At this point we must pause to consider the nature and bearing of
the Epistle to the Pisos, which has unfortunately come to be known
by the later and question-begging name of 'Ars Poetica'.[1] Round
it has centred the most pronounced activity in Horatian scholarship
during the last twenty years, and no agreement has been reached,
or is likely to be reached, as to its originality and its plan. The
controversy began with a discovery at Herculaneum. There in a
villa, possibly that of Lucius Piso Caesoninus,[2] were found a few
fragmentary columns of Book V of a treatise *On Poems* by
Philodemus,[3] who combined a capacity for composing erotic epigrams of great charm with a love of dry and vigorous polemic.
In these fragments he attacked, among others, one Neoptolemus
of Parium, a writer who had been dead for two hundred years;
and this is of unusual interest because of a remark, long neglected,
which the scholiast Porphyrion prefixed to his notes on Horace's
Epistle to the Pisos. 'He has collected in this poem the precepts of
Neoptolemus of Parium, not all indeed, but the most conspicuous';[4]
or Jensen has claimed to show, even from the scanty fragments of
Neoptolemus which Philodemus picks out to punish, that both
in arrangement and in substance Horace did follow this model.
Rostagni's edition of the 'Ars Poetica'[5] accepted and enlarged upon
this assumption, on which Horace becomes simply the brilliant
'Classicist' exponent of Hellenistic ideas, so that his poem can only
be taken as reflecting his own views and relating to his own poetry
in so far as he chose one treatise rather than another as his model.

But reaction was not long delayed, and in 1932 Immisch published
a commentary[6] emphasising the contemporary bearing of the

1 First so called by Quintilian, VIII, 3, 60.
2 The identification is uncertain: see Rostagni, *op. cit.* p. xxvi, n. 2.
3 Published by C. Jensen, *Abh. d. Berliner Akademie*, 1918, Nr. 14;
Philodemus über die Gedichte (1923).
4 '—in quem librum congessit praecepta Neoptolemi τοῦ Παριανοῦ
e arte poetica, non quidem omnia, sed eminentissima.'
5 *Arte Poetica di Orazio* (1930). The Introduction is especially worth
reading for its elucidation of Epicurean poetic theory as held by Philodemus,
which proves to be remarkably sensible and enlightened. Cf. J. W. H.
Atkins, *Literary Criticism in Antiquity*, II (1934), pp. 55–6.
6 *Horazens Epistel über die Dichtkunst* (*Philologus*, Supplementband XXIV,
Pt. 3).

'eclogae', or selected subjects, which Horace chose to treat. Ac
cording to him Horace was actually a member of the eclectic Ne
Academy during his residence at Athens;[1] but while his own ide
of poetry, like the academic Cicero's ideas of rhetoric, were coloure
by those of the school,[2] the Epistle to the Pisos is no less topic
and no less a personal expression of views than Cicero's rhetoric
works.[3] It was through the Academy that he could have come t
know Neoptolemus' work.

No justice can be done to Immisch's learned arguments in a boo
such as this, but an opinion must be given. His view that the poem
is not founded simply on Neoptolemus has been strengthened b
a change of view on the part of Jensen himself, who now attribut
less of the quotations in Philodemus to Neoptolemus than he d
originally.[4] And to some extent he has vindicated Horace from th
charge of refurbishing anachronistic wares. But the chief questio
he had to answer was, why did Horace choose only one type
poetry to discuss, and that the drama,[5] and why did he devote thir
lines (220-50) to the Satyr-play, a form unknown, if not also u
thinkable, at Rome? Even if we were to accept his theory (it is i
more than a theory) that Augustus was anxious to revive the dram
above all, can we really suppose that the Satyric drama, a plant th
sprang peculiarly from Greek soil, was to be included?[6] It is f
easier to believe that Horace devoted space to this, and to the dram
in general, because drama was the form that chiefly interested th
principal literary critics of the Hellenistic age, the Peripatetics, who
fountain-head was the *Poetics* of Aristotle. There are also some deta

1 P. 26.   2 Pp. 27 ff.

3 On Cicero's *De Oratore* and Horace's *Ars Poetica* see G. C. Fiske an
M. A. Grant, *Harvard Studies*, xxxv, 1924, pp. 1 ff.; *Univ. of Wiscons
Studies*, No. 27, 1929.

4 *Sitz. Berl. Akad.* 1936, pp. 292-320.

5 Why not his own special province of lyric, or the fashionable epi
Immisch discusses the question, pp. 7 ff., 139 ff. His explanation hard
carries conviction. Dating the work, partly on this very ground, as ear
as 20/19 B.C., he suggests that it would have been an impertinence for Hora
to publish rules for Epic at a time when, as everyone knew, Virgil was
work on the *Aeneid*.

6 Immisch, *op. cit.* pp. 139-58. Satyric drama and stage music were,
the other hand, favourite topics of discussion in the early Hellenistic peric
Atkins, *op. cit.* 1, p. 160. See further Rostagni, *op. cit.* p. 64 n.

in the poem which are certainly borrowed from Neoptolemus, and not a few which betray an origin neither Roman nor contemporary.[1] The personality of the Pisos affects it no more than that of Memmius affects the *De Rerum Natura*, though the elder boy seems to have had the itch to write.

Perhaps we should not be far wrong if we characterised the 'Ars Poetica' in some such terms as these: in form it is an Epistle, addressed nominally to Piso and his two sons, though really, and at times openly, to the reading public in general;[2] but in essence it is a *sermo*, a piece treating of a single general subject but gliding from one selected aspect to another by a natural process of thought-association just as we do in conversation, the lack of strict arrangement being intentional;[3] both in matter and treatment, it is strongly influenced by Hellenistic works, if not by a single treatise, so that the selection of topics is not necessarily indicative of the poet's own interests; on the other hand we may presume that he consulted authorities with whom he was in sympathy.[4]

The Romans, notoriously an unphilosophic race, were more interested in examples than in generalisations. In art they excelled in vividly individualised portraiture, whereas the Greeks pursued

1 *Ib.* pp. 23 ff.; W. Kroll, *Sokrates*, VI, 1918, pp. 81 ff. K. Latte, *Hermes*, LX (1925), pp. 1 ff. A notable example is the mention of *male* hired mourners; these were a feature of Alexandrian, not Roman, funerals. At l. 357 Horace gives as example of a bad poet the obscure Choerilus of the *fourth century*.

2 E.g. l. 38.

3 Heinsius and others were mistaken in trying to introduce order by transpositions.

4 Scholars are still discussing whether the poem has any plan. E. Norden (*Hermes*, XL, 1905, pp. 481–525) discerned one analogous to that of Hellenistic handbooks on other arts, with two parts entitled 'Ars' and 'Artifex'. Jensen (*Neoptolemos und Horaz*) found traces of a tripartite arrangement in Neoptolemus; and Immisch gives the three divisions as, *poesis* (general precepts) 1–152, *poemata* (the recognised *genres*) 153–294, *poeta* 295–end (*ib.* p. 20). W. Steidle (*Studien zur A.P. des Horaz*, 1939) reverts to Norden's two divisions (1–294, 295–end), and even so the distinction is hard to maintain; thus 335–340, if not also 347–365, are a trespass of 'ars' on 'artifex'. See Vahlen's criticisms of Norden's theory, *Sitz. Berlin. Akad.* 1906, pp. 589 ff., esp. p. 613. Klingner (*Ber. Sächs. Akad.*, Bd. 88, H. 3, 1936) finds one main thread, 'Amateur poets and the art of poetry'; others would say it was the doctrine of appropriateness, τὸ πρέπον, *decorum* (L. Labowsky, *Der Begriff es πρέπον in der Ethik des Panaitios*, 1934). See now C. O. Brink, *Horace on Poetry* (1963); G. Williams, *J.R.S.* 1964, pp. 186–96.

the ideal. In poetry they excelled in didactic, illuminating with images and colour drawn from their own experience the genera precepts they inherited from the Greeks. It is not enough fo Lucretius to assert simply the well-known fact that things become worn away imperceptibly by time: he gives us a series of pictures 'moreover with many revolutions of the sun's year a ring on the finger is worn away underneath, the dripping of water hollows ou a stone, the curved ploughshare in the fields diminishes unperceived we notice how the paving of streets is worn away by the footstep of men; and bronze statues set at doorways have their hands wor away by the frequent touching of them that kiss and them tha pass by'.[1] It is this quality which illuminates the *Georgics* with so many vivid Italian landscapes; and it is this which makes the Epistl to the Pisos such lively reading.[2] I believe that Horace se out to amuse at least as much as to instruct, and we shoul bear this constantly in mind when we are tempted to take th poem too seriously. The details, not the precepts, are the cream τὸ πάρεργον κρεῖττον τοῦ ἔργου. If didactic purpose had bee uppermost, he would surely have been at pains to make his wor more methodical.

The fame and influence of this jaunty Epistle have been out o all proportion to its merits as literary criticism. Stripped of it trimmings, what does it teach in its 476 lines? The precepts ar not many, and I will enumerate them because, amid the dust o controversy, it is well to keep in view what the poet does in fac say. Baldly speaking they are as follows:

(1) *Poems should be homogeneous.*   (1–23

(2) *Do not carry good tendencies to excess.*   (24–31

---

1 I, 311 ff. Cf. I, 159 ff., illuminating a generalisation of Epicurus (Diog Laert. x, 38).

2 E.g. The characterisation of the ages of man (ll. 158–74). (Note th Horace includes small children, though they seldom appeared as characte in plays.) Macaulay remarks in his Essay on Bunyan, 'there can be n stronger sign of a mind truly poetic than a disposition to reverse th abstracting process and make individuals out of generalities'. This facult may not be *essentially* poetic, but it is extremely valuable in enlivening lon poems which are bound to have what Coleridge called 'flats between th heights'.

(3) *Good detail cannot redeem a bad whole.* (32–37)

(4) *Choose a subject within your powers.* (38–41)

(5) *Arrange your material carefully.* (42–45)

(6) *Common words in uncommon association are good.* (46–48), cf. 240–3

(7) *New words may be coined (when needed, and with discretion); Usage is the final judge of words.* (49–72)

(8) *Each form has its proper metre.* (73–92)

(9) *But the words and tone must suit the situation and speaker.* (93–118)

10) *Characters, if traditional, must conform to tradition; if new, they must be self-consistent.* (119–127)

11) *A traditional subject is safest, but it must not be treated slavishly.* (128–135)

12) *Do not begin with what should be a climax.* (136–145)

13) *Select and recast one episode from the saga.* (146–152)

14) *Remember the age of your characters.* (153–178)

15) *Keep violent action off the stage.* (179–188)

16) *Have five acts and three actors; and divine intervention only where necessary.* (189–192)

17) *The Chorus should be 'an actor', and on the side of the angels.* (193–201)

18) *Music should be only a soft accompaniment.* (202–219)

19) *Even in Satyr-plays vary your diction to suit the characters.* (220–250)

20) *Be careful over metre, and indeed in all your art.* (251–308)

21) *'Sapientia' (implying high morals) is the secret of writing well.* (309–334)

22) *Be brief in your precepts.* (335–337)

23) *Fictions should be credible.* (338–340)

24) *The best poems edify as well as delight.* (341–346)

25) *We should not always demand impeccability.* (347–365)

26) *But an artistically mediocre poet is intolerable.* (366–407)

27) *Both genius and art are essential, but art is too often neglected.* (408–418)

28) *Make use of candid critics.* (419–452)

29) *Shun the mad poet.* (453–end)

It will be seen that most of the precepts are sensible enough, thoug rather obvious to us. Behind many stands the authority of Aristotl Some, like the prescription of five acts for a play, are mere fossilisations of post-Aristotelian tradition. The most fundamental, whic are also the most debatable, are (21) and (24), a complementar pair; and they alone shall be treated here. They assert that soun morality based on moral 'wisdom' is the first essential for poet,[1] and that the best poems are those which edify as well please.

This idea of literature can be traced to the age of the Sophists and is found at its extreme in Plato's *Republic*. Aristotle set again it (for tragedy) his theory of *catharsis*, but the germ of its futur revival may be discerned in the *Poetics*, where it is said that poetr is more philosophic and serious than history since it treats of th universal, not the particular.[3] For this profound and true observa tion might suggest to shallower *epigonoi* that poetry should useful in a more direct way. And so it happened. We find Phil demus' Hellenistic victim maintaining that 'the virtue of poetr consists in the true representation of reality, *which is of itself instru tive and educative*'.[4] It followed too that the good poet (or orato must be a good man, a view implied in Plato's *Gorgias* and Isocrate *Antidosis* (277) and taught by the Stoics. 'An orator', said Cat 'is a good man skilled in speaking.' 'It is impossible', said Strab 'to be a good poet without first being a good man.'[5]

To the utilitarian minds of the Romans this doctrine was sure appeal. There is no better illustration of its effect than Quintilian judgment on Alcaeus: 'In his political poems he contributes muc to morality; but he descends to trifles *and love-poetry*, though f for higher things.'[6] The evidence for its prevalence in the Graeco Roman world is considerable, but these few examples must suffic

1 'Scribendi recte sapere est et principium et fons.' The parallel passag on oratory in Cicero (*Orator*, 70) asserts: 'Est eloquentiae sicut reliquarur rerum fundamentum sapientia.'

2 See esp. Aristophanes, *Frogs*, 1008 ff.

3 IX, 3. Rostagni, *op. cit.* pp. xlv ff.

4 Περὶ ποιημάτων, v, fr. 2 (Jensen), p. 7. This harks back to the Platon doctrine that virtue is knowledge.

5 I, 2, 5. Longinus, IX, 3; Tacitus, *Dialogus* 31.

6 X, 1, 63. Cf. Cicero in Seneca, *Epistles*, 49, 5; Strabo, I, 1, 19.

Let us now turn to the passage in which Horace expounds it (309 ff.):

> Scribendi recte sapere est et principium et fons.
> rem tibi Socraticae poterunt ostendere chartae,
> uerbaque prouisam rem non inuita sequentur.
> qui didicit patriae quid debeat et quid amicis,
> quo sit amore parens, quo frater amandus et hospes,
> quod sit conscripti, quod iudicis officium, quae
> partes in bellum missi ducis, ille profecto
> reddere personae scit conuenientia cuique.
> respicere exemplar uitae morumque iubebo
> doctum imitatorem et uiuas hinc ducere uoces.[1]

'Rem' in the second line is odd. It can hardly mean that the dramatist should actually take his *matter* from the writings of the followers of Socrates; it must mean that these are the sort of works that teach observation of human nature and instil the right attitude to life, the true morality, which the poet must reflect.[2] But what are we to make of the next remark, that he who has learnt what is the *duty* of man in every station

> reddere personae scit conuenientia cuique?

If it means that he will be a good delineator of character, it is plain nonsense; if on the other hand it means that he will be a delineator of good character, that may be so (if we accept the principle that 'who drives fat oxen should himself be fat'), but his play is not likely to be the better for that. The idea that dramatic characters

---

1 'Wisdom is the first principle and source of good writing. The Socratic literature will be able to guide you as to subject, and subject once envisaged, the words will follow easily. Whosoever has learnt what he owes to his country and friends, what love he should have for parent, for brother and guest, what is the duty of a senator and a judge, and what the part of a general sent to the wars, he knows therewith how to give the proper treatment to each character. I will bid the represer who has learnt this to look at life and conduct for his pattern and thence derive the language of life.'

2 The next line is not so irrelevant as it might seem. The corollary of Cato's remark 'orator est uir bonus dicendi peritus' was his 'rem tene, uerba sequentur': literature has a serious purpose, and the art that commends the subject should not be sought for its own sake. This was the Stoic view.

should be 'good' (χρηστά) was once indeed countenanced by
Aristotle himself[1]—there is no getting away from it—but Horace'
exposition of it here is a sufficient *reductio ad absurdum*. One canno
help suspecting that he has really confused the two meanings o
conueniens (πρέπον)—moral and dramatic propriety.

The poet, then, must be virtuous, and it is but one step furthe
to say that his poems should be edifying:

> Aut prodesse uolunt aut delectare poetae
> aut simul et iucunda et idonea dicere uitae…
> omne tulit punctum qui miscuit utile dulci
> lectorem delectando pariterque monendo.[2]

The principle of simple mathematical addition as applied to ar
is no more valid here than in lines 341–2, where it is assumed tha
the best work will appeal to all classes of spectator, the elderly
for instance (*centuriae seniorum*), and the haughty young knight
(*celsi Ramnes*).[3]

So long as Horace simply postulates for his poet the *mens diuinior*
he might hold his own. In the words of Milton: 'He who would
not be frustrate of his hope to write well hereafter in laudable things
ought himself to be a true poem.'[4] And if life is 'three parts conduct', then most poems are likely to bear on conduct and so, in a
sense, to be useful, as every widening or deepening of experience
is useful. But this quality is not an *essential*. Thus while Shelley
was an intensely moral poet, Keats was remarkably non-moral; ye
even if we refuse the highest merit to the description of scenery
in the *Ode to Autumn*, are we to refuse it to the description of moods

---

1 *Poetics*, xv. See Butcher, p. 327 f.

2 Ll. 333–4, 343–4: 'Poets wish either to benefit or to delight, or at
once to say things pleasing and helpful in life.…He wins every vote who
mingles the useful with the pleasant, equally delighting and admonishing
the reader.'

3 Victor Hugo made the same mistake when he divided audiences into
(1) Thinkers, who demand characterisation, (2) Women, who demand
passion, (3) The mob, which demands action, and concluded that every
great play should satisfy all three. The orators with their λόγος πρὸς τοὺς
ἀκροατάς may have influenced Horace. *Si plausoris eges* (l. 154) points the
same way.

4 *Apology for Smectymnuus*. E. M. W. Tillyard, p. 361.

in the *Ode to the Nightingale*?[1] We need not deny that there are poems which are successful by arousing in us emotions which are largely moral. Such is the Regulus ode (III, 5), in which our poetic pleasure is bound up with our admiration for the hero's courage. But even morality in its deepest and most spontaneous form need not be involved. And as for *conventional* morality, if we may define it as a tissue of repressions of primitive instincts which has been evolved by society for its own protection, it is unlikely to evoke the deepest emotions in individuals.[2]

In siding with the moralists Horace was not simply accepting a universal belief of his age. We are too apt to talk glibly of the 'ancient view' of this and that when we mean simply the majority view, or the view of which we have heard most because it was put forward by writers who have survived through literary merit or sheer accident. Aristotle was not the only Greek who attributed to poetry a non-moral function. Eratosthenes asserted that every poet aimed at charming, not instructing, which was certainly the case at Alexandria.[3] Still more important for our present inquiry is the attitude of those whose views are reflected by Philodemus, the philosophic mentor of the poets who later formed Maecenas' circle. He declared roundly that it was not the function of poems to be profitable;[4] and that even when they were so, it was not *qua* poetry.[5] Now it is quite probable that Horace knew Philodemus,[6] and was aware

1 'We dislike a poem', said Keats, 'which has a palpable design upon us.'

2 Here I must disagree entirely with Campbell's thesis in his *Horace* (see esp. pp. 54–5). I do not think that the 'moral sense' is analogous to the other senses; it is, to begin with, so much younger and less 'instinctive'; and to make it the basis of a whole theory of poetry is to neglect the many masterpieces which can only be called 'moral' by begging the question. And how *good* a man, by ordinary moral standards, was Catullus or Propertius or Villon or Marlowe or Verlaine or Baudelaire or Swinburne? But the problem is obviously too large for discussion here.

3 ποιητὴν ἔφη πάντα στοχάζεσθαι ψυχαγωγίας, οὐ διδασκαλίας: Strabo, I, 2, 3. Horace did indeed assume that the object of poetry was to please, *oblectare* (*A.P.* 321). But he suggests that it pleases *by* edifying (319–22), whereas Philodemus said bluntly οὐκ ἔστι τέρπειν δι' ἀρετήν (Jensen, *op. cit.* p. 7).

4 εἰ δὲ ὡς ἐπὶ παιδείαν ζητῶ. περὶ ποιημάτων, v (Jensen), p. 7.

5 κἄν ὠφελῇ, καθὸ ποιήματ' οὐκ ὠφελεῖ, col. 29, ll. 18 ff. On the whole subject see Rostagni, *op. cit.* pp. lxxxiii–cvii.

6 See Rostagni, *op. cit.* p. xxvii.

that he disagreed violently with Neoptolemus; we may therefore suppose that he chose his model for the Epistle with his eyes open. And this brings us to the question, how far Horace's practice conformed to this theory of the moral function of poetry.[1]

Insueuit pater optimus hoc me: Horace tells us (Sat. I, 4, 105 ff.) that it was his father who taught him the habit of observing the virtues and faults of individuals. That sounds like the truth. And when he translated his observations into satire, he defended his work on the ground that it was 'fair comment on matters of public interest', like the Old Comedy and Lucilian Satire (*ib.* 1–6). Even Congreve, when pressed, claimed that he benefited society by his comedies; but was that his object in writing them? Horace, on his own showing, was not so public-spirited as to court unpopularity by public recitations (*ib.* 23); his object was surely to entertain a circle of friends by an amusing form of literature, whose ultimate motive is presumably amiable *Schadenfreude*, not missionary zeal. Juvenal enjoyed being indignant, Horace enjoyed mocking. *Risi, iocosius, risu diducere rictum*—these are the terms in which he speaks of Satire. Barton Holyday, a seventeenth-century critic, protested that 'a perpetual grin, like that of Horace, doth rather anger than amend a man'. Much he would have cared! When he represents Trebatius in Satires II, I as scolding him for writing satire, his defence is that it pleases him to write verse in the style of Lucilius, not that he is a public benefactor: indeed he would prefer to keep his sharp edge solely for self-defence (39–42).

The Epodes are in a different case. True, the 'genuine moral *reasonableness*' discovered in them by Campbell[2] is not visible to the naked eye, and the attacks on individuals, with the dubious exception of the fantastic Canidia, cannot seriously claim to be in the public interest. On the other hand there does emerge in a few pieces (VII, IX and XVI) an anxiety for the condition of Rome and a feeling that a poet may speak of this to his countrymen at large. The *poeta* is becoming *uates* once more.

1 Horace's statement at *A.P.* 86–7 that a poet must observe the 'colour' appropriate to each metrical form is patently belied by his practice. See R. K. Hack, *The Doctrine of Literary Forms*, in *Harvard Studies*, XXVII, 1916, pp. 27 ff.; W. Kroll, *op. cit.* pp. 209 ff.

2 *Op. cit.* p. 92. It is interesting to note that Quintilian considered that Horace needed expurgation if he was to be read in schools: I, 8, 6.

As the avowed priest of the Muses Horace comes forward in the first stanza of Book III of the Odes, usurping the priestly versicles 'procul este, profani' and 'fauete linguis', and he addresses himself to the future hope of the nation:

> Odi profanum uolgus et arceo.
> fauete linguis. carmina non prius
>   audita Musarum sacerdos
>   uirginibus puerisque canto.[1]

The six odes that follow, and a number of others in Books I–III, are in this vein. They are evidence of the new prestige of poetry under Augustus and of Horace's public spirit and sense of responsibility.[2] But their relative weight is sometimes exaggerated. Not only are they numerically quite a small proportion: their total effect is by no means predominant in the impression made by a reading of the first three books as a whole. The other odes, miscellaneous as they are, constitute the main fare; they cannot be treated simply as relief or padding. And even though many of these are couched in terms of advice,[3] this is often a mere disguise for self-expression.[4]

It was in the period that followed their publication in 23 B.C. that Horace became a serious student of moral philosophy. He tells us so in the first Epistle:

> Nunc itaque et uersus et cetera ludicra pono;
> quid uerum atque decens curo et rogo et omnis in hoc sum;
> condo et compono quae mox depromere possim.[5]

'Depromere' suggests that he intends to write again when he has set his philosophic house in order. This new state of mind corre-

---

1 'I abhor the unhallowed throng and bid it keep afar. Hold your peace. The Muses' priest, I sing songs unheard before for girls and boys.'

2 The defence of poets in the *Epistle to Augustus* (II, 1, 118–38) is not to be taken so seriously; Horace rakes together anything he can think of that might show an assumption that poets are useful to the state.

3 It is worth noting that Alcaeus had given such advice in his poems: fr. 73, ἀλλ' ἄγι, μὴ μεγάλων ἐπιβάλλεο.

4 E.g. I, 7; 9; 11; 13; 24; 33.

5 Ll. 10–12: 'Now, therefore, I am laying aside verse and all other such trifling; what is right and seemly—that is my study and inquiry and all my thought. I am storing up and gathering material that I may soon produce.'

sponds well with the standpoint of the Epistle to the Pisos, which may, as Immisch thinks, have been begun about this time:

> Scribendi recte sapere est et principium et fons.[1]

There is no need to suppose that this principle was more than spasmodically in his mind before his fortieth year. The second and sixth Epistles are specimen products of his new resolution; but it cannot be said to have heralded any fundamental change in his work or character—only the development of his more serious side at the expense of youthful spontaneity. It may, however, have accounted for his choosing Neoptolemus as the chief model of the Epistle to the Pisos in spite of the damaging criticisms of Philodemus.

TRADITION

In most ages poets have made free of what Seneca called the 'commonalty of letters'; Chaucer plundered the *Roman de la Rose*; Shakespeare versified considerable passages of North's Plutarch; and Coleridge drew on amazingly variegated sources in creating that most original of poems, *The Ancient Mariner*.[2] But Greek and Roman writers went further than modern; they had no law, and very little sense, of copyright,[3] and most of them did not prize originality of subject. If a poet preferred to treat a traditional theme, the test was whether he could transfigure it by his own individual treatment—ἡ ἰδία κατασκευή, as Philodemus called it.[4] This Classical principle was formulated by Isocrates in the fourth century: 'I believe that the study of oratory as well as the other arts would be much improved if we admired and honoured, not those who aspire to speak about subjects never treated before, but those who speak in a way that others cannot emulate.'[5]

At Rome especially the imitation of specific models was common, since Roman literature emerged but slowly from its original role of transmitting Greek. One instance from Horace will suffice

1 Cf. *Ep.* II, 2, 141: 'Nimirum sapere est abiectis utile nugis.' Rostagni, *op. cit.* pp. cx–cxii.

2 See J. Livingstone Lowes, *Convention and Revolt* and *The Road to Xanadu*, the latter a unique study of a poet's psychological processes.

3 For a good example see Seneca, *De Ben.* VII, 6, 1.

4 Horace states the principle at *A.P.* 131 ff. (*Publica materies*, etc.).

5 *Panegyricus*, 10.

to show how even a record of personal experience could be invaded by traditional matter. In 37 B.C. he made a journey to Brundisium in company with Maecenas, Virgil and others. Yet when he described it in Satires I, 5, although his fellow-travellers would be the kernel of his audience, he introduced two incidents that came, as they all knew, from Lucilius' account of *his* journey to the Sicilian Straits![1]

The fact that Horace, like Virgil, used traditional matter freely is too well known to need discussion here, but the way in which he used it, and his remarks on the subject, are worth attention. In the nineteenth Epistle he defends himself against the taunts that the Epodes were unoriginal, claiming that although, like Sappho and Alcaeus, he borrowed metre and spirit from Archilochus, he did not copy his subject-matter.[2] As far as we can tell this is substantially true; but, as Leo has shown,[3] the *mise en scène* of several of the poems was suggested by his model; and in the Odes he used Alcaeus and others in the same way. In the great political odes he invested the form of the Lesbian personal lyric with the dignity of Greek choral lyric. Occasionally he wrote a poem consciously in the manner of some poet, as I, 15 (*Pastor cum traheret*) is in the manner of Bacchylides, IV, 4 (*Qualem ministrum*) in that of Pindar; occasionally he wrote one corresponding more closely, without being an actual paraphrase, to a Lesbian original, such as I, 10 (*Mercuri facunde*) and I, 14 (*O nauis, referent*), which recall poems of Alcaeus;[4] but more often he adapted a line or two from the Greek to start his poem and then developed the theme on lines of his own, giving it ἡ ἰδία κατασκευή, as in I, 9 (*Vides ut alta*) and I, 37 (*Nunc est bibendum*).[5] The audience, *doctus utriusque linguae*, would enjoy spotting the reminiscences, and they served to create the desired

---

[1] The contest of the *scurrae*, where even the details are borrowed, and the incident in ll. 82–5 (Fiske, *op. cit.* p. 308). Tenney Frank (*Catullus and Horace*, p. 179), in belittling the extent of Lucilius' influence, omits just those incidents common to both pieces which cannot be dismissed as coincidence.

[2] Ll. 19–34.

[3] *De Horatio et Archilocho* (1900).

[4] Fr. 2 and 30 D.

[5] Fr. 90 and 39 D. All this has been amply demonstrated by Pasquali in his great work *Orazio Lirico*. See esp. pp. 104 ff.

atmosphere for the poem:[1] thus the cry of triumph over Cleopatra's fall echoes Alcaeus' joy at the overthrow of the tyrant Myrsilus For us Horace's poems are a sufficient achievement in themselves but he himself took pride especially in having introduced new metres with their wedded forms to Latin Literature:

> Libera per uacuum posui uestigia princeps,
> non aliena meo pressi pede. qui sibi fidit
> dux reget examen. Parios ego primus iambos
> ostendi Latio....[2]

and again:

> Princeps Aeolium carmen ad Italos
> deduxisse modos.[3]

His mastery of the Lesbian metres, which seems so effortless, probably cost him more toil than we should suspect.

Let us now consider as specimens two of the longer odes which illustrate respectively the confined and the free use of tradition the Epinicion for Drusus (IV, 4) and the Archytas ode (I, 28) When asked by Augustus to write in praise of his stepson Horace' thoughts naturally turned to Pindar. One suspects that the task wa not altogether congenial, and rather than strike out on a line of hi own the poet settled down to the facile but dangerous alternative o reproducing the Pindaric form.[4] What, he seems to have asked himself, is the recipe for a Pindaric epinicion in honour of a boy victor? We must have a long and involved sentence, so he start off with one of twenty-eight lines, unparalleled in the Odes. W must have a simile about an eagle, so that is put in the forefront Pindar would have a discursive parenthesis, with a γνώμη of naïv

1 We have here the rudiments of T. S. Eliot's elaborate technique. had already been employed by the Greeks. Reitzenstein, *Neue Jahrb.* 1922 p. 26.

2 'I planted free footsteps first on virgin soil, it was no other's domai that I trod. He who trusts himself will be leader and king of the hiv I first displayed Parian iambics to Latium....'

3 '(I shall be said) to have been the first to compose Aeolian songs t Italian music.' Catullus composed two poems in Sapphics, but these ar hardly enough to invalidate Horace's claim (*Odes*, III, 30, 13–14).

4 He knew the hazard, for a few years earlier he had spoken of or Titius (*Ep.* I, 3, 10):

> 'Pindarici fontis qui non expalluit haustus.'

iety attached, so we are given a few lines which would indeed
be admirable as burlesque if we could take them as such:

> ...Vindelici (quibus
> mos unde deductus per omne
> tempus Amazonia securi
>
> Dextras obarmet quaerere distuli;
> nec scire fas est omnia)....[1]

Pindar could 'get away with' such sentiments in a way denied to
poets of a more sophisticated age.) Next the father (or trainer) is
duly praised, and the inevitable question of φύσις and μάθησις,
inborn talent and training, broached. Finally we come to the 'myth'
recounting the heroic deeds of the boy's ancestor, Claudius Nero,
the victor of the Metaurus.[2] Here Horace lets himself go and for
nine stanzas[3] pours out some of the finest rhetoric he wrote, which
almost redeems the poem from its initial frigidity.

The championship of the claims of *doctrina* as being necessary for
the development of *uis insita* is Horatian, being in fact a departure
from Pindar's haughty standpoint; it corresponds to the emphasis
on *ars* as the necessary adjunct to *ingenium* that we find in the Epistle
to the Pisos. The way in which Augustus is thus worked in as
trainer and the conversion of the story of Claudius Nero into an
eulogy of Rome are most skilful. But the ode as a whole remains
tour de force, with the ingenuity and competence of a prize poem
and none of the spontaneity of Horace's best work.

The other ode, I, 28, is on a higher level of poetry, its subject
being nearer to Horace's heart, and for this reason I will quote it
in full. Unfortunately the *mise en scène* is rather obscure to us, as
in Epode IX, though in reciting the poet would be able to make it
all clear. Most scholars are now agreed that it is a dramatic mono-

1 'The Vindelici (the origin of whose age-long custom of arming
their hands with the Amazonian axe I have deferred inquiring; nor is
it right to know everything).' These lines are of a piece with the rest of
the Pindaric pastiche, and scholars who bracketed them as spurious had no
justification.

2 Hannibal's speech, as Heinze points out, is more Epic than Pindaric
in its affinities.

3 The final stanza is surely the poet's closing comment, not part of
Hannibal's speech.

logue; but the train of thought, and in particular the connection
between lines 1–20 and 21–36, is not transparent. One important
clue, discovered by Wilamowitz and followed more whole-heartedly
by Oates,[1] is the influence of Simonides. Let us take this as our
starting-point and try to trace the association of ideas by which
Horace may have come to write the ode; for in this case the difficulties can so be best explained.

Let us suppose that Horace conceived the idea of a dactylic poem
on his favourite subject, human mortality, perhaps having in mind
some words of Simonides to which we will recur. To start with,
there were two *communes loci* of funeral-elegy ready at hand, the
vanity of even the noblest gifts and actions to save a man from
death,[2] and the recollection of greater men who have died. These
old ideas had been expanded by Lucretius at the climax of his Third
Book, where the famous names of Ancus,[3] Xerxes, the Scipios,
Homer and Democritus lead up to Epicurus himself. Searching for
a suitable name Horace hit upon Archytas of Tarentum, mathema-
tician, astronomer and friend of Plato, whose grave by the Matine
shore in his own Apulia must have been a familiar sight to him.
Archytas was a Pythagorean, a believer in survival by transmigra-
tion; thus a hint of irony creeps in; but I do not think that it is
right to find it in the first six lines; these, like their parallels in the
Consolationes, suggest only 'the pity of it':[4] for all his genius and
sublime pursuits Archytas perished like any other:

> Te maris et terrae numeroque carentis harenae
> mensorem cohibent, Archyta,

1 Wilamowitz, *De Tribus Carminibus Latinis* (1893); W. J. Oates, *The
Influence of Simonides of Ceos upon Horace* (1932), ch. II. In what follows
I accept Oates' view of the genesis of the poem. See, however, the criticism
of F. Jacoby, *Gnomon*, 1934, pp. 483 ff.

2 Cf. Prop. III, 18, 27; IV, 11, 11; *Consol. ad. Liviam*, 41 ff.; Ovid, *Am.* III
9, 19. For the oratorical *Consolationes* see M. Siebourg, *Neue Jahrbücher*
1910, p. 267.

3 1025 ff. Ancus' name in this context at *Odes*, IV, 7, 15 must be a reminiscence of Lucretius or of a common source. The earliest example of this
locus is in Homer, *Il.* XXI, 106 ff.:

> ἀλλά, φίλος, θάνε καὶ σύ· τίη ὀλοφύρεαι οὕτως;
> κάτθανε καὶ Πάτροκλος, ὅ περ σέο πολλὸν ἀμείνων.

4 Cf. esp. Simmias' beautiful epitaph for Sophocles, *A.P.* VII, 21.

Pulueris exigui prope litus parua Matinum
    munera, nec quidquam tibi prodest
Aerias temptasse domos animoque rotundum
    percurrisse polum morituro.[1]

Horace adds other great names, choosing those whom legend
credited with approaching to immortality, and ending with the most
significant for his purpose, the type of all believers in survival,
Archytas' own master, Pythagoras. Pythagoras claimed to be the
reincarnation of a hero who fought at Troy, Euphorbus son of
Panthus, and 'proved' it by identifying Euphorbus' shield among
those hung up in the Heraeum of Argos; the shield was taken down
and the name found on the back. Curtly the whole legend is dismissed, not without some irony at The Master's expense:[2]

Occidit et Pelopis genitor, conuiua deorum,
    Tithonusque remotus in auras
Et Iouis arcanis Minos admissus, habentque
    Tartara Panthoiden, iterum Orco
Demissum, quamuis clipeo Troiana refixo
    tempora testatus nihil ultra
Neruos atque cutem morti concesserat atrae,
    iudice te non sordidus auctor
Naturae uerique. *sed omnes una manet nox*
    et calcanda semel uia leti.[3]

1 'Thou the measurer of sea and earth and the countless grains of
sand, art confined, Archytas, in a scanty tribute of a little dust beside
the Matine shore, nor does it aught avail thee that thou didst explore
the mansions of heaven and traverse its vault with thy mind, being
mortal.'

2 Cf. *Sat.* II, 6, 63: *faba Pythagorae cognata*.

3 'The father of Pelops died, that feasted with the gods, and Tithonus
that was borne up into the air, and Minos that was admitted to the secret
counsels of Jupiter; and Tartarus holds the son of Panthus sent down again
to the Underworld, although, having given proof of his presence at Troy
when the shield was taken down, he had claimed to yield nothing save
flesh and sinews to dark death—in thy judgment no mean authority on
nature and truth. But one same night awaits us all, and once for all the
way of death must be trod.' (N.B. Tithonus' bid for immortality, not his
shrinkage into a cicala, is in point here.)

This thought is strikingly expressed in two fragments of Simonides 8 and 9D, especially the former:

πάντα γὰρ μίαν ἱκνεῖται δασπλῆτα Χάρυβδιν,
αἱ μεγάλαι τ' ἀρεταὶ καὶ ὁ πλοῦτος.

It was evidently characteristic of the *Cea nenia*, but is too common to justify our assuming forthwith that Horace had Simonides in mind. But now follows another *locus communis*, the varied form of death, which leads up to the revelation of the *mise en scène*, concealed at first for the sake of surprise, as in Epode II: the speaker is not Horace, but the ghost of a man shipwrecked near Archytas' tomb on the Matine shore; and this ghost has connections with Simonides:

> Dant alios Furiae toruo spectacula Marti;
> exitio est auidum mare nautis;
> Mixta senum et iuuenum densentur funera; nullum
> saeua caput Proserpina fugit.
> Me quoque deuexi rapidus comes Orionis
> Illyricis Notus obruit undis.[1]

Let us pause for a moment and take stock. The poem has revealed itself as an expansion of the sepulchral epigram-form, and beside the fragment already quoted there are several things to suggest that Simonides lies behind it. He wrote an epigram on a ship-wrecked man (*A.P.* VII, 496) and made a dead man speak (VII, 516). In so doing he had followers enough. But the latter epigram quoted as part of an anecdote at *A.P.* VII, 77: 'Simonides finding a corpse on an island and burying it, wrote over it:

οἱ μὲν ἐμὲ κτείναντες ὁμοίων ἀντιτύχοιεν,
Ζεῦ ξένι', οἱ δ' ὑπὸ γᾶν θέντες ὄναιντο βίου.[2]

---

1 'Some the Furies present as a spectacle to grim Mars; the hungry sea is the sailor's doom; thick crowd the funerals of old and young; cruel Proserpina avoids no head. I too have perished, overwhelmed in the Illyrian waves by Notus, the swift comrade of setting Orion.'
The fifth line here means simply that he is, like Archytas, dead, but need not imply that Archytas met his death by drowning. This ambiguity has caused much of the trouble.

2 'May those who killed me meet with a like fate, Zeus of Strangers, but may those who buried me live and prosper.'

Attitude to Poetry

The buried corpse then appeared to Simonides and warned him not to sail. Therefore, since his companions could not be dissuaded, he alone survived.' So the passing 'nauta', whom the corpse in Horace now proceeds to address,[1] is conceived as being in the same situation as Simonides on the island:

> At tu, nauta, uagae ne parce malignus harenae
>   ossibus et capiti inhumato
> Particulam dare: sic, quodcumque minabitur Eurus
>   fluctibus Hesperiis Venusinae
> Plectantur siluae te sospite, multaque merces
>   unde potest tibi defluat aequo
> Ab Ioue Neptunoque sacri custode Tarenti.
>   neglegis immeritis nocituram
> Postmodo te natis fraudem committere? fors et
>   debita iura uicesque superbae
> Te maneant ipsum: precibus non linquar inultis
>   teque piacula nulla resoluent.
> Quamquam festinas, non est mora longa; licebit
>   iniecto ter puluere curras.[2]

Horace may, then, have used Simonidean associations as a basis for a new poem of his own, as he probably did elsewhere.[3] This, and the realism that forbids dramatic monologue to be too logical,

[1] He corresponds to the ξεῖνος or ὁδίτης so often addressed in Greek epitaphs.

[2] 'But do thou, sailor, grudge not spitefully to put a morsel of loose sand on my unburied bones and head: thus, however Eurus threatens the western waves, when the woods of Venusia are smitten mayest thou be safe, and may a rich reward redound to thee from whence it can, from Jupiter and Neptune the guardian of sacred Tarentum. Is it a small thing to thee to commit a crime that will harm thy innocent children after thee? Perchance due retribution and the reward for thy contumely may await thee thyself. My prayers will not be left unavenged, and no expiations shall release thee; though thou hastenest, it is only a moment to stop; throw dust on me thrice and thou mayest run thy ways.'

[3] Esp. Odes, III, 2 (Angustam amice); Oates, op. cit. ch. I. Many scholars have been worried because this ode turns suddenly from 'valour' to 'faithful silence'. The link may well be Simonides. Line 14 in the first part, 'mors et fugacem persequitur uirum', translates his fr. 12D, ὁ δ' αὖ θάνατος κίχε καὶ τὸν φυγόμαχον, and line 25 that begins the second part, 'est et fideli tuta silentio merces', is from his fr. 38D, ἔστι καὶ σιγᾶς ἀκίνδυνον γέρας (a favourite quotation of Augustus). Oates makes out a plausible case for

are sufficient in Oates' opinion to 'cause the apparent lack of unity to disappear'. But there is a further thought which gives the poem a positive unity, not merely an excuse for apparent incoherence. It is striking how the dead man, for all his uncompromising talk about the finality of death, on which he has a right to be as dogmatic as Callimachus' Charidas, shows nevertheless a pitiable anxiety for even a symbolic burial. I suspect that Horace is once more looking ironically at human inconsistency, just as in Epode II he poked fun at the city man who praises the country as the only place worth living in but ends by staying in the city, and in Odes III, 26 at the lover who thanks Venus that he is free at last but betrays in his prayer that he is not so free as he makes out.

So far I have been dealing with the imitation of particular poets; but Horace was equally indebted to commonplaces of literature and oratorical *schemata*. Even the best Greek poets had drawn freely on such material,[1] and even so inventive a Roman poet as Lucretius often had recourse to it in his less philosophical passages.[2] 'The treatment of *communes loci*', said Nettleship, 'was the main, if not the only, exercise of originality known to the educationalists of Cicero's day.'[3] The elder Seneca tells a story of one Albucius, who once, while pleading at the bar, produced a gambit he had learnt at school: 'Do you agree to settle the matter by oath? Swear then, but I will dictate the oath. Swear by your father's bones, which lie unburied, swear by your father's memory'—and he went through the whole *locus*. When he had ended, opposing counsel rose and said: 'We accept your oath: my client will swear.' Albucius ex-

---

Simonides' having written an Ode on Civic Virtue from which both lines would come (see fr. 37D). So whatever Simonides' motive for switching from 'valour' to 'discretion', we need not look for topical reasons to explain why Horace did so.

1 E.g. Sophocles, *O.C.* 1225 ff. Cf. Theognis, 425, Bacchylides, v, 160–2.
2 E.g. The flattering euphemisms of lovers, IV, 1160 ff. Cf. Plato, *Rep.* v, 474 D. Horace (*Sat.* I, 3, 43 ff.) and Ovid (*Ars Am.* II, 657 ff.) also treated this 'locus'.
3 *Lectures and Essays*, pp. 111–2. Gorgias and Protagoras established the practice in oratory (Quintilian III, 1, 12); it was transplanted to Rome in the middle of the second century B.C. by one Servius Galba (Cic. *Brutus*, 82). Cicero compares the orator's stock-in-trade of *loci* to the letters of the alphabet, a game-preserve, a mine and a treasure-house (*De Orat.* II, 130, 147, 174; *De Fin.* 4, 10).

ostulated, 'I was not making a proposal; I was using a figure of
ratory'. But he lost his case on it.[1]

One of the commonest of all *schemata* was that known as ἐκ τοῦ
δυνάτου. Instead of saying 'for ever' the poet detailed a list of
blue moons' and 'months of Sundays' which would occur before
ome particular change—πρίν κεν λύκος οἶν ὑμεναιοῖ—or which were
ccurring metaphorically because of some change—ἄνω ποταμῶν
ερῶν χωροῦσι παγαί.[2] Or he might use the positive form: there will
e no change while nature goes on in her course—ὄφρ' ἂν ὕδωρ τε
άῃ καὶ δένδρεα μακρὰ τεθήλῃ.[3] Horace's use of this *schema* may
erve as an illustration of his practice.

In the sixteenth Epode (25–34) the Phocaean oath of this pattern
s strung out to ten lines with no apparent object, and the ἀδύνατα
re a mere collection of proverbial instances. The poetic effect is
ot half so good as in the lover's oath in the fifteenth:

> Dum pecori lupus et nautis infestus Orion
> > turbaret hibernum mare
> Intonsosque agitaret Apollinis aura capillos,
> > fore hunc amorem mutuum.[4]

There is no more point in the instances here, but the fatal prolixity
s avoided, and the third line, with its weak caesura and its double
l's', is both beautiful in sound and expressive of what it describes.[5]
But how much more impressive is the mature art of Odes III, 30:

> Usque ego postera
> crescam laude recens dum Capitolium
> scandet cum tacita uirgine pontifex.[6]

---

1 'Non detuli condicionem, schema dixi.' *Controv.* VII, Intr. 6 f.

2 Aristoph. *Peace*, 1076; Eur. *Medea*, 410.

3 Epigr. *ap.* Plato, *Phaedr.* 264D; attributed to Cleobulus of Lindos
Diog. Laert. I, 6, 2).

4 'That so long as the wolf should be a peril to the flock, and to sailors
Orion that troubles the wintry sea, and so long as the breeze should fan
the unshorn locks of Apollo, our love should be mutual.'

5 The effect of the weak caesura is to make the stress and metre coincide
in a steady, undulating rhythm; and the double l's, both sounded as in
talian, suggest somehow the gentle lifting of the hair. Oaths such as this
were actually used; see Diodorus, IX, 10, 3.

6 'I shall grow, kept ever fresh by the praise of posterity, so long as the
Pontifex climbs the Capitol with the silent Vestal.'

Here is no tarnished convention, but a striking image which add
to the effect of the context: the poet from Apulia has raised a monu
ment in Rome which shall last as long as Rome's splendour shal
last. Virgil made the same progress from the naïve ἀδύνατα of th
Eclogues to the noble apostrophe to Nisus and Euryalus in the *Aeneid*

> Fortunati ambo! Si quid mea carmina possunt,
> nulla dies umquam memori uos eximet aeuo,
> *dum domus Aeneae Capitoli immobile saxum*
> *accolet imperiumque pater Romanus habebit.*[1]

These few examples may suffice to illustrate the various ways i
which Horace used traditional matter. In the Odes at least, howeve
many borrowings the source-hunters may have discovered, on
rarely feels that a poem is anything but his own; and that is hi
justification.

ART AND ALEXANDRIA

It was a peculiar feature of Roman Literature that it had a perio
of decadence before reaching maturity. For the political and socia
bankruptcy of the Republic coincided with a wave of enthusiasn
for late Greek poets like Euphorion, whose fragments bear out hi
reputation of being decadent. Of the poems written under Alex
andrian influence by the *Neoteroi* few specimens survive, sinc
Catullus' lyrics scarcely come under this heading; at most we car
count only his *tour de force* in Galliambics, the *Attis*, supposedl
based on a Hellenistic poem, his 'epyllion', the *Peleus and Theti*
and one or two of his longer elegiac poems. And yet althoug
Calvus and Catullus died when Virgil and Horace were still boys
the influence of their school persisted into Augustan times. It wa
in their metres that Maecenas wrote. It was the Alexandrian
Theocritus and Callimachus respectively that Virgil and Propertiu
chose to imitate. The sixteenth Epode, perhaps one of the earlies
poems that Horace wrote, has not only the romantic longing fo
escape but also the metrical cadences[2] of the *Peleus and Thetis*. An

1 *Ecl.* I, 59 ff.; V, 76–8; VIII, 52 ff.; *Aen.* IX, 446–9. For a similar effec
Housman chose the central feature of his Shropshire landscape:
> 'The lads you leave will mind you
> Till Ludlow tower shall fall.'

2 E.g. of its last six hexameters five have the molossus in the middle, a
arrangement common in Catullus, but later reserved by Virgil for special effec

the *curiosa felicitas* of the Odes, the *urbanitas* and wit, the directness, the cunning use of ordinary words,[1] all these are symptoms of a literary temperament which had found expression in the plain-style oratory of Calvus.[2] But the Augustans profited by the technical refinements of the *Neoteroi* without being obsessed with them; and by degrees the *poeta* became *uates*, composing poetry more to convey social, political and moral ideas, and less for its own sake.

The term 'Alexandrianism' as conventionally applied to the poetry of the *Neoteroi* is a term of abuse. What people really mean by it is the characteristic faults of some Alexandrians. Recent years have brought a juster appreciation of other Hellenistic poetry besides the romantic Idylls of Theocritus, which the Victorians also found congenial. Too often it had been condemned on *a priori* grounds which are insufficient. It was non-moral, but what of that? The Hylas-poem of Propertius and the Aristaeus-episode in Virgil's *Fourth Georgic* show what could be made of the purely narrative elegy and 'epyllion' of the Alexandrians. It was sometimes obscurely learned, but what of that? How many readers of *Lycidas* who thrill at the mysterious suggestiveness of

> the fable of Bellerus old
> Where the great vision of the guarded mount
> Looks towards Namancos and Bayona's hold

could explain the references?[3] It was highly artificial, but what of that? 'There is only one kind of verse that is not artificial,' said Lytton Strachey, 'and that is, bad verse.'[4] What is objectionable is triviality of subject, obscurity which is enigmatic without being suggestive, learning which is unassimilated, and artistry which is self-consciously paraded. Of this some Alexandrians were sometimes guilty, and Horace was not. But we are told so often that

---

1 *A.P.* 46–8; 240–3; Cic. *Orator*, 77 ff.

2 See Tenney Frank, *Catullus and Horace* (1928), pp. 126–7.

3 Bellerus seems to be a figure invented by Milton from Bellerium, the classical name for The Lizard (substituted for the 'Corineus' of the first draft). 'The guarded mount' is St Michael's Mount off Penzance, 'the great vision' being the apparition of the Archangel reputedly seen on the rock there called 'St Michael's Chair'. See Masson's *Milton*, p. 475.

4 Lecture on Pope, *Characters and Commentaries*, p. 289.

Horace was the enemy of Alexandrianism,[1] that some warning i
necessary. It is true that he was free from the faults mentioned above
but turn to the other side of the balance-sheet. Whence did he
derive most of the ideas in his lyrics that are not his own? Either
from lost Hellenistic lyrics or from Hellenistic epigrams. That is the
conclusion to be derived from the investigations of Reitzenstein
and from Pasquali's great work *Orazio Lirico*.[2] And where in Greek
poetry do we find the closest parallel to the short Horatian lyric?
Surely in the epigrams of Callimachus.[3]

Callimachus was the outstanding figure in Alexandrian poetry
and men like Wilamowitz and Headlam have endeavoured to
secure him due recognition.[4] The bulk of his work does not concern us here, and his lyrics survive only in tantalising fragments
but in those fifty consummate epigrams we see anticipated the
studied perfection, the economy, the restraint, the wit, the irony
and the sense of situation that are characteristic of Horace's odes
Take, for example, the scene at the riotous party in Odes I, 27
where Horace obtains silence and then continues:

> Voltis seueri me quoque sumere
> partem Falerni? dicat Opuntiae
>   frater Megillae quo beatus
>   uolnere, qua pereat sagitta.
>
> Cessat uoluntas? non alia bibam
> mercede. quae te cumque domat Venus
>   non erubescendis adurit
>   ignibus ingenuoque semper

1 E.g. Glover, *Horace*, pp. 69–70: 'Horace despised the Alexandrians,
as a matter of fact—a very significant antipathy; they posed, they displayed
their art, and paraded their obscurity—no poets for a man with a sense of
humour.'
Cf. Syme, *op. cit.* p. 255; D'Alton, *op. cit.* pp. 282–4.

2 Allowance must be made for the fragmentary nature of early Greek
lyric poetry. But it is noteworthy that 140 pages of Pasquali suffice for
Aeolic influence and 68 for Roman, while no fewer than 500 are required
for Hellenistic.

3 The publication of the *Garland* of Meleager shortly before Horace's
time probably did much to bring Greek epigrams to the notice of
Romans.

4 *Hellenistische Dichtung*, passim; *A Book of Greek Verse* (1907), pp. 302–3.

Amore peccas. quicquid habes, age,
depone tutis auribus. a miser,
    quanta laborabas Charybdi,
        digne puer meliore flamma!...[1]

Where in ancient literature have we been present at such a moment?
In Callimachus.

ἕλκος ἔχων ὁ ξεῖνος ἐλάνθανεν· ὡς ἀνιηρὸν
    πνεῦμα διὰ στηθέων (εἶδες ;) ἀνηγάγετο
τὸ τρίτον ἡνίκ' ἔπινε, τὰ δὲ ῥόδα φυλλοβολεῦντα
    τἀνδρὸς ἀπὸ στεφάνων πάντ' ἐγένοντο χαμαί·
ὤπτηται μέγα δή τι. μὰ δαίμονας, οὐκ ἀπὸ ῥυσμοῦ
    εἰκάζω, φωρὸς δ' ἴχνια φὼρ ἔμαθον.[2]

Not only the dramatic *mise en scène* but the humour of the confession
at the end are thoroughly Horatian.[3]

There are instances enough in Horace of direct influence by
Callimachus;[4] but what I want to stress here is, that in his conception of the kind of poetry that he wanted to write he was, no doubt
consciously, a disciple of the Callimachean school. The views of
that school are now best represented for us by the recovered Prologue
to the *Aetia*, in which the poet attacks the practitioners of Grand

1 'You would have me too take my share of the potent Falernian? Then
let Opuntian Megilla's brother say of what wound, what shaft, he is the
happy victim. Reluctant? On no other terms will I drink. Whatever Venus
enslaves you, you need not blush for the fire in which she burns you; you
never go astray with a low-born love. Whatever it is, come, entrust it to
safe ears.—Ah, poor wretch, in what a Charybdis you were struggling,
you that deserved a better flame....'

2 *Ep.* 43. Pasquali, *op. cit.* p. 515. 'Our friend was nursing a wound
unnoticed. What a sigh (did you notice?) he heaved from the bottom of
his heart when he drank the third cup, and the roses in the man's wreath
all dropped their petals on the floor. He must be on fire indeed. Good God,
I can guess and no mistake! Set a thief to catch a thief!'

3 There is something of the baroque spirit of Alexandria, which we find
also in Ovid's *Metamorphoses*, in the Europa-ode (III, 27, *Impios parrae*...),
especially in the extravagance of 'speciosa quaero pascere tigres'.

4 E.g. *Sat.* I, 2, 105 f.; Call. *Ep.* 31. *Odes*, I, 3, 5 ff.; Call. fr. 114. *A.P.*
131 ff.; Call. *Ep.* 28. See further E. Englmaier, *Was ist in des Horaz Satiren
und Episteln auf griechischen Einfluss zurückzuführen* (1913), p. 37.

Epic.[1] In words that became famous he there described how Apollo spoke to him when first he began to write poetry (lines 21–32):

'For when first I set the tablet on my knees, Lycian Apollo said to me: "Poet, you should rear the fattest victim you can for me but a slender Muse (λεπταλέην). And this too I bid you, to tread the path that wagons do not wear, and not to drive your chariot in the common tracks of others nor along the broad highway; but you shall drive a path of your own, though it be narrower." Him I obeyed. For I sing among those who love the cicala's sweet sound and not the noise of asses. Let others bray like the long-eared beast but may I be the dainty, the winged creature.'[2]

Horace remembered this passage when he wrote the last poem of his last book of odes:

> Phoebus uolentem proelia me loqui
> uictas et urbes increpuit lyra
> ne parua Tyrrhenum per aequor
> uela darem.[3]

And when he says that the Fates have given him

> spiritum Graiae *tenuem* Camenae,[4]

that *tenuem* represents the Greek λεπτός, 'subtle', a favourite Callimachean epithet of praise.[5] These writers, like Jane Austen, would not desert their 'small square, two inches, of ivory'. They took infinite pains to secure that perfection which is only to be achieved by luck after a long process of trial and error. Their ambition was

---

1 Horace also satirised bombast (*Sat.* II, 5, 41), substituting 'Furius' for 'Iupiter' in Furius' line:

> 'Iupiter hibernas cana niue conspuit Alpes.'

2 Text: *Ox. Pap.* XVII, 2079; E. Lobel, *Hermes*, 1935, p. 32. Commentaries: A. Rostagni, *Riv. Fil.* 1928, 1 ff.; R. Pfeiffer, *Hermes*, 1928, pp. 302 ff.

3 IV, 15, 1: 'When I wished to tell of battles and the conquest of cities Phoebus sounded his lyre in warning not to set my little sails over the Tyrrhenian deep.'

4 II, 16, 38.

5 *Ep.* 29, on Aratus' *Phaenomena*:

> χαίρετε, λεπταὶ
> ῥήσιες, Ἀρήτου σύντονος ἀγρυπνίη.

Cf. *Ars Poetica*, 46 (45): 'In uerbis etiam *tenuis* cautusque serendis....'

o give an impression of ease while straining every muscle, like a
ballet-dancer.[1] Horace once mentions, among the disappointments
he and his friends suffer when they recite their poems at inopportune
moments,

> lamentamur non apparere *labores*
> nostros et *tenui* deducta poemata filo.[2]

He shared Callimachus' contempt for the common herd and sought
the approval only of the few who could appreciate refinements:

> Saepe stilum uertas iterum quae digna legi sint
> scripturus, neque te ut miretur turba labores,
> contentus paucis lectoribus;[3]

and as Dryden thought it worth while to rewrite Chaucer, so
Horace was moved to emulate Lucilius, because by ill luck that
great *ingenium* had been sent into the world before the days of
refined art.[4]

It was the more irritating that there had developed in some circles
a positive taste for the rugged and archaic. Cicero and Varro had
been *fautores ueterum* in the days of the *Neoteroi* partly out of dislike
for 'musical trifles', but Horace, who for the same reason was no
advocate of the *Neoteroi*—and no amount of faith that one good
poet must really have appreciated another can entirely sweeten
the line

> Nil praeter Caluom et doctus cantare Catullum—[5]

felt that the time for reaction was now past. The Augustans, his
own circle, were writing poetry which had all the polish of the
Neoteroi and something worth saying as well; and he quickly dismissed as merely jealous anyone who still professed to like the old,
unpolished poets better. This is the burden of his spirited Epistle[6]

1 *Ep.* II, 2, 124–5.
2 *Ep.* II, 1, 224: 'We lament that our toil goes unnoticed and the fine-
spun fabric of our poems.'
3 *Sat.* I, 10, 72–4: 'You must often reverse your pen [rub out], if you
will write lines worth a second reading, nor strive to win the admiration
of the crowd, being content with few readers.'
4 *Ib.* 56–71. Cf. *Sat.* I, 4, 6–13.
5 *Sat.* I, 10, 19.
6 *Ep.* II, 1; esp. ll. 50–89.

to Augustus. No great name, not even that of Ennius, can impres̄
him unduly. In his view the Roman poets of earlier ages deserve
indulgence rather than honour, and he speaks as patronisingly c̄
them here as he did of Lucilius in the Satires. The most Horatia̅
element in the Epistle to the Pisos is the insistence that *ingeniu̅*
without *ars* is nothing.[1] And art involves time and labour. Rathȳ
than publish an unpolished poem you should keep it for nine years̄
as long, in fact, as Cinna, the admirer of the Alexandrians, kept h̄
Zmyrna. 'I wrote it thirteen times,' said Housman of one of h̄
stanzas, 'and it was more than a twelvemonth before I got it right.'

1 See esp. ll. 263–74 (where Plautus is again criticised for carelessness)̄
289–98; 366–90; 408–52.
2 *The Name and Nature of Poetry*, p. 50.

CHAPTER V

THE HORATIAN ODE

PERHAPS it will be best to clear the way for the study of what Horatian lyric is by recollecting what it is not In the first place, it is rarely 'lyrical', being the product of meditation rather than immediate emotion. There are, of course, exceptions, in tone if not in inspiration—I, 19 (*Mater saeua Cupinum*), I, 26 (*Musis amicus*) and IV, 3 (*Quem tu, Melpomene*), for instance—but they are not many.[1] Though Horace himself constantly speaks of his lyre and the Latin word 'ode' had not then been invented, the longer pieces are nearer in feeling to what we call 'odes' (our associations with the word being no doubt coloured by his work) than to what we call 'lyrics', while the shorter pieces are sometimes akin to hymns, sometimes to Miltonic sonnets.[2] And the fact that many of the poems are addressed to an individual gives them a hortatory turn which is alien to the free self-expression of lyric. It takes two to make a normal Horatian ode.

Again, the Horatian lyric is rarely suggestive or imaginative. The Roman mind was practical, not visionary, and Roman poetry, however intense the feeling that inspires it, is normally that of statement, not of suggestion.[3]

> Odi et amo. Quare id faciam, fortasse requiris.
> Nescio, sed fieri sentio, et excrucior.

1 Occasionally the true lyrical note is heard in the hexameter poems; e.g. in the outburst of enthusiasm for country life at *Sat*. II, 6, 60-7: 'O rus, quando ego te aspiciam....'

2 'Horace elaborated a form of ode which it is easier to recognise than in few words describe; and a number of Milton's sonnets may be referred to his ode form. If we compare, for example, his *Cyriack, whose grandsire with Martiis caelebs* or *Aeli uetusto*, there can be no doubt that Milton was deliberately using the sonnet form to do the work of Horace's tight stanzas.' Robert Bridges, *Keats* (Collected Essays, Vol. I), p. 136. Cf. Campbell, *. cit.* p. 11. A. Quiller-Couch, *Studies in Literature*, pp. 61 f.

3 On the distinction see E. M. W. Tillyard, *Poetry Direct and Oblique* (1934).

The Horatian Ode

That is simple, even colloquial, statement; but it is also poetry
In the poetry of Horace it is only very occasionally that the word
suggest more than the literal meaning. There are glimpses, but onl
a few, that go beyond the picturesque:

> Nuper in pratis studiosa florum et
> debitae Nymphis opifex coronae
> *nocte sublustri nihil astra praeter*
> *uidit et undas.*[2]

Here and there an image, even a personification, may sudden
come to life:

> Contracta pisces aequora sentiunt
> iactis in altum molibus: huc frequens
> caementa demittit redemptor
> cum famulis dominusque terrae

> Fastidiosus: *sed Timor et Minae*
> *scandunt eodem quo dominus, neque*
> *decedit aerata triremi et*
> *post equitem sedet atra Cura.*[3]

What is no more than vivid fancy in the first stanza merges in th
second into real imagination. We feel in this case that the po

---

1 Walter Headlam once wrote: 'The Athenians were Ionian, and th
quality they inherited and developed was lucidity; an admirable qualit
and by its help the Athenian mind expressed itself eventually in admirab
prose; but the defect of it is that by leaving nothing to the imagination, b
abolishing suggestion, it becomes the death of poetry' (*C.R.* XVI, 190
p. 439). There *is*, nevertheless, a poetry of statement, and it is not har
to think of examples of the highest quality.

2 *Odes*, III, 27, 29–32: 'But lately intent upon flowers in the meadov
and designer of a bouquet owed to the Nymphs, in the glimmering nigl
she saw nothing but stars and billows.'

3 *Odes*, III, 1, 33–40: 'The fishes feel the sea shrink as the piles are throw
into its depths: into it the contractor with his crowds of slaves and th
owner tired of the land pour their rubble: but Fear and Foreboding clim
where the owner climbs, and black Care forsakes not the bronze-plate
trireme and sits at the horseman's back.' Horace seems to have been please
with these images, for he uses them again, less successfully, at *Odes*,
16, 21 f.

visualised what he wrote. But his personifications have not always this quality:

> Virtus recludens immeritis mori
> caelum negata temptat iter uia.[1]

In the first line here Virtue seems to be a goddess opening the gates of heaven for her devotee, while in the second she represents the man of virtue entering them; the image is confused and unreal.

Metaphor too, which springs from the imagination, plays no great part in Roman poetry. The orators and critics, both Greek and Roman, were very severe in this respect, and their asceticism may have affected poetry.[2] We must remember, however, that metaphors which seem tame to us, with our increased nimbleness of association, may have been exciting to them. Macrobius praises Virgil for examples we should hardly notice, such as 'aquae mons' and 'ferreus imber'.[3] In a well-known passage of the Epistle to the Pisos (46 ff.) Horace gives this advice:

> In uerbis etiam tenuis cautusque serendis
> dixeris egregie, notum si callida uerbum
> reddiderit iunctura nouum.[4]

And he repeats it at line 240 ff., adding,

> tantum series iuncturaque pollet,
> tantum de medio sumptis accedit honoris![5]

---

1 *Odes*, III, 2, 21–2.

2 In Aristotle's day it was considered extravagant to call the Odyssey a good mirror of human life'. Cicero would not allow the Senate to be called 'orphaned' by the death of Cato without a ponderous 'ut ita dicam'. Arist. *Rhet.* III, 3, 4; Cic. *de Orat.* III, 41, 164 and 167. Cf. Longinus, *On the Sublime*, XXXII.

3 *Sat.* VI, ch. VI, 7.

4 'Subtle and wary in combining your words too, you will have used them excellently if clever combination has made a well-known word new.' On this see my article in *C.Q.* 1959, 181–92.

5 'Such is the power of arrangement and combination, such the distinction imparted to ordinary words!' The context shows that, as Rostagni insists, the second passage also refers to choice of words for their meaning, not for their *concinnitas*.

What was meant by 'making a word new'? There is a passage in the treatise on rhetoric *Ad Herennium* which throws some light on this (IV, 42). The author quotes a sentence: 'Postquam iste in rem publicam impetum fecit, *fragor* ciuitatis ruentis es auditus.'[1] 'Fragor' becomes a metaphor by being applied to 'ciuitatis', and it is referred to as *nouum uerbum*. So that those have been on the right track who have held that *iunctura* includes 'metaphor-making'. It means the use of old words in such a context that they acquire a new aura of associations.

It might be said that in these passages Horace was only once more repeating the words of a Hellenistic writer.[2] But even to-day we can detect phrases in his poems, such as *diuites insulae* at Epod. XVI, 42,[3] which illustrate this *callida iunctura*. And there is a remarkable piece of contemporary evidence which bears on the subject, a saying of Agrippa recorded in Donatus' *Life of Virgil* (180) 'Marcus Vipsanius said that Virgil was suborned by Maecenas to introduce a new kind of affectation (κακοζηλία), neither turgid nor plain, but consisting of ordinary words, and therefore unnoticed.' Marx has illustrated what Agrippa must have meant with regard to Virgil's diction, and shown how he might have included Horace as well.[4] There must be many cases in which we fail to detect what sounded 'new' to an Augustan: more than we can recapture lies behind Quintilian's 'uerbis felicissime audax'.

An element of suggestion is also introduced by the Augustan quasi-allegory to which I have already referred (p. 69), and in one particular trait which occurs several times in his lyrics and which deserves special attention, the depicting of natural phenomena as symbolic of human experience. This has become so common a feature of modern literature that there is a danger of our projecting

1 Compare Horace's own phrase (*Odes*, II, 1, 31), *auditumque Medi Hesperiae sonitum ruinae*.

2 Cf. the view quoted by Philodemus, περὶ ποιημάτων, fr. 9: ποίημα. . γίγνεσθαι ἐξ ἰδιωτικῶν τε καὶ εὐτελῶν, συγκειμένων δὲ καλῶς, χρηστόν.

3 A play on the normal 'beatae', which was misused to mean 'rich', like our 'prosperous'.

4 *Rhein. Mus.* LXXIV (1925), pp. 184 ff. Agrippa's tone of hostility does not concern us here; but it is surprising that he should have accused Maecenas whose own poetic diction, to judge by the fragments, was flamboyant, of introducing this particular subtlety.

t into ancient when it was not intended to be there;[1] but as there
are some cases in Horace which are generally acknowledged, there is no
ground for initial scepticism. Take the opening stanzas of Odes II, 9:

> Non semper imbres nubibus hispidos
> manant in agros aut mare Caspium
>   uexant inaequales procellae
>   usque, nec Armeniis in oris,
>
> Amice Valgi, stat glacies iners
> menses per omnes, aut Aquilonibus
>   querceta Gargani laborant
>   et foliis uiduantur orni:
>
> Tu semper urges flebilibus modis
> Mysten ademptum.[2]

As Page remarks: 'Throughout these two stanzas Horace selects
illustrations from nature which admirably fall in with the idea of
grief: "rain", "disorder", "storms", "lifelessness", "winds",
"groans", "desolation".' Epode XIII provides another example. The
poet exhorts his friends to drink because there is bad weather outside:

> Horrida tempestas caelum contraxit, et imbres
>   niuesque deducunt Iouem; nunc mare, nunc siluae
> Threicio Aquilone sonant. Rapiamus, amici,
>   occasionem de die....[3]

1 Shakespeare, in his 104th Sonnet, uses the words:
      'Three winters cold
Have from the forests shook three summers' pride',
where the context is about the passing of human beauty. They are strikingly
reminiscent of *Epode* XI, 5-6:
    'Hic tertius December ex quo destiti
      Inachia furere siluis honorem decutit',
but I doubt if we should here attribute a symbolic intention to Horace.

2 'Not for ever do showers stream upon the shaggy fields or gusty
storms vex the Caspian sea unceasing, nor throughout the year, friend
Valgius, does the ice stay motionless on the Armenian shores, or the oaks
of Garganus labour in the wind and the ashes stand bereft of their leaves.
You for ever pursue in mournful strains your lost Mystes....'

3 'The sky is lowering with a rough storm, and showers and snow bring
down the heavens; here the sea, there the woods are loud with the Thracian
North Wind. Let us snatch our chance, friends, from the day...'

The simple idea is found in Anacreon (fr. 6 D). But the tone of what follows is unusually serious; lines 7–8,

> Cetera mitte loqui; deus haec *fortasse* benigna
> reducet in sedem uice,[1]

and the *dirae sollicitudines* of line 10 suggest something more than the sad reflections on human life which are the commonplaces of such poems. This epode is far from Archilochus and very near to Odes 1, 7 and 9, and is therefore to be placed among the latest. In that case it will belong to the late thirties, and the storm may be intended to suggest the political storm which blew up in 33–32 and burst at Actium.[2]

A less conventional example occurs, I think, in Odes II, 3. The theme here is the familiar one, 'We must all die, so enjoy life while you may'. After suggesting drinking *in remoto gramine* as a suitable occupation the poet continues (l. 9):

> Quo pinus ingens albaque populus
> umbram hospitalem consociare amant
> ramis? Quid obliquo laborat
> lympha fugax trepidare riuo?
>
> Huc uina et unguenta et nimium breues
> flores amoenae ferre iube rosae
> dum res et aetas et sororum
> fila trium patiuntur atra.[3]

On *nimium breues* Page again remarks: 'Notice the pathos of the epithet thus introduced in an ode on the short life of man; cf "gather ye rose-buds while ye may..."'. But it has not been sufficiently noticed that there are suggestive overtones in the previous

---

1 'Of the rest be silent; God *perhaps* will right these things with a merciful change.'

2 So Campbell, *op. cit.* p. 143. It is noteworthy, in view of 'Threicio Aquilone', that Θρηίκιος Βορέας was used symbolically for a storm of love by Ibycus (fr. 6D) and that Alcaeus (fr. 73) uses Boreas as a symbol for the political trouble caused by the Thracian-born tyrant Pittacus.

3 'To what end do the tall pine and the white poplar love to entwine their branches in hospitable shade? Why does the fleeting water strain to hurry down its twisting course? Bring hither wine and unguents and the petals of the lovely rose that die too soon, while means and age and the dark threads of the three sisters permit.'

anza also. Ostensibly the answer to the two rhetorical questions
simply, 'to provide an ideal place for drinking'. The scholiast
orphyrion duly explains, 'subaudiendum, "si ea non utimur"'.
ut Orelli alone, to my knowledge, has seen the further point.
Horace', he says, 'has attributed to the trees themselves the feeling
f love, as with branches entwined they unite in forming a shade,
that the traveller may enjoy a single shade under the two trees.'
ut he does not say why. Surely the picture of the tall pine and
e white poplar intertwined, as well as the use of the words *consociare
nant*, is meant to give a hint that Horace seldom omits when his
eme is the brevity of life, that love-making as well as drinking
ould not be neglected. The second question suggests the other
de of the picture, with the significant juxtaposition of *laborat* and
epidare, words that recall the feverish toil of worldly affairs,
d *fugax*, which had some of the associations of our word
leeting'.

There is one ode of which the appreciation is vitally affected by
wareness of its nature-symbolism, 1, 9. The ostensible trend is as
ollows: 'It is so cold outside, that we must do our best to enjoy
urselves indoors. Leave the rest to the gods. Enjoy yourself while
oung, not neglecting the pleasures of Campus and piazza.' The
ange of scene between the beginning and end is certainly re-
arkable, or would be so in any other poet. Campbell's comment
this:[1] 'That the ode which begins with a picture of snow-capped
oracte should end with an account of outdoor sports that must be,
the best, highly inappropriate to such a season, is so characteristic
f Horace's practice that we must regard it as intentional; and in
oint of fact the third stanza itself implies a transition from winter
spring; the advice thereafter becomes general.' And in a footnote
e attributes the change of mood to 'the desire to give an *appearance*
spontaneity'. But there is, I think, another explanation. Let us
rn to the poem:

> Vides ut alta stet niue candidum
> Soracte, nec iam sustineant onus
>   siluae laborantes, geluque
>   flumina constiterint acuto?

[1] *Op. cit.* p. 224.

Dissolue frigus, ligna super foco
large reponens, atque benignius
 deprome quadrimum Sabina,
  O Thaliarche, merum diota.[1]

The idea, as is generally recognised, comes from Alcaeus (fr. 90 D)

ὔει μὲν ὁ Ζεύς, ἐκ δ' ὀράνω μέγας
χείμων, πεπάγαισιν δ' ὑδάτων ῥόαι...

κάββαλλε τὸν χειμῶνα κ.τ.λ.

But of the details only the frozen rivers are common to both
Horace seems to envisage, not a storm, but a clear, icy landscape
Some suppose him to be describing a real winter at Rome of excep-
tional severity.[2] It may be so, though in that case the absence o
any reference in contemporary writers is to be noted. But suppose
on the other hand, that Soracte is simply local colour, and that th
whole scene is a fiction symbolic of old age. Everything falls into
line: snow is used as a symbol for old age at Odes IV, 13, 12 (*capiti*
niues); *nec iam sustineant onus siluae laborantes* recalls the symboli
use of *querceta Gargani laborant* at II, 9, 7, and *geluque flumina consti*
terint acuto the *stat glacies iners* of the same passage.

The second stanza follows Alcaeus closely; but the third intro
duces a new picture:

Permitte diuis cetera, qui simul
strauere uentos aequore feruido
 deproeliantes, nec cupressi
  nec ueteres agitantur orni.[3]

Why does Horace choose this particular illustration of the powe
of the gods? Heinze says, rather lamely, that it is because thei

1 'You see how Soracte stands deep in snow, and the labouring wood
can now scarce bear their burden, and the rivers are halted with ice. Me
the cold, piling logs generously on the fire, and fetch out a mellowe
vintage, four years old, Thaliarchus, in a Sabine jar.'

2 Pasquali, *op. cit.* p. 78.

3 'Leave the rest to the gods; when they have stilled the winds that d
battle over the raging sea, neither the cypresses nor the old ashes are shake
any more.'

power is most strikingly displayed in the stilling of storms. But
the stanza gains enormously in significance, and unites the whole
poem, if we feel the storm to be the storm of life, and the calm the
calm of death.[1]

The thought of death then leads on naturally to the next stanza:

> Quid sit futurum cras fuge quaerere, et
> *quem fors dierum cumque dabit lucro*
> *adpone*, nec dulces amores
> sperne puer neque tu choreas,

when the snow-theme of the opening lines is picked up again and
made explicit by

> Donec *uirenti canities* abest
> morosa....[2]

The poem, then, is not intentionally formless; on the contrary
it derives a subtle unity of feeling from the undercurrent of nature-
symbolism. The suggestive effect is: 'Old age will come, so enjoy
yourself now. Your life is in the hands of fortune. So before old
age comes, enjoy yourself.' And the poem is, after all, to use a
simile of Campbell's, a circle and not a parabola.

Horace may have found such symbolism in Greek lyric poetry.
An elaborate example occurs in the sixth fragment of Ibycus.[3])
One ancient critic at least thought he detected it in Virgil.[4] But
I have only dwelt on it because it has been little noticed, not because
it is at all common in Horace's work.

---

1 For this symbolism see Housman, *A Shropshire Lad*, XXXI:
> 'The gale it plies the saplings double,
> It blows so hard 'twill soon be gone:
> To-day the Roman and his trouble
> Are ashes under Uricon.'

2 'What to-morrow will bring do not stop to inquire, and each day that
fortune grants you, count it gain, nor despise sweet loves and dancing while yet
you are young, while yet your green youth is free of gloomy white hairs—.'

3 C. M. Bowra, *Greek Lyric Poetry*, p. 272.

4 See Servius on *Aen.* XI, 183. His name was Asinius Pollio, and he
may be the great Augustan. (See, however, Ribbeck, *Prolegomena*, p. 116;
Fronto, *Ep.* I, 6 *fin.*) Cf. Heinze, *Vergils Epische Technik*, pp. 366 ff.

Nor does Horace summon to his aid a rich or rare diction. His epithets aim at being just (*propria*) rather than striking;[1] they help the artistic symmetry more than the sense. The magniloquent compound-words that enrich Pindar's odes were alien to the genius of the Latin language,[2] and 'tauriformis'[3] is his sole attempt at such coining. The Italian dialects were too remote from Latin for extensive borrowing, and there was no attempt, so far as we know, to interbreed them as Greek dialects were interbred by the Alexandrian poets. *Ex noto fictum carmen sequar*, said Horace, and his decision was wise.

Finally, Horace did not write what is now known as 'beauty-poetry'.[4] His object was to give the most lively expression he could to his thoughts and feelings, and everything was subordinated to this. Propriety (τὸ πρέπον—*decorum*) was his cardinal principle, and in this he followed the main stream of Graeco-Roman opinion. The very first section of the Epistle to the Pisos deprecates the irrelevant introduction of 'purple patches'—Diana's grove and altar, swift streams winding through lovely meads, the Rhine or the rainbow:

> *sed nunc non erat his locus.*[5]

Horace will describe with equal faithfulness the limpid beauty of the Bandusian spring or the unpleasant symptoms of dropsy. If he sought to create beauty it was not through his choice of subject-matter, but rather through the perfection of his art.

So much for what Horatian lyric was not; now let us consider what it was. The absence of lyric spontaneity was compensated to

---

1 A notable exception is *splendida arbitria* at *Odes*, IV, 7, 21. Vollmer unnecessarily shrinks from it, and reads with Hartman, 'et de te, splendide, Minos', etc.

2 Quintilian remarked on this fact (1, 5, 70; cf. 1, 6, 28).

3 *Odes*, IV, 14, 25.

4 The idea that certain subjects are peculiarly poetical appears in Demetrius (*On Style*, 132-3), though he disclaims it to some extent (135).

5 Ll. 14-19. A strange exception occurs in his own earliest known work, *Sat.* I, 7, 27, where we are told that the voluble Persius

> 'ruebat
> flumen ut hibernum, *fertur quo rara securis*'.

It is hard to see how the romantic afterthought is appropriate to the ribald context.

ome extent by the perfect control under which the poems were
levised. They were cunningly contrived, and display to a high
legree the quality of 'wit' in the seventeenth-century connotation
f the word. That Horace had an unusually good sense of situation
s apparent from some of the Satires, witness the encounter with a
ore (I, 9), and the cross-examination of Agamemnon (II, 3, 187 ff.).
One can well imagine that he loved the Comedy of Manners: we
now that on one occasion he took the Comic poets Plato and
Menander to the country to read,[1] and he adapted ten lines straight
ut of Terence.[2] This sense of situation served him well in many
f the odes; as in the scene at a rowdy party (I, 27, *Natis in usum*),
n the triangular love contest (III, 20, *Non uides quanto*), above all
n the perfect dialogue-piece (III, 9, *Donec gratus eram tibi*). In these,
nd in many others, we see the satirist, the spectator of the human
omedy, turned poet.

He could also be dramatic in the commonplace sense of the word.
Alcaeus' storm-scene[3] is an armchair piece compared with Horace's
daptation, and other poems, such as the seventh Epode, are vividly
dramatic. One of the most important branches of the study of
oratory was 'actio', which comprised a good deal of the histrionic
rt,[4] and we know that reciters of poems reinforced their words
with a wealth of appropriate gesture.[5]

The element of surprise plays a large part in some of the odes.
Horace will lull us into security by a pretty picture of spring, to
wake us suddenly with the knocking of death at the door (I, 4);
r he will beguile us with an orthodox song of triumph which slips
nperceptibly into a panegyric of the vanquished queen (I, 37).

1 *Sat.* II, 3, 11.

2 II, 3, 262. He also refers explicitly to a scene in Terence. *Sat.* I, 2,
0 ff.

3 Fr. 30D; *Odes*, I, 14. Alcaeus' poem has too many particles to be
ruly dramatic. As Demetrius rightly remarked (*On Style*, 194), πολλὴν
πάθειαν τοῖς συνδέσμοις συνεμβαλεῖς. Cf. Longinus, *On the Sublime*,
XI.

4 So pronounced were the gestures employed that Quintilian had to tell
rators how theirs should differ from those of actors. Cicero (*Or.* 55) called
ctio 'quasi corporis quaedam eloquentia'.

5 Stat., *Silv.* III, 5, 64 ff. Pasquali (*op. cit.* p. 413) notes that in the epigram
f Philodemus *A.P.* v, 46, the word καταμάνθανε requires a gesture to
xplain it.

And indeed he loved contrasts for their own sake,[1] as in his apostroph
to Bacchus (II, 19, 17):

> Tu flectis amnes, tu mare barbarum,
> tu separatis uuidus in iugis
>   nodo coerces uiperino
>   Bistonidum sine fraude crines,[2]

or where he sets the peace of rural life beside the turmoil of politics.

At first sight a few of the pieces seem to lack unity of subjec
and to go off at a tangent. But on closer inspection most will b
found to have a single idea behind them, however inconsequen
they may seem on the surface.[4] An exception is the Europa od
(III, 27): the myth is ostensibly told as a cautionary tale for Galatea
but the happy ending is hardly consistent with this; it looks a
though the situation, Galatea's departure, were simply a makeshif
excuse for introducing the story.

But it is not the wit, the charm and the cleverness of Horace'
mind that give the Odes their unique quality. That is due more t
words than to thought, and for it we have ultimately to thank th
Roman training in oratory. In virtue of this all educated Roman
(and their Greek contemporaries) were connoisseurs in the artisti
use of language, sensitive to sounds and rhythms and to the archi
tectural construction of sentences as few other peoples have been
Even the uneducated were aware of rhythmical faults, and it is o
record that when an orator fell into a monotonous series of cadence
the audience began to shout the rhythm in anticipation.[5] The per
fection of the oratorical 'period',[6] which we often miss in Lucretius

---

1 The exploitation of contrasts was a particular feature of the poets o
the Parnasse. As Cicero remarks of metaphor (*Or.* 134), 'swift transitio
of thought is in itself pleasant'.

2 'Thou dost sway rivers, thou the foreign sea, thou tipsy on the se
questered mountain-ranges dost confine in a knot of serpents the hair o
the women of the Bistones without harm.'

3 III, 29, 21–8; IV, 5, 25 ff.

4 I have already cited instances in *Odes*, I, 9 (pp. 129 ff.) and III,
(pp. 70 ff.). See Campbell, *op. cit.* pp. 6–7.

5 Cic. *de Or.* III, 197; Demetrius, *On Style*, 15.

6 On the 'periodic' style see Aristotle, *Rhet.* III, 9; Cic. *Or.* 204 f
Aristotle stresses the pleasurable effect of inevitability which it gives.

was introduced by Virgil into Latin hexameter poetry and by Horace into lyric. Sound was even more important than it is in modern poetry, because Roman poetry was designed for recitation, and it is also worth remembering that such evidence as there is suggests that, even when reading alone, the Romans read aloud.[1] (See further my *Golden Latin Artistry*, 1963.)

One result was that sentences tended to be limited so as to be easly uttered in one breath.[2] Cicero prescribes the equivalent of four hexameters as the normal limit for prose, and Virgil rarely exceeds this.[3] And within the sentence the 'limbs' (*cola*) were so weighted and arranged that the period became a work of art independently of the sense. There is a passage in Longinus about this which is most striking in a critic who lays such stress on the value of content: 'Nothing is of greater service in giving grandeur to such passages than the synthesis of the various members. It is the same with the human body. None of the members has any value in itself apart from the others, yet one with another they constitute a perfect organism. Similarly if these elements of grandeur are separated, the sublimity is scattered to the winds. Whereas if they are united into a single system, and embraced moreover by the bonds of rhythm, then merely by being rounded into a period they acquire a living voice'.[4]

The Odes of Horace are as carefully constructed as the periods of Virgil. In the shorter pieces at least I believe that, if a stanza could be removed without impairing the sense, we should still feel something to be lacking, even though we were unfamiliar with the poem. What Demetrius said of prose periods applies well to them: 'The members in a period may be likened to the stones which press upon one another and hold together a vaulted roof.'[5] Each

---

1 Most of the evidence is derived from exceptions that prove the rule. See J. Balogh, *Voces Paginarum*, *Philologus*, LXXII (1926–7), pp. 84–109, 202–40. Cf. Norden, *Kunstprosa*, p. 6.

2 Arist. *Rhet.* III, 9, 5; Cic. *de Or.* III, 175.

3 *De Or.* III, 181 f.; *Or.* 222. Lucretius has a sentence of no less than 16 lines (I, 935–50). Norden, *Aeneis*, VI³, p. 376.

4 *On the Sublime*, ch. XL. The rhythm, weighting and grouping of the petitions in the Anglican Litany provide an excellent illustration.

5 *On Style*, 13. Compare Nietzsche's characterisation of the Horatian ode (p. 4).

individual sentence or stanza in the ode is also arranged with carefu
art. Take the first stanza of I, 21:

> Dianam tenerae dicite uirgines;
> intonsum, pueri, dicite Cynthium,
> Latonamque supremo
> dilectam penitus Ioui.

This follows the principle familiar in music by which the last o
three related phrases is longer than the other two and sums then
up.[1] But detailed analysis of the periodising of the Odes would
contribute no more to our enjoyment than the elaborate numerica
schemes which have been extracted from Virgil's work. He tha
hath ears to hear, let him hear.

Another characteristic of the periodic style was smoothness.[2] Two
things cause roughness, hiatus and agglomeration of consonants, and
except when it was desired for special effects this was avoided by
the orators from Isocrates onwards. Cicero enjoins that the juncture
between words be neither 'aspera' nor 'hiulca', but such as to rende
the style 'aequabiliter fluentem'.[3] This, it may be said, refers only
to prose; but Dionysius, in the fullest discussion of the subject tha
has come down to us, gives as his example of this smooth style a
poem, Sappho's Hymn to Aphrodite (a circumstance to which we
owe its preservation).[4]

Horace's lyric poetry is certainly 'aequabiliter fluens', and it may
be noted that he tended gradually to eliminate hiatus between lines,
while his consonants are hardly ever crowded.[6] He seems also to

1 This principle is stated by Demetrius, *On Style*, 18. On 'tricola' is
general see Norden, *Aeneis*, VI, App. II, p. 370 f.

2 For the connection see Dion. Hal. *De Comp.* XXIII. (To him this styl
embraces all the virtues of good prose.)

3 *De Or.* III, 172; cf. *Part. Or.* 21; Auctor *ad Her.* IV, 18.

4 *Ibid*. He finds only seven rough junctures in the 28 lines. Dionysiu
was in Rome at the time when Horace began to write his Odes.

5 To this rule of 'synaphia' there are only six exceptions in the Alcaic
of Books I–III, and none in the Sapphics of Book IV. Cf. Verrall's observations, *Studies in Horace*, pp. 179 ff.

6 This is partly due, of course, to the comparative scarcity of consonant
in the Latin language. Sapphics in German, scanned by stress, have no
the Horatian flow. In the Oberammergau Play I noticed one stanza which
ended with a rare mouthful of consonants:

> 'Schmeīchĕlnd zŭr Schāu trāgt.'

have taken some care that consonants which clashed at the end of one word and the beginning of the next were such as followed easily in the mouth.[1]

The music of the sounds themselves, though again a detailed analysis would contribute little to our enjoyment, is an element of immense importance, and Horace's taste was no less exquisite in this. The natural assonance of Latin case endings can lead even to regular rhyme:

Terrarum domin*os*	euehit ad de*os*
hunc, si mobil*ium*	turba Quirit*ium*
certat tergeminis	tollere honoribus;
illum, si proprio	condidit horre*o*
quicquid de Libyc*is*	uerritur are*is*.[2]

Alliteration too, an embellishment that abounded in a rather crude form in early Roman poetry and was, perhaps for that reason, less common in the *Neoteroi*, was restored with discretion by the Augustans.[3] Horace used these graces particularly in the opening lines of odes:

*Angustam amice pauperiem pati
robustus acri militia puer…*

and

*Motum ex Metello consule ciuicum
bellique causas et uitia et modos…*

are two examples of very similar pattern.

Quem tu, Melpomene, semel,

the opening line of iv, 3, is striking enough, but still more so is the 'chiasmus' of sounds with which the next ode begins:

Qualem ministrum fulminis alitem.[4]

Often, we may suppose, the choice of a particular word or name was influenced more by sound than sense. Why, asked Verrall,

1 An Australian doctor who knew his Horace by heart remarked to me that he had noticed this trait, without being aware that the ancients had discussed such matters. Dionysius (*loc. cit.*) gives instances of smooth and rough collocations and shows an amazing degree of fastidiousness.

2 I, 1, 6–10. Cf. the many internal rhymes in Ovid's pentameters. See J. Marouzeau, *Horace artiste de sons* (*Mnemosyne*, iv, 1936), 85–94.

3 Norden, *Aeneis*, vi, p. 416, surprisingly belittles the amount of alliteration in Horace.

4 Cicero seems to have been experimenting in assonance in his much-abused lines

'O fortunatam natam me consule Romam'

and

'Cedant arma togae, concedat laurea linguae'.

does Horace appeal to the Muse of *tragedy* at the end of the first three books?[1] Surely the answer is, not that they are a concealed tragedy, but that she of all the Nine had the name which created the most euphonious assonance:

> et mihi De*l*phica
> lauro cinge u*ol*ens, Me*l*pomene, co*m*am.

We have only to substitute the alternatives he suggests as having been open to the poet, 'Mnemosyne' or 'Musa precor', to see how the music is destroyed.

The Romans liked the effect of Greek words interspersed with Latin,[2] and certainly there is a peculiar grace in lines such as

> nec Polyhymnia
> Lesboum refugit tendere barbiton.

It is the Greek names combined with the alliterative 'd's' that tune what I have always found one of the most haunting of Horace's stanzas:[3]

> Doctor argutae fidicen Thaliae,
> Phoebe, qui Xantho lauis amne crines,
> Dauniae defende decus Camenae,
>   leuis Agyieu.

But the general euphony of the Odes is subject to the law of propriety. The letter 's' has always caused discomfort from the time of Lasus of Hermione, Pindar's master, who wrote poems from which it was excluded altogether, to that of Tennyson, who in his revised version of *In Memoriam* cut out every case (save one) in which it occurred at the end of one word and the beginning of the next.[4] When Horace speaks of dropsy his words are as ugly as his subject, and hiss with sibilants:[5]

> Cre*s*cit indulgen*s s*ibi diru*s* hydrop*s*,
> nec *s*itim pellit nisi cau*s*a morbi
> fugerit ueni*s* et aquo*s*u*s* albo
>   corpore languor.

---

1 *Op. cit.* p. 5.   2 *Sat.* I, 10, 20; Quint. XII, 10, 33.   3 IV, 6, 25–8.
4 Cf. Dion. Hal. *De Comp.* XII; Longinus, *On the Sublime*, XLIII. Norden, *Kunstprosa*, p. 58 n. It should be remembered that the Latin 's' was hissed. Euripides was wrongly abused for the ugliness of a line spoken by Medea to Jason (*Med.* 476):
> ἔσωσα σ' ὡς ἴσασιν Ἑλλήνων ὅσοι—
The sibilants represent the hissing of her hatred.   5 II, 2, 13–16.

Ancient critics from Democritus[1] onwards were much interested in the aesthetic effect of the various sounds and letters. Without ascribing to Horace too much attention to theory we may suppose that he was fully conscious of the possibilities that the Latin language offered.

The law of propriety demanded also that language should be as far as possible imitative—μιμητικὸν τῶν πραγμάτων, or, as we should say, onomatopoeic. Under this term I would include any device of sound or rhythm or technique that reinforces the sense. It is generally agreed that a good style is one which accommodates itself to the meaning, but although onomatopoeia is clearly a corollary of this principle, in modern times it has come to be regarded as at best a *tour de force*, at worst a childish trick. Now we may grant that when it is too obvious and self-conscious it may be tiresome by distracting our attention from the object to the poet's cleverness; but when it helps to present a relevant image to the inward eye, giving colour to what would otherwise be mere black and white, then it belongs to the realms of the imagination. In its subtler forms it merges into that pervading rightness and felicity of expression which characterises those poets to whom poetry is above all a means of communicating experience.[2]

There is a remarkable passage in the *Cratylus* of Plato in which Socrates discusses the mimetic effect of various letters of the alphabet, claiming that ρ suggests motion, ι penetration, λ liquidity or smoothness, γλ glutinousness, ν inwardness, ο rotundity.[3] Of course the sounds cannot suggest the meaning in themselves, but they can reinforce it. To some this may seem fantastic; yet I believe that Plato is on the right lines, even when he finds that a sound suggests

---

1 He wrote περὶ καλλοσύνης ἐπέων, περὶ εὐφώνων καὶ δυσφώνων γραμμάτων (Diog. Laert. IX, 48), and had many followers. See Norden, *Kunstprosa*, I, pp. 57 ff.

2 On the subject of onomatopoeia in ancient poetry see *C.Q.* XXXVI (1942), pp. 121–33. For some curious examples from English poetry see A. Platt, *Nine Essays*, pp. 178–9.

3 For a similar list see the elder Scaliger, *Poetics*, IV, ch. 47 f. According to him, A suggests breadth, U obscurity, I length, O greatness, softness. On onomatopoeia in general see the admirable chapters of Dionysius of Halicarnassus, *De Comp.* 14–20, presumably based on Theophrastus.

some quite abstract quality.[1] The matter is highly subjective, bu
if one reader points out examples which seem significant to him
it may at least awaken others to the possibilities and lead them t
discoveries of their own.

In the art of onomatopoeia Virgil is outstanding among Lati
poets, as Tennyson is among English.[2] As in the case of alliteration
he was reviving a popular trait of early Latin poetry which th
Neoteroi had generally neglected, and using it with finer skill an
sensibility. And Horace, though his poetry was less descriptiv
and so gave less scope for it, has also many striking examples.[3]

In the hexameter poems he takes any obvious opportunity. Thu
stammering is represented by repeated 'p's',

> Infans namque pudor prohibebat plura profari,[4]

whispering by repeated sibilants,

> Stridere secreta diuisos aure susurros.[5]

And perhaps we are meant to hear the whirring of the potter'
wheel in

> *cur*rente rota *cur urc*eus exit?[6]

Horace drives lumbering up to the hills in his carriage in a lin
full of 'm's' and elisions,

> Ergo ubi me in montes et in arcem ex urbe remoui.[7]

In a more complex example the rustic on the river-bank

> expectat dum defluat amnis, at ille
> labitur et labetur in omne uolubilis aeuum.[8]

Not only do the repeated verb and the coincidence of ictus an
accent suggest the steady flow of the river; we also wait, like th

---

1 The state or configuration of the mouth when the sound is made seem
to play almost as much part in the suggestion as the sound itself. See Si
Richard Paget, *Human Speech*, esp. pp. 174–5, on the origins of language.

2 See R. Maxa, *Wiener Studien*, XIX (1897), pp. 78 ff., for examples fror
the *Aeneid* (the *Georgics* would be still more worth study); Norden, *Aene*
VI[3], App. VII, pp. 413–24.

3 Norden surprisingly belittles the amount of onomatopoeia, as c
alliteration, to be found in Horace; *ib.* p. 421.

4 *Sat.* I, 6, 57.   5 *Sat.* II, 8, 78.
6 *A.P.* 22. See J. Marouzeau, *op. cit.* pp. 85–94.
7 *Sat.* II, 6, 16.   8 *Ep.* I, 2, 42 f.

rustic, for the expected break in the line, the caesura,[1] and it never comes. This may seem far-fetched, but I believe it accounts for the effectiveness of the line. Virgil likewise slips a caesura when he wishes to represent a chariot out of control:[2]

> Fertur equis auriga neque audit currus habenas.

It is as though he were thinking of himself here, as he does explicitly in two other places,[3] as a charioteer driving a team of hexameters

> with necks in thunder cloathed and loud-resounding pace.

In the lyric poems there are a few instances of simple sound-imitation. Like Virgil, Horace uses the letters 'c', 'l' and 'i' to suggest running water:

> Mella caua manant ex ilice; montibus altis
> leuis crepante lympha desilit pede,[4]

and again:

> Me dicente cauis impositam ilicem
> saxis unde loquaces
> lymphae desiliunt tuae.[5]

Coincidence of ictus and accent suggests a steady undulating motion, and the lingering double 'l's' suggest hovering, in the lovely image in the fifteenth Epode of the breeze fanning Apollo's hair,

> Intonsósque ugitáret Apóllinis aúra capíllos.[6]

Such sound-imitation gives a pleasure which is appreciable, if not very important, like Tennyson's

> Myriads of rivulets hurrying through the lawn.

More interesting is the art with which Horace contrives to work rhythmic imitation even into the fixed metre of his stanzas. Addressing Iullus on the expected triumphal return of Augustus to Rome, he wrote in Sapphics:[7]

> Tum meae, si quid loquar audiendum,
> uocis accedet bona pars, et 'o sol
> pulcher, o laudande', canam recepto
> Caesare felix.

---

1 I.e. the regular 4½ as well as 2½ in lines with no 3½ caesura.
2 G. I, 514.   3 G. II, 540; III, 17–18.   4 *Epodes*, XVI, 48.
5 *Odes*, III, 13, 14–16.   6 *Epodes*, XV, 9.   7 *Odes*, IV, 2, 45–8.

The Horatian Ode

It was Heinze, I believe, who pointed out that 'ó sol púlcher, ó laudánde' suggests the trochaic rhythm of the popular verses shouted at triumphs. The love-sick poet in the eleventh Epode[1] sets out resolutely for home, but soon his feet betray him:

> Iussus abire domum ferebar incerto pede.

The elisions help to entwine the branches in the line

> Umbram hospitalem consociare amant,[2]

since slurring runs the words together. The relentless pounding of the sea is well represented by the reiterated quadrisyllables of

> Quae nunc oppositis debilitat pumicibus mare,[3]

the stamping of feet by the repeated 'ter' in

> Gaudet inuisam pepulisse fossor
> ter pede terram,[4]

and the faltering of the tongue by the slurred hypermetron of

> Cur facunda parum decor(o)
> inter uerba cadit lingua silentio ?[5]

In the Eleventh Aeneid Virgil has a vivid onomatopoeic picture of a tumult, in which he contrasts hot-headed youth and murmuring but powerless age:

> Arma manu trepidi poscunt, fremit arma iuuentus:
> flent maesti mussantque patres.[6]

But this is surpassed by Horace's description of the tyrant's fear of fortune's fickleness:

> Iniurioso ne pede proruas
> stantem columnam, neu populus frequens
> ad arma cessantes, ad arma
> concitet imperiumque frangat.[7]

'Aux armes, citoyens!' cries the mob, but the moderates, the solid molossus of 'cessantes', hold it back at first, till with a second cry it sweeps them along in a torrent of dactyls. To put a comma before

1 L. 20.   2 Odes, II, 3, 10.   3 Odes, I, 11, 5.
4 Odes, III, 18, 15–16.
5 Odes, IV, 1, 35–6. Cf. the boiling over of the cauldron in Georgics, I, 295:   'Aut dulcis musti Volcano decoquit umor(em).'
6 Ll. 453–4.   7 Odes, I, 35, 13 ff.

'cessantes' and not after, as Vollmer does in the Teubner text, destroys the effect.

The alternation of wide 'a' sounds and obscure 'u' sounds at the opening of the Archytas ode[1] struck me as somehow suggesting the contrast between his wide ambitions and his obscure and common fate long before I found that Scaliger had attached such associations to those letters:

> Te maris et terrae numeroque carentis harenae
> mensorem cohibent, Archyta,
> Pulueris exigui prope litus parua Matinum
> munera.[2]

Propriety of metre is a more complicated subject. It would be fascinating to know why Horace chose the metre he did for each particular piece, for it would reveal how he conceived his poetry. Sometimes an ode had its germ in a line or a poem of some Greek lyric poet, and the metre naturally, though not inevitably, followed suit.[3] But the majority have no such literary associations. The Alcaic soon established itself as the most weighty and serious medium at the poet's command; it is interesting to note that the earliest specimen (I, 26, *Musis amicus*)[4] is a light poem of only three stanzas, whereas those written later are nearly all much longer.[5] Conversely the Sapphic soon established itself as the lightest medium, capable even of doing the work of the short Greek epigram;[6] and while one early specimen, I, 2 (*Iam satis terris*), is a long and serious poem, most of the later odes in this metre are not. But why a poem so slight as III, 26 (*Vixi puellis*) should be in Alcaics, or one

---

1 I, 28.

2 The inferior reading 'latum' for 'litus', accepted by Vollmer, incidentally mars this fine effect.

3 As in I, 9; 10. But I, 14, in the Fourth Asclepiad, is modelled on a poem in Alcaics (Alc. fr. 30D), and I, 27, in Alcaics, was probably suggested by an Anacreontic poem (Anac. fr. 43D).

4 See pp. 11 ff.

5 In Tripos Latin Verse papers at Cambridge eight lines of English are usually set for Lyrics. Many candidates compose an Alcaic poem of two stanzas, but it is safe to say that such a poem could never be an artistic success as a whole.

6 As in I, 30; III, 22.

so weighty as I, 12 (*Quem uirum aut heroa*), in Sapphics, is hard to say. The stately Alcaic is used in II, 19 (*Bacchum in remotis*) for the simulation of Bacchic frenzy, which seems to be more suitably conveyed by the headlong Second Asclepiad, as in III, 25 (*Quo me, Bacche, rapis*). The love-poems are nearly all in the graceful Asclepiadic metres. It may be that in some cases odd lines or stanzas tended to form themselves spontaneously in Horace's head and that he later constructed poems round them, so that a large element of chance would enter in; a phrase like 'quid leges sine moribus uanae proficiunt', or 'O fons Bandusiae splendidior uitro', flashing across the mind, might well be the starting-point of a poem whose metre it would determine.

The metre once chosen, Horace knew well how to exploit its possibilities:

> Tutus bos etenim rura perambulat;
> nutrit rura Ceres almaque Faustitas;
> pacatum uolitant per mare nauitae;
>   culpari metuit fides;
>
> Nullis polluitur casta domus stupris;
> mos et lex maculosum edomuit nefas;
> laudantur simili prole puerperae;
>   culpam poena premit comes.[1]

So he counts on his fingers the blessings of Augustan rule, each in a single line. Everything is regular, orderly, peaceful, in the rhythm as in the land.[2] Of all his metres only the Third Asclepiad[3] could achieve just this effect. It requires a stanza in which all the lines are alike. (The Glyconic fourth line is not different in rhythm from the three lesser Asclepiads that precede it.) Sapphics would not do because the short Adonic fourth line is incapable of bearing a

---

1 IV, 5, 17-24: 'For in safety the ox treads up and down the fields; Ceres nurtures the fields, and benign Prosperity; over a peaceful ocean the sailors fly; loyalty keeps clear of reproach; no scandal stains the chaste home; custom and law have purged away the taint of guilt; mothers are praised for children like their fathers; punishment treads on the heel of crime.'

2 The asyndeton helps this effect. The mind is relieved of all effort, even that of following a constructed period.

3 With the possible exception of the First Asclepiad.

elf-contained idea, besides being rhythmically different from the
aree it rounds off.[1]

In I, 3 (*Sic te diua potens Cypri*) he accustoms us for twenty-eight
nes to a rhythm in which the stop comes after the second, longer
ne of the metre (Second Asclepiad); then he continues:

> Post ignem aetheria domo
>> subductum macies et noua febrium
> Terris incubuit cohors
>> semotique prius tarda necessitas
> Leti corripuit gradum.[2]

he metre, like death, has caught up a line—*corripuit gradum*.

It is not surprising that there are many who value the Odes
hiefly as a storehouse of memorable phrases, 'jewels five words
ong' whose economy and perfection would be impossible in
nost languages—*miseri quibus intemptata nites*—*non sine dis animosus
nfans*—*debitae Nymphis opifex coronae*—*munitaeque adhibe uim
apientiae*—*spes animi credula mutui*. They are so clean-cut, so
ree from the fussy little words that blur our uninflected English.
he terseness of which Latin was capable had to be discovered;
vhat Sallust did for prose, Horace did for verse, long after the
ther outstanding quality of the language, its sonority, had
ren recognised and exploited by writers. For every phrase of
Catullus that sticks in the memory there are a score from Horatian
yric.

I need not discuss at length the various rhetorical devices which
elped to create the artistic harmony which the Romans called
concinnitas'.[3] Horace, like Virgil,[4] had them all at his fingers' ends,
nd we may note, for instance, how he uses anaphora in the short
de I, 26 (*Musis amicus*) both to bind the poem together and to

---

1 Something of the same effect is, however, achieved in Sapphics at
Odes, III, 8, 17-24.

2 'After fire was purloined from the halls of heaven, wasting and hosts
f fevers unknown before descended upon the earth, and what was formerly
he slow necessity of distant death quickened its pace.'

3 See Cic. *Or.* 80-4.

4 Macrobius (*Sat.* IV) analyses passages from Virgil, giving each sentence
s rhetorical label.

impart swiftness.[1] But in him they never seem unnatural, recalling what Cicero well remarked of 'color' in prose, that it should be diffused in the blood, not plastered on as 'make-up'.[2]

There was one artistic effect which Latin, with its flexible word-order, could achieve, while in other languages it is scarcely possible—the arrangement of words in grammatical patterns.[3] As I know of no English term for this, let us call it 'word-placing'. It consists chiefly in the separation of nouns from their epithets. In hexameters the most conspicuous example is 'that verse which they call Golden, of two substantives and two adjectives with a verb betwixt to keep the peace'.[4] This arrangement has a monumental effect and was generally reserved by Virgil for special purposes, such as the summing up of a period, while by lesser artists its value was frittered away through over-use.[5] Horace rounds off the second Satire of Book II with a brave Golden Line,

> Fortiaque aduersis opponite pectora rebus.

He also uses the type twice running for mock-grandiose effect in describing the impressiveness of the house entered by the town mouse and the country mouse:

> Rubro ubi cocco
> *tincta super lectos canderet uestis eburnos*
> *multaque de magna superessent fercula cena.*[6]

---

1 *Quis—quid, necte—necte, hunc—hunc.* For this binding effect of anaphora cf. Landor's poem:

> 'Ah what avails the sceptred race?
> Ah what the form divine?
> What every virtue, every grace?
> Rose Aylmer, all were thine;
> Rose Aylmer....'

2 *De Or.* III, 199. Cf. II, 149–209 for a detailed discussion.

3 On the whole subject see Norden, *Aeneis*, VI, App. III. In elegiac poetry this word-placing often gave something of the effect of rhyme, balancing the halves of the lines.

4 Dryden, Preface to Translations. (Prepositions, etc. are disregarded.)

5 It is a sign of the immaturity of *Epode* XVI that no fewer than six of the last nine hexameters are of this or similar construction, recalling the monotonous rhythm of Catullus' *Peleus and Thetis*.

6 *Sat.* II, 6, 102–4.

And with a splendid example,

> Nobilis ut grandi cecinit Centaurus alumno,

he lifts the thirteenth Epode from the contemporary atmosphere of the beginning to that of the Heroic Age.

This form of artistry, already familiar in dactylic verse, was transferred by Horace to lyric. His words are often so interwoven that the pattern is only complete at the end of the clause or sentence, and the whole is subtly bound together, as in

> Nunc et latentis proditor intimo
> gratus puellae risus ab angulo[1]

or

> Qui fragilem truci
> commisit pelago ratem
> primus....[2]

We are so familiar with the word-placing of Latin poetry that it is hard to realise how much rarer it is in Greek. Gorgias, the great experimenter, had attempted such effects in prose, but no one had followed him. In the whole of the Anthology there is scarcely a couplet that attempts the intricate Roman style.[3]

The flexibility of Latin word-order also enabled the poet to arrange his ideas exactly as he would:

> Truditur dies die
> nouaeque pergunt interire lunae.[4]

How perfectly the sequence of words brings out the relentless passing of time! And how well the alternation of words in the line

> Inuicte mortalis dea nate puer Thetide[5]

suggests Achilles' double nature, half human, half divine, and the dilemma that was his tragedy! Nietzsche was right in holding that it is the cunning arrangement of words that is the chief cause of the inimitability of the Odes.[6]

---

1 *Odes*, I, 9, 21–2.   2 *Odes*, I, 3, 10–12.
3 Norden, *ib.* The only significant exception, in VI, 165, he attributes to a Roman, Statilius Flaccus by name.
4 *Odes*, II, 18, 15–16.   5 *Epodes*, XIII, 12.
6 See p. 4.

The Horatian Ode

I make no apology for having given so much space to details of form and technique. Few modern critics—Robert Bridges is a conspicuous exception—have cared to discuss such matters. But the ancients were far more interested in them, and if we try to see ancient poetry through their eyes, we are more likely to achieve a full understanding of their work. I will conclude this chapter by taking a single ode and trying to analyse the secret of its charm, one which displays many of the typically Horatian characteristics. I have purposely chosen a poem which seems to me to rank high in beauty and perfection without having any of that conventional 'importance' of subject-matter that some consider to be essential to Horace's best work.[1] It is Odes III, 28:

> Festo quid potius die
>   Neptuni faciam? Prome reconditum,
> Lyde, strenua Caecubum
>   munitaeque adhibe uim sapientiae.
>
> Inclinare meridiem
>   sentis, ac ueluti stet uolucris dies
> Parcis deripere horreo
>   cessantem Bibuli consulis amphoram.
>
> Nos cantabimus inuicem
>   Neptunum et uirides Nereidum comas;
> Tum curua recines lyra
>   Latonam et celeris spicula Cynthiae;
>
> Summo carmine quae Cnidon
>   fulgentesque tenet Cycladas, et Paphon
> Iunctis uisit oloribus
>   dicetur, merita Nox quoque nenia.[2]

1 See p. 2.
2 'What better can I do on Neptune's day? Quick, Lyde, bring out the treasured Caecuban, and storm the fortress of wisdom. You know the sun has passed its zenith, yet as though the fleeting day stood still, you hesitate to pull down from the store the loitering wine-jar of Bibulus' consulship. We will chant in turn of Neptune and the Nereids' sea-green tresses; then to your curved lyre you will sing again Latona and the shafts of swift Cynthia; in our final song she who is queen of Cnidos and the shining Cyclads and visits Paphos with her swan-drawn car shall be sung, Night too in a hymn deserved.'

This is, of course, a light occasional poem. Horace's humour eeps through in the idea of wine besieging wisdom, in the choice f Bibulus' suggestive name for its vintage-year, and in the word cessantem' that makes the jar itself reluctant to leave its dignified clusion at the back of the shelf. But there is also, I fancy, an over-one in the second stanza of a kind we have noted before;[1] Horace ives a warning like Herrick's:

> The glorious lamp of heaven, the sun,
> The higher he's a-getting,
> The sooner will his race be run
> And nearer he's to setting,

ut he is too delicate to point the moral explicitly, 'Then be not oy...'. He leaves Lyde in no doubt, however; for the final song to be of Venus, and Night is to deserve her hymn. Yes, this is love-poem, but the poet's tact is perfect.

Perfect, too, is his art. The design is of the favourite type—two qual units (in this case the first two stanzas), completed by a longer ird (the remaining two);[2] and this form is repeated within the nal unit—but not mechanically; for the third *colon* breaks off, and ith a quiet coda—*merita Nox quoque nenia*—the music dies away; he sparkling brightness of the islands of Greece gives way to the usk, and the lovers are left together. The sounds are beautiful too, ith the responsive alliterations, each pair divided by a word, which une the verse like rhyme—*sentis—stet, ueluti—uolucris, cessantem—nsulis, Neptunum—Nereidum, celeris—Cynthiae, carmine—Cnidon, Nox—nenia*. As Giorgione throws over a simple landscape with gures a strange, indefinable beauty, so Horace has made of a simple ccasion a poem which has the subtle significance of a consummate ork of art.

1 See p. 131.   2 See p. 136.

CHAPTER VI

TRANSLATION

THE repeated assertion of some critics that Horace is un
translatable has not daunted his admirers, for translation
continue to appear. The problem in his case is recognised to
be peculiar, so that it merits a short chapter to itself.

The Satires and Epistles present no special difficulty, but on
warning is necessary. Though Horace himself insisted that they wer
not poetry, and they are both in matter and diction *sermoni propior*
yet they are written in a metre associated with epic. Liberties ar
taken with that metre which bring it down a step or two from i
pedestal, but it is still far from the common earth of prose. Indeed
the verse-form gives a certain mock-grandiose flavour to the homel
sentiments. Moreover the rules remain stringent compared wit
those of many modern metres, and ensure a certain vigour an
tautness, so that epigrams can be clinched in a memorable way:

> Rem facias, rem,
> si possis, recte, si non, quocumque modo rem.[1]

> Credat Iudaeus Apella,
> non ego.[2]

> Laudes, lauderis ut absens.[3]

Particularly memorable are the single-line *sententiae*:

> Quicquid delirant reges, plectuntur Achiui.[4]
> Naturam expellas furca, tamen usque recurret.[5]
> Caelum, non animum, mutant qui trans mare currunt.[6]

Now English blank verse, at first sight the obvious choice becaus
it is nearest to common speech, is not adequate to the task.[7] It ca
indeed be heroic, but only when the words themselves are heroic

---

1 *Ep.* 1, 1, 65–6.   2 *Sat.* 1, 5, 100–1.
3 *Sat.* II, 5, 72.   4 *Ep.* 1, 2, 14.
5 *Ep.* 1, 10, 24.   6 *Ep.* 1, 11, 27.
7 Mr R. C. Trevelyan's version (*Translations of Horace*, 1940), using th
loosest of blank verse, is faithful to the matter, but misses the manner whic
is essential to the commending of it.

here is nothing inherently stately in it, as there is in the hexameter. The peculiar blend of every-day matter and elevated form, which Horace learnt from Lucilius, escapes it. And more important, it can give little help to epigram. It is not because of the metrical form that stray lines and phrases of Shakespeare stick in the memory.

But English has in rhyme a device which does give to common-place matter just that fillip which the hexameter gives to Horace's talk, as can be seen in the poetry of Crabbe. Where the couplets are enjambed, the effect is so slight that the colloquial tone is not lost; where they are self-contained, as in Pope, they can be as epigrammatic and memorable as you please. I would suggest, then, that the best medium for translating Horace's hexameter poems is rhymed couplets, which should normally be enjambed, but should drop into the style of Pope wherever the original becomes vigorous or epigrammatic enough to justify it.[1] The single-line *sententiae* should generally be given a couplet to themselves.

It is when we turn to the lyrics that the barriers begin to arise; and if I criticise the attempts of others, it is only because the detection of their difficulties reveals to us what it is in Horace that is inimitable. To say that the translators ought to have realised that these were insuperable and left well alone, might be true, but it would also be inhuman. Yet we cannot help being sorry if poems that we love suffer in public esteem through inadequate translation. Of course one can give up the attempt to reproduce Horace's art, and concentrate on conveying his spirit. This has been done with notable success by Sir Edward Marsh,[2] who does not scruple, for instance, to render a Sapphic ode[3] into blank verse; shaking himself free from the *ductus uerborum*, he has produced a volume of poems which are enjoyable in themselves, apart from any comparison with the originals, and which bring out particularly well the light-hearted side of Horace's character. But that is not translation.

Choice of metre is the first and most vital consideration. Obviously we must find some medium that gives an effect like that of the

1 Conington's version, though slightly *too* like Pope throughout to reflect the original faithfully, is not likely to be surpassed. For the two styles, Popian and naturalistic, compare his first and last paragraphs of *Sat.* 1, 6.
2 *The Odes of Horace* (1941).
3 III, 27 (*Impios parrae...*).

original. But there is no short cut. Quantitative imitation is ou
of the question:

> Whatsoever virtues, whatsoever charities

may be a correct pentameter by Latin rules, but it cannot be suc
to English ears. More successful have been the attempts made i
various languages to acclimatise the Horatian metres by making
stressed syllable equivalent to a long syllable.[1] But a stressed syllabl
automatically weakens its neighbours, even when they are mono
syllables: we have no way of exactly imitating *ēlabōrābūnt* o
ēnāuigāndā or *triūmphātīsque*. And there is a more fundamenta
objection. Latin quantity was practically fixed; English stress is b
no means fixed, and the reader's taste may obstinately insist o
conflicting with the poet's.

In rendering stanza-poems we must choose or invent some stanz
that recalls the movement of the original. Horace's stanzas progress
they cannot be represented by a pair of couplets. And the relativ
weight and speed of the several lines that compose them should b
preserved as far as possible. With Sapphics this is easy; but wit
Alcaics it is no light task to reproduce the gathering wave of th
first two lines, the thundering fall of the third and the rapid back
wash of the fourth:

> Regum timendorum in proprios greges,
> reges in ipsos imperium est Iouis
> clari Giganteo triumpho
> cuncta supercilio mouentis.

There is no easy way of reproducing that effect.

Then there is the question of rhyme. Conington says modestl
in the introduction to his translations that he has adopted it, believin
it to be 'an inferior artist's only chance of giving pleasure'.[2] Bu
we are seeking counsels of perfection, and must determine whethe
this pleasure is offset by serious drawbacks. Latin verse was tune
by the clear beauty of the language itself, with the aid of alliteratio
and assonance; English ears are accustomed to expect rhyme i
lyric, and to miss it when it is absent. Now there are certain o
Horace's metres, notably those which fall into couplets, whos

1 E.g. by A. H. Clough in *The Classical Museum*, IV (1847), pp. 347 ff
2 P. xi.

ature is not alien to rhyme.[1] But here the rhyme must be alternate
f it is not to jar:

> Mater saeua Cupidinum
> Thebanaeque iubet me Semelae puer
> et lasciua Licentia
> Finitis animum reddere amoribus.[2]

That is rendered by Conington:

> Cupid's mother, cruel dame,
> And Semele's Theban boy, and Licence bold,
> Bid me kindle into flame
> This heart, by waning passion now left cold.

say nothing of the words, but the rhyme is unobjectionable. Now
here are four more lines in the same metre:

> Nil mortalibus ardui est:
> Caelum ipsum petimus stultitia, neque
> per nostrum patimur scelus
> Iracunda Iouem ponere fulmina.[3]

Conington renders these in the same metre with a different rhyme-
scheme:

> Nought is there for man too high;
> Our impious folly e'en would climb the sky,
> Braves the dweller on the steep,
> Nor lets the bolts of heavenly vengeance sleep.

In this case the rhyme cuts across the couplet–effect and perverts the
movement of the poem.

But with four-line stanzas the case is different:

> Omnes eodem cogimur, omnium
> uersatur urna serius ocius
> sors exitura et nos in aeternum
> exilium impositura cymbae.[4]

---

1 These cover the Epodes, the dactylic Odes (I, 4, 7, 28; IV, 7), and the
second Asclepiad.

2 I, 19, 1–4. 3 I, 3, 37–40. 4 II, 3, 25–28.

Here it might be harmless to rhyme the first two lines, but the third
and fourth *must* move on. Conington's version,

> One way all travel; the dark urn
>> Shakes each man's lot, that soon or late
> Will force him, hopeless of return,
>> On board the exile-ship of Fate,

is inadequate not only because the metre and words are commonplace, but because the unrolling of the Alcaic stanza, and the impression it helps to convey of a relentless movement towards death
is completely spoilt by the fact that both the metre and the rhyme
of the last two lines hark back to those of the first two.

But can English lyric verse be written successfully without rhyme?
The answer is that it can—if the writer is a poet. As proof of this
we have one masterpiece, truly Horatian in tone though not in
matter, Collins' *Ode to Evening*, a poem so beautifully tuned by
assonance, that it is easy to forget in reading it that it has dispensed
with the aid of rhyme.[1] In the best anthology of Horatian rendering
known to me[2] the pieces that stand out are those by Lord Lytton
which are not rhymed. Here is his version of Odes II, 14:

> Postumus, Postumus, the years glide by us,
> Alas! no piety delays the wrinkles,
>> Nor old age imminent,
>>> Nor the indomitable hand of Death.
>
> Though thrice each day a hecatomb were offered,
> Friend, thou couldst soften not the tearless Pluto,
>> Encoiling Tityos vast,
>>> And Geryon, triple giant, with sad waves—
>
> Waves over which we all of us must voyage,
> All whosoe'er the fruits of earth have tasted;
>> Whether that earth we ruled
>>> As kings, or served as drudges of its soil.

1 See Sir A. Quiller-Couch's admirable essay, *The Horatian Model in
English Verse* (*Studies in Literature*, 1920), p. 75. For a good analysis of the
sounds of this poem see James Sutherland, *The Medium of Poetry*, pp. 132–4.

2 *The Odes of Horace*, Selected Metrical Translations, ed. S. A. Courtauld
(1908). In the latest edition (1929) he prints a version of II, 14 by L. L.
Shadwell.

Vainly we shun Mars and the gory battle,
Vainly the Hadrian hoarse with stormy breakers,
    Vainly, each autumn's fall,
        The sicklied airs through which the south wind sails.

Still the dull-winding ooze of slow Cocytus,
The ill-famed Danaids, and, to task that ends not
    Sentenced, Aeolides;
        These are the sights on which we all must gaze.

Lands, home, and wife, in whom thy soul delighteth,
Left; and one tree alone of all thy woodlands,
    Loathed cypress, faithful found,
        Shall follow to the last the brief-lived lord.

The worthier heir thy Caecuban shall squander,
Bursting the hundred locks that guard its treasure,
    And wines more rare than those
        Sipped at high feast by pontiffs, dye thy floors.

There is here, especially in the last two stanzas, much of the Horatian dignity and distinction, undisturbed by the tinkling of rhyme; and though the third lines are too light to suggest the effect of those three long syllables in the middle that concentrate the force of the Horatian Alcaic stanza, yet the total impression is not unfaithful to the original.

So much for metre and tuning. The problems they present to the translator are difficult, but not insuperable. We now come up against the peculiar advantages of the Latin language which I discussed in the last chapter. But we must recognise at the outset that Horace wrote in two styles; one is straightforward, and is associated mainly, though not exhaustively, with the dactylic metres, the Epodes and the First and Fifth Asclepiads; the other is intricate, and found principally in the odes in four-line stanzas.

    Laudabunt alii claram Rhodon, aut Mytilenen,
        aut Epheson, bimarisue Corinthi
    Moenia, uel Baccho Thebas uel Apolline Delphos
        insignes, aut Thessala Tempe;
    Sunt quibus unum opus est....

That is perfectly straightforward speech, λέξις εἰρομένη, and ther
is no reason why it should not be successfully rendered into Englis
couplets with alternating rhyme, like those in Housman's versio
of IV, 7 (*Diffugere niues*), which I have already quoted.[1]

> Exegi monumentum aere perennius
> regalique situ pyramidum altius,
> quod non imber edax non Aquilo impotens
> possit diruere aut innumerabilis
> annorum series aut fuga temporum.

That again is straightforward, and could go into some form c
couplet, this time with successive rhymes.[2] But what of this?

> Tu pias laetis animas reponis
> sedibus uirgaque leuem coerces
> aurea turbam, superis deorum
> gratus et imis.

Or this?

> Me dulces dominae Musa Licymniae
> cantus, me uoluit dicere lucidum
> fulgentes oculos et bene mutuis
> fidum pectus amoribus.

Here we have an artistic pattern, a 'mosaic of words'; and ther
is really no way of producing quite the same effect in English witho
doing violence to the language as a natural conveyer of meaning.

Through being inflected Latin dispenses with many preposition
and it has no articles; and by its free use of apposition it gets r
of other such jostling little words; so that it can give the impressic
of being built up of clean-cut blocks of stone. This quality w
appreciated by Horace more than any other writer, and it can rare
be compassed in natural English. The English for *non sumptuo
blandior hostia*[3] is 'which would not be made more pleasing by
sumptuous offering'; a poet might save a few of the words, b
could hardly reduce the eleven to four.

1 P. 41.
2 Or the whole poem, with skilful compression, might be made in
a sonnet.
3 III, 23, 18.

Translation

Milton once set out to show translators where the difficulty lay. He chose for his experiment an ode in which this intricate quality is most marked, I, 5 (*Quis multa gracilis*). He rejected rhyme, and invented a metre designed to reproduce for English ears the effect of the original (the very metre that Collins borrowed for his *Ode to Evening*). Where he could, he rendered word for word, at the risk of ambiguity in an uninflected language.[1] Though Courtauld rejects his version as 'hardly satisfactory',[2] it is the only one that even attempts to convey what it is in the Latin that is unique:

> What slender youth bedewed with liquid odours
> Courts thee on Roses in some pleasant cave,
>   *Pyrrha*, for whom bind'st thou
>   In wreaths thy golden hair,
>
> Plain in thy neatness? O how oft shall he
> On Faith and changèd Gods complain: and Seas
>   Rough with black winds and storms
>   Unwonted shall admire:
>
> Who now enjoyes thee credulous, all Gold,
> Who always vacant, always aimiable
>   Hopes thee; of flattering gales
>   Unmindfull. Hapless they
>
> To whom thou untry'd seem'st fair. Me in my vow'd
> Picture the sacred wall declares t' have hung
>   My dank and dropping weeds
>   To the stern God of Sea.

I cannot tell how this would sound to anyone ignorant of Latin, but, apart from its merits as poetry, as an object-lesson it is of great value; and strange it is that, in face of this *caveat* from so high an authority, translators can still be found who think that such a poem can be rendered in a familiar couplet-form. Sir Arthur Quiller-Couch has rightly insisted that, whatever medium is chosen, it must

[1] In line 9 anyone ignorant of the original would take 'all gold' to be parallel to 'credulous', referring to the boy.
[2] The translation by Thomas Hood that he prints instead is not unpleasing; the long third and short fourth lines of the stanzas upset the movement of the original. 451 versions known; Storrs, *Ad Pyrrham* (1957), p. 191.

not be easy.[1] Yet no English stress metre is so difficult as Latin quantitative metre, for none can be so confined; ultimately what is difficult, what will distinguish a good from a tolerable version is the achievement of that harmony of sound which only the ear of a true poet can feel after and find.

To sum up, while we may admit that rhyme is valuable in tuning a language less automatically musical than Latin, it must not be allowed to interfere with the spirit or movement of the original and for a large number of the poems it must be rejected outright. The metres chosen or invented should not be commonplace when the original is not commonplace, and they should follow the variations of weight and speed in the Latin metre. Above all, no one who is not sure that he has the ear of a poet should attempt to translate Horace; and for this reason I shall deny my readers the pleasure of watching a pageant of Icarian flights.

1 *Op. cit.* p. 70.

CHAPTER VII

EPILOGUE

LIKE Virgil and Cicero, Horace is not merely a poet and character of two thousand years ago, but an international institution, a strand in the literary, social, and even political, fabric of European history. More of him escaped Libitina than he could himself have conceived possible. While it would be beyond the scope of this book to do full justice to his influence, and it would require the reading of a life-time to do so, yet to close an account of him at 27 November, 8 B.C., would be like omitting the last act of a play. I will content myself therefore with indicating a few of the ways in which his influence spread over the whole continent,[1] begging the reader not to expect a balanced or adequate account, which I am not equipped to give.

It is safe to say that after the *Ludi Saeculares* of 17 B.C. Horace's works were known and appreciated by all educated Romans, as they were in due course also thumbed by schoolboys,[2] so long as pagan literature was valued in the Western Empire. The last ancient recension of his text was made by Mavortius in 527; but already the barbarian invasions had distracted men's minds from literature, and it withered under the disapproval of ecclesiastics like Gregory the Great, which only Virgil, gladly accepted as a Christian Prophet, could escape. That Horace survived at all was due first to the Benedictine zeal for copying manuscripts of all kinds, and later to the schools founded by Charlemagne, in which he fortunately played the part he had wryly anticipated.[3] And even then he was known

1 In this I am much indebted to a series of lectures delivered before the Istituto di Studi Romani at Rome in celebration of Horace's bimillennium in 1935 by representatives of thirteen nations and published (1936) under the title *Orazio nella Letteratura Mondiale.* I shall refer to this as 'O.L.M.' Other sources of material are: M. Manitius, *Analekten zur Geschichte des Horaz im Mittelalter, bis* 1300 (1893); E. Stemplinger, *Das Fortleben des Horazischen Lyrik seit der Renaissance* (1906) ('F.H.L.'); *Horaz im Urteil der Jahrhunderte* (1921) ('H.U.J.'). For a short general account see G. Showerman, *Horace and his Influence* (1922), pp. 69–169.

2 Quint. I, 8, 6; Juv. VII, 225 ff.

3 *Ep.* I, 20, 17–8.

chiefly from improving excerpts, derived mainly from the Satires and Epistles,[1] in the Anthologies (*Florilegia*) which the boys learnt by heart. He was valued only as 'poeta ethicus', and to Dante, who put him third after Homer and Virgil in Limbo, he is still 'Orazio satiro'.[2] Like all other personalities of antiquity he was little more than *magni nominis umbra*; his life and personality were not known, nor was he read as a whole. Perhaps the nearest approach to a true Horatian in the Middle Ages was Alcuin, the Anglo-Saxon monk who played a leading part in organising the schools of Charlemagne; besides writing a commentary on the hexameter poems he appreciated the lyrics, which he echoes more than once in his own poetry; and in the Carolingian academy he went by the pseudonym of Flaccus.[3] In the next two centuries Horace is often quoted, but the Schoolmen stifled this incipient Renaissance in the twelfth century; and in general it may be said that for close on a thousand years the wonder is that any of the pagan writers survived at all. Our subject does not really begin before 28 November, 1347, the day on which Petrarch bought his Horace.

Petrarch ranks as 'the first modern man' because he reasserted the importance of individual personality. He not only wanted to know all about others, but assumed that they would want to know all about himself. 'You will perhaps wish to hear', he says at the beginning of his autobiographical memoir, 'what sort of a man I think I was, and what was the success of my works, especially of those whose renown has reached you, or of those which are known to you only by name.' Centred in himself, he cared passionately for individual fame, for his own *gloria*, and hence for that of others who had sunk undeservedly into oblivion. His rediscovery of ancient writings thrilled him not only because he was a true poet capable of appreciating great literature, but because he was finding personalities where before there had been only shadowy names.

1 Hugo of Trimberg refers to the existence of two other works of his (the Odes and Epodes) as 'minus usuales, quos nostris temporibus credi ualere parum' (thirteenth century). Manitius, *op. cit.* p. 108.

2 *Inferno*, IV, 89. Even as a satirist he appealed to the spirit of the age less than the fiery Juvenal.

3 Manitius, *op. cit.* p. 18. The commentaries are in an eleventh-century MS. in the Palatine Library at Vienna.

Of all the ancients there were two who stood out as flesh and
blood beyond the dark gulf of fourteen hundred years because they
had revealed themselves—Cicero and Horace. Cicero's was the
more perfect revelation because it was for the most part uninten-
tional; but Petrarch yearned not only to know but to admire, and
in that Correspondence, whose discovery was perhaps the most
exciting event of his life, he found a lack of resolution which dis-
turbed him—so much so that he taxed Cicero with it in an open
letter. Horace, on the other hand, was more like himself; he told
the world so much as he chose, and was a student of character who
had enjoyed Lucilius for the same reason that Petrarch enjoyed
Cicero:[1]

> Ille uelut fidis arcana sodalibus olim
> credebat libris, neque si male cesserat usquam
> decurrens alio, neque si bene: quo fit ut omnis
> uotiua pateat ueluti descripta tabella
> uita senis.

And, like Cicero, Horace had cared intensely for personal glory,
or the glory of poets and the immortality that they could in turn
bestow.[2] Petrarch's love was too much tinged with veneration for
him to treat Horace as a companion rather than a master. But the
adjustment came with time and familiarity. In 1437 we find Gregorio
Corraro writing to his teacher Vittorino just as a modern might
write: 'I am sending you your Horace, that has now shared my
travels for ten years and been a great stand-by; when I was in
Germany I dressed him in a red tunic, in case he should suffer from
the cold.'[3] But the man of the Renaissance who made him most
truly a friend, perhaps the most Horatian of all the literary figures
that we know, was Montaigne.[4] He quotes him, perhaps, no more
than he quotes other great Classical writers, but it was from Horace
that he received the stimulus to write about himself; and blessed

---

1 *Sat.* II, 1, 30–4: 'He entrusted his secrets to his book as to trusted
friends, turning aside neither when things went badly for him nor when
they went well; so that the whole life of the man lies open as though it were
painted in a votive picture.'
2 It seems that in Rumania 'Non omnis moriar' is the motive in Horace
which has oftenest been echoed. N. J. Herescu in *O.L.M.* p. 183.
3 Stemplinger, *H.U.J.* p. 52.
4 See esp. Essay III, 5.

like him with a country estate and a love of good literature, he achieved the same calm, sane, detached outlook on life, and the self-knowledge that can be derived from the observation of others.

After the Renaissance and the substitution of Horace's entire works for the *Florilegia* in schools, backed by men like Celtis and Erasmus, the influence of his personality becomes merged in the general enlightenment; but although it can no longer be traced it must have been continual and enormous ever since then. Boredom and inattention can only in part shut out the subtle influence of the books boys read in school, and Horace is in any case one of the authors whom schoolboys find least boring. We have one means however, of estimating at least what his influence was believed to be we can study the attitude of those in authority towards him, particularly that of the Church.

The official attitude of the Church to pagan literature was always severe.[1] It took its tone from St Augustine. The Renaissance only modified it in the sense that the writing of a good Latin style was now considered important, and for that the ancients were the acknowledged models. Laxity that grew up in practice in Humanist circles was condemned at the Counter-Reformation. The Council of Trent (1545) and the edict of the Jesuits on *literae humaniores* (1599) both insisted that the Classics must be read for style and style alone.[2]

Nevertheless there had been a liberal party in the early Church descended from such Fathers as Clement and Basil,[3] which held that many of the pagan writers had had a partial revelation. And in the Dark Ages, while some of the Monastic Orders frowned on secular literature, others, notably the Benedictines, who were set in this path by Cassiodorus in the sixth century, did at least preserve it. The peace of the cloister drew into it all men, religious-minded or not, who still cared for letters, and in time these made their influence felt there. When the Renaissance came there were many prelates who shared the new enthusiasm for the classics, as there were many Humanists who remained good Christians. The Counter

1 'Quid facit cum psalterio Horatius?': St Jerome.
2 Stemplinger, *H.U.J.* p. 11.
3 See especially St Basil's *Address to the Young on the Right Use of Greek Literature.*

Reformation could not reverse the trend of world opinion, and the Church, as usual, settled down to a policy of compromise. As for Horace, much of his work was of positive value in the moral sphere, and he was taken heartily under the wing of the Jesuit schools. Where he offended against good morals, he could be expurgated, where he was too pagan, Christianised.

The first expurgated edition was produced by the Jesuits of Dillingen in 1570, and it had many successors. As usual, the expurgators concentrated on women as the chief danger. Schoolboys were preserved from reading whole masterpieces, such as *Donec gratus eram*; the harmless Lalage of *Integer uitae* was supplanted by the still more harmless 'Charites'; and a healthy Arnoldian turn was given to the injunctions to youth in *Vides ut alta*:

> Nec *caros sodales*
> sperne puer neque *sperne ludos*.[1]

Much less concern was shown over what might well have been considered a more insidious peril, Horace's outlook on life as a whole. The qualities in him which the Humanists had liked, besides his mastery of language, were just those which the Medieval Church had condemned—self-sufficiency, self-reliance and trust in reason. But the time had gone by when the Church could afford to require so complete a renunciation of individuality.

As for religious scruples, the idea of turning Horace to Christian account had occurred to a monk, Metellus of Tegernsee, as early as the twelfth century. He used his model as Horace had used Alcaeus, taking the opening lines of odes as starting-points for poems of his own.[2] Celtis, the great apostle of Humanism north of the Alps, mingled Christian with pagan motives in his Horatian lyrics, and many of his successors aspired to the name of *Horatius*

---

1 For
> 'nec dulces amores
> sperne puer neque tu choreas'.

In other editions tantalising gaps were left, regardless of metre. Stemplinger, *N.U.J.* p. 55. Desmond MacCarthy on Horace (*Portraits*, 1, p. 130) has an amusing passage on the contrast between the morals reflected in the Classical poems boys are taught to admire in class and those impressed upon them in other times, in which he quotes this very passage.

2 He wrote *Quirinalia*, Horatian odes about Quirinus, the patron saint of his convent.

Christianus.[1] Protestants and Catholics competed in this quaint form
of composition, which flourished everywhere except in England.
In the seventeenth century quaintness degenerated too often into
absurdity.

> Laudabunt alii iustum Noam aut Abrahamam,[2]

begins one monstrosity. The associations of the original were
naïvely expected to be forgotten: it was quite common to begin a
sacred poem with a disastrous reminiscence, such as

> O nate in usum laetitiae Puer,[3]

or even

> Cum tu, Magdala, liuidam
> Christi caesariem, cum male pendula
> Spectas brachia—[4]

The last Christianised Horace appeared in 1886 at Salins, entitled
'Horatius Christianus seu Horatii odae a scandalis purgatae,
scopulis expeditae, et sale Christiano conditae'.[5]

But the world at large went on its way heedless of such aber-
rations.[6] At first, no doubt, Horace was read for the sage reason
set out by Landinus in the dedicatory epistle of the *editio princeps*
(1482): 'His works are so written that, provided they are rightly
understood, his lyric poetry can help greatly in stimulating the
youthful mind and in polishing and ennobling style, while his
Satires and Epistles are not only allowed to have great influence in
purging the human character of all stain and inspiring it with good
morals, but also equal the books of many philosophers in their
teaching.'[7] Macaulay, in his essay on the Restoration Dramatists,

1 Rettenbacher the Benedictine in Austria, Balde the Jesuit in Bavaria,
Luis de León in Spain, Petrycy in Poland, Tasnádi in Hungary. *O.L.M.*
pp. 87, 161, 242.

2 Hoppe (German), Stemplinger, *H.U.J.* p. 122. *Odes*, I, 7.

3 Balde (German), *ib.* p. 126. *Odes*, III, 21; I, 27.

4 Sarbiewski (Polish), *ib.* p. 125. *Odes*, I, 13.

5 Ed. J. F. Bergier, *ib.* p. 56.

6 The crowning absurdity was the theory of J. Hardouin (1646–1729),
that the lyric poems were Christian allegories written, not by Horace, but
by medieval monks. Lalage stood for the Church, and so forth.

7 Petrarch used to say that the reading of no ancient author improved
him so much as Horace.

8 P. 1. *Works* (Longmans, 1920), p. 570.

tated well the justification of Christian societies for allowing their
boys to read pagan authors: 'It is unquestionable that an extensive
acquaintance with ancient literature enlarges and enriches the mind.
It is unquestionable that a man whose mind has been thus enlarged
and enriched is likely to be far more useful to the state and to the
church than one who is unskilled, or little skilled, in Classical learning.
On the other hand we find it difficult to believe that, in a world so
full of temptation as this, any gentleman whose life would have
been virtuous if he had not read Aristophanes or Juvenal will be
made vicious by reading them.' But in due course Horace came to
be read simply because he was readable, and people cared less and
less whether he was a good moral influence; or rather, they were
less and less whole-hearted in their acceptance of the specifically
Christian values and their defence of a 'fugitive and cloistered virtue'.

'Epicurean' was a very ugly word throughout the Middle Ages,
and even after the Renaissance, bearing connotations both of de-
bauchery and atheism; and Horace, a self-confessed Epicurean, was
from time to time attacked on this score.[1] Yet it was the Epicurean
side of his character in the better and juster sense of the word, his
quietism and love of a simple country life, that most attracted the
growing company of his devotees. Petrarch himself in later life had
his Sabine farm, much on the same scale as Horace's, which he
built for himself in the Euganean Hills about ten miles from Padua;
and all over Europe, when men had this fortune—Ronsard in the
Loire valley, Herrick in his Devonshire vicarage—they began to
compare themselves with Horace. It was not that they learnt from
him a new enthusiasm, but that they found in him the best expression
of what they already felt. It was generally so with his poetry. The
most striking illustration is the immense popularity at the Renaissance of the Second Epode (*Beatus ille*). Few people would now
rate this among the more remarkable of Horace's poems. For all
its charm, the picture of country life which it gives is, and was in
his own day, conventional; indeed, since it is put into the mouth
of an usurer who turns out to believe in it only in theory, it may
even be to some extent ironically conventional.[2] Quite probably

---

1 His reputation suffered unjustly from a canard in the Suetonian life,
which attributes to him an extravagance of a man of similar name, Hostius.
2 See p. 55.

it was written before Horace received his Sabine farm; at all event
it is inferior in real feeling for the country to such Odes as I, I
(*Velox amoenum*) and III, 13 (*O fons Bandusiae*), and to more tha
one of the hexameter poems. Yet what echoes it raised throughou
all Europe! It was the first Horatian poem to be translated int
German, by Johann Fischart (1550–90), who took 145 rhyme
couplets to do it.[1] An imitation of it by the Marquis de Santillan
inaugurated the Horatian vogue in Spain in the early fifteent
century, and it was echoed several times by Lope de Vega.[2] I
Holland its fame was extraordinary in the seventeenth century, a
age of action and turmoil, and no less so in the eighteenth century
an age of ease and exhaustion; in the former it reflected a commo
mood of reaction, in the latter a whole attitude to life.[3] In Swede
too it was a great favourite.[4] And it was set to music for fiv
voices by no less a composer than Orlando di Lasso.[5] Its popularit
was partly due to its straightforward syntax and its easy metr
(the difficulty of some of the Horatian metres has always bee
an obstacle), but chiefly to the universality of its theme; for
expresses simply and fully the recurrent nostalgia, felt especially i
troubled or commercial societies, for a simpler life, the life of th
Golden Age. As often as not the usurer was left out in the translatio
and adaptations. He had nothing to do with what men wanted t
find, faithful presentation of an emotion they already felt.

The political poems have been rather less popular until rece
times. But many princes have been an Augustus to some poet,
the King of Poland to Rettenbacher after the defeat of the Turk
Gustav III of Sweden to Kellgren, Frederick the Great to Ramle
and Louis XIV to his court poets. Deification, which sounds strang
enough on Horace's lips, becomes a grotesque convention whe
Ronsard promises to sacrifice on the altar of Henri II, or Matthe
Prior pleads with the great god William III to exert his influenc
on high. His attitude to the Principate was sympathetic to ages
recovery which followed after religious or political upheaval, suc

1 Showerman, *op. cit.* p. 116.   2 Showerman, *op. cit.* p. 118.
3 H. Wagenvoort in *O.L.M.* pp. 136, 142, 148. The poem was par
phrased and Christianised by D. V. Coornhert in the sixteenth century.
4 A. Forström in *O.L.M.* p. 230.
5 See Stemplinger, *F.H.L.* p. 435.

as the eighteenth century in England. As for the more constructive and patriotic poems, there is one country at least which seems to have valued them most of all, and it is also the country in which Horace has played relatively the greatest part—Hungary.[1] In England too the Augustan ideals he proclaimed must have had considerable influence on the men who, in the century of his highest popularity, built up the greater part of the Empire.

On the other hand his acquiescence in absolute rule was distressing to the age of romantic idealism and struggle for liberty which followed the French Revolution. Even admirers like Ugo Foscolo held that it would have been better for him if he had never been given his farm, and had never, out of gratitude, had to renounce his freedom of thought.[2] Leopardi, while still recognizing his importance, could refer to him parenthetically as 'uomo di poco valore in quanto poeta', and 'uomo di basso ma sottile ingegno'.[3] Both his admirers and his detractors thought of him too crudely as a court poet, a subservient propagandist, buying patronage with his pen.

So much for the influence of his mind and personality, sketchy though the account must remain. As a man he has appealed most to three ages, the early Renaissance, when the Humanists hailed a kindred spirit with too much enthusiasm for any questionings of Christian conscience; the eighteenth century, enjoying the lull between the religious and the class struggles; and the decades that followed the Rationalistic Movement of the last century. The eighteenth century accorded him the greatest vogue, but it probably did not understand him best. In England at least it appears to have put the satirist above the poet, and also to have failed to appreciate the *seriousness* of his character except in its more obvious manifestations. The favourite of the Elizabethans was Catullus. It was Ben Jonson who taught the English to relish Horace, Ben Jonson, who, driven by need to follow his father-in-law's trade of a bricklayer after going down from the University, worked at Lincoln's Inn 'with a trowel in his hand and a Horace in his pocket'.[4] Even if we take

1 J. Huszti in *O.L.M.* pp. 247–8.　　2 L. Pietrobono in *O.L.M.* p. 127.
3 *Pensieri*, 54; 751.
4 He translated the *Ars Poetica*, and his *Ode to Lucius Carey* on the death of their friend Morison, though called Pindaric, is far more Horatian, especially

the lighter poems alone, there is more of the true Horatian spirit in Ben Jonson, Marvell and Herrick than in such *epigonoi* as Matthew Prior or the German Anacreontics who passed for Horatians in the eighteenth century, gay poets of women, wine and song who were in reaction from the Puritans and Pietists of the preceding age. No wonder that the prophets of the *Sturm und Drang* and the Romantic Revival found him so inadequate. But although the Golden Mean appeals neither to the romantic nor to the religious nor to the social reformer, humour, reasonableness and kindness will win a man friends enough in any age, and Horace's popularity never sank low even in the nineteenth century. Characters which strike one as Horatian are often to be met with in real life, but unless they are writers they leave no trace on the world at large. Many men of letters have inherited a portion of his spirit, as Montaigne, Molière, Voltaire and Anatole France in France, Ben Jonson, Herrick, Fielding and a host of others in England. Dr Glover rightly mentioned Charles Lamb in this connection, and certainly his gentle humour, his love of homely detail and his disarming egotism are essentially Horatian.

* * * *

It remains to consider his influence as a poet. I will deal first with that of his form, because at the Renaissance it was invariably the formal merits of ancient literature that first attracted the Humanists, and only later the content. In his case form means primarily metre. Of the ancients who borrowed his metres by far the most important was Prudentius, the fourth-century hymn-writer, because through him some of them remained familiar throughout the Middle Ages. In this he did Horace a great service, by removing one of the chief obstacles to the enjoyment of his poetry. He must have had a rare enthusiasm for the Odes to conceive the idea of

the famous stanza beginning

> It is not growing like a tree
> In bulk doth make man better be.

In his *Poetaster* he brings on Horace to discuss with Augustus his view of Virgil. I am indebted to the late Lord Keynes for drawing my attention to the primary influence of Jonson.

pressing their metres into the service of Christianity. Music was written for his hymns, and in due course for Horace's Odes themselves; medieval settings of III, 9 (*Donec gratus eram*) and one or two other have survived.[1]

The Renaissance Humanists delighted in writing Latin poems in the various Horatian metres. Celtis wrote four books of Odes, a book of Epodes and a Carmen Saeculare.[2] Cardinal Bembo and his circle were especially fond of this pursuit. Most of the poems of these Neo-Latinists that I have read are metrically correct, but almost all, save a few by Celtis, have the stiffness of prize compositions. They are generally too long, the language is not musically attuned, and the periodising is clumsy: in fact, they could not have been written by Horace. Clearly it was enough of a feat for these writers to compose in such metrical strait-jackets at all.

When it was found that the difficulty of the lyric metres was a barrier to appreciation, Celtis led the way in making his schoolboys at Ingolstadt and Vienna sing the Odes according to metre, in settings for four voices. This inaugurated a vogue which flourished in the sixteenth century, when several settings for all the Odes were composed, for use mainly in schools.[3] There were some, notably the Swiss scholar Glareanus, who objected to such part-singing as unclassical, and composed unison-settings on the lines of Gregorian chants.[4] After the sixteenth century the practice unfortunately died out, but not before it had made its mark on Christian hymn-singing, particularly in the Protestant Church.[5]

The next step was the acclimatisation of the metres to the various tongues of Europe. Quantity is not a natural basis for verse in many modern languages, and in nearly every case the adaptation was made by treating a stressed syllable as equivalent to a long.

1 Stemplinger, *H.U.J.* p. 202, n. 25; E. Castle in *O.L.M.* p. 23.

2 He was followed by Rettenbacher, Balde, the Pole Sarbiewski, Bernardo Tasso and many others. At first strict Classicism prevailed, but later on Latin words of all ages were used indiscriminately.

3 Tritonius (1507), Senfl (1543), etc. Stemplinger, *H.U.J.* p. 108.

4 Stemplinger, *F.H.L.* p. 43. Judenkünig was another; he came into line with ancient practice by adding instrumental accompaniment.

5 E. Castle in *O.L.M.* pp. 30–1. From time to time since then music has been composed for odd poems. In 1757 Arne and five other English composers published settings of twelve of the Odes for voices and instruments. P. Dancian's setting of the *Carmen Saeculare* (1787) had a great success.

Epilogue

In France, where stress was hardly distinguishable, quantitative imitations were made by Ronsard, Baif and Rapin, but the correspondence amounts to little more than equivalence in the number of syllables.

> Luy qui peut des morts rallumer le flambeau,
> Et le nom des Roys retirer du tombeau,
> Imprimant ses vers par un art maternel
> d'un stile éternel.[1]

If that is to sound like a Sapphic stanza, the long and short syllables must be distinguished with the help of music, and with the encouragement of Ronsard French composers did write settings that followed Horace's metre faithfully. But the soil was not suitable, and the metres were never acclimatised.[2] Nor were they in England, though the presence of a stress accent made it possible, and attempts have occasionally been made, from Sir Philip Sidney[3] down to A. H. Clough.[4] The English stress accent is a sentence-accent, and is left to such an extent within the discretion of the individual speaker that it is no fit basis for verse-forms so rigid as those of Horace. The German language, however, proved well able to bear them, with its heavy, well-defined stresses. The metres which emerge are thoroughly German in character, rarely attaining to the Horatian neatness and flow; but, thanks to Klopstock, Hölderlin and many others, and not least to certain well-known hymns,[5] they have made themselves a valuable element in the national poetry. Abriani in Italy (1680), Adlerbeth in Sweden (1817), translated all the Odes into the metres of the originals. But the language best fitted for their adaptation is probably Hungarian, which distinguishes rigidly between short and long syllables; all the Horatian metres had been reproduced in it by the end of the eighteenth century.[6]

There is one metre, the Sapphic, which calls for special treatment for a very peculiar reason. The rules which Horace imposed upon

---

1 Note that Rapin has felt the need of rhyme to help out the verse.
2 P. Eickhoff, *Der Horazische Doppelbau der Sapphischen Strophe* (1895), p. 51.
3 Sapphic stanzas in *Arcadia*.   4 See p. 152, n. 1.
5 E.g. the Alcaic hymn:

> 'Nún preíset álle Góttes Barmhérzigkeit.'

6 J. Huszti in *O.L.M.* p. 245.

t, particularly the caesura after the fifth syllable, had a curious ffect which has no analogy in his Alcaic stanza: they introduced, oncurrently with the Lesbian quantitative metre, a more or less egular stress rhythm:

> ínteger uítae scélerísque púrus.

he fourth stress was sometimes barely perceptible, as in

> íactat ultórem uágus ét sinístra.

A monosyllable could throw the rhythm out of gear, as in

> nec vénenátis gráuida sagíttis.

But taking the poems as a whole this undercurrent is insistent and nmistakable, when we remember that, so far as can be judged or the development of Latin metre, the Romans allowed the stress-ccent of their normal speech to be heard concurrently with the netrical scheme imported from Greece.

I have stated elsewhere my reasons for thinking that the intro-uction of this rhythmical undercurrent was no part of Horace's ntention.[1] His rules were made for other reasons.[2] But the more ne Latin stress accent asserted itself in later Latin Poetry, as it begins o do already in the *Peruigilium Veneris*, the more this rhythm ncroached on the metre, until in the Dark Ages we find specimens n which it has gained the upper hand.[3] The quantitative metre e-established itself in the ninth century with the revival of Classi-sm, was lost again in the twelfth, and again emerged in the fifteenth. But however much the Classicists might expel the lilting stress-iythm with a pitch-fork, it would always return. It might be as Carducci called it) 'barbarous', but it was easy for the untrained ar, and remarkably pleasing. In Spain, for instance, it became very

1 *C.R.* LIV (1940), pp. 131–3.
2 See p. 10.
3 In Eugenius Migne, Isidore of Seville, and Alcuin. P. Eickhoff, *op. cit.* 38. Rhyme, internal and final, was also introduced; and Hilary of Poictiers nvented a variant by resolving the last syllable, of which here is a specimen, ne opening of a threnody to the abbot *Hug*, dated 844 (*ib.* p. 41):

> 'Hug, dulce nomen, Hug, propago nobilis
> Karli, potentis ac sereni principis,
> insons sub armis tam repente saucius
>   occubuisti.'

popular in the seventeenth century (with the third stress weakened
in favour of the fourth), as in Villegas' famous *Ode to the Zephyr*:

> Dúlce vecíno de la vérde sélva,
> Huésped etérno del abríl florído,
> Vítal alíento de la mádre Vénus,
> Céfiro blándo.[1]

But above all it became familiar through Christian hymns, th
fountain-head of which was J. Heermann's

> Hérzliebster Jésu, wás hast dú verbróchen?

of the sixteenth century. How many of those who sing in ou
churches such hymns as

> Lord of our life and God of our salvation

and

> Nocte surgentes vigilemus omnes

realise that these are in the accentual Sapphic stanza accidentall
invented by Horace? The only setting of an Horatian ode sti
regularly sung, the German Flemming's *Integer Vitae*, follows th
accentual rhythm, not the quantitative metre.[2]

Translation of Horace began comparatively late, but has mad
up for this with a vengeance. The whole of the Odes have bee
translated over 100 times in England and France, 75 times i
Germany, 50 times in Italy.[3] But he lent himself also to a peculia
form of travesty or modernisation, because his poems are so largel
made up of universal sentiments illustrated by topical example
Pope's spirited imitations of the Hexameter poems are the speci
mens best known to us,[4] but long before him the practice ha
flourished on the Continent. Kochanowski, for instance, th
greatest of Polish poets, had written in 1558 a poem on the Floo
adapted from Odes I, 2 (*Iam satis terris*), in which Pyrrha become
Noah and the Tiber the Vistula.[5] Zachariä rewrote Odes I, 3 (*S*

1 C. Riba in *O.L.M.* p. 209.
2 So also the modern music for Latin Sapphic hymns, such as the
    'Régis Henríci púeri togáti'
sung at King Henry VI's Foundations of Eton and King's College, Cambridg
3 Stemplinger, *F.H.L.* p. 40, with allowance for later additions.
4 In England Nicholas Rowe had already so adapted some of the Ode
5 L. Sternbach in *O.L.M.* p. 158. He had a follower in Petrycy, *ib.* p. 16.
Kellgren and other Swedish poets of the eighteenth century did the sam

te diua potens), with Columbus and Captain Cook as the types of overweening mortals and the Lisbon earthquake as the equivalent of the angry thunderbolts of Jove.[1] How happy such adaptations could be, may be seen from Ronsard's of Odes III, 30 (*Exegi monumentum*):

> Je volerai tout vif par l'univers,
> Eternisant les champs où je demeure
> De mon renom engressés et couvers,
> Pour avoir joint les deus harpeurs divers
> Au dous babil de ma lire d'ivoire,
> Se conoissans Vandomois par mes vers.

It is worth noting that just as Horace was spared by Nicolò Niccoli (along with Virgil and Plato) in his study of the imperfections of writers, so he has escaped completely from being parodied with malicious intent.

But the most important kind of influence, the working of his spirit and his artistic sensibility in other poets, is also the most intangible. The industrious collection of echoes of his phrases may show how much he was loved and studied, and how his works became part of the background of many poets' minds, but it does not touch the main issue. A poem may be full of Horatian tags, yet thoroughly un-Horatian. On the other hand few of the English poems which I have had occasion to mention as parallels, Collins' *Ode to Evening*, some of Milton's Sonnets, stanzas from Gray's *Elegy* and Fitzgerald's *Omar*, for instance, have anything for the hunter of quotations.[2] Of conscious imitations few have been so successful as Marvell's *Ode on Cromwell's Return from Ireland*, either in feeling or in form; but there is also much that is Horatian in another poem of his with no direct reminiscence—*To His Coy Mistress*, with its urgent, reasoning tone, its touches of ironic humour ('Till the conversion of the Jew', 'The grave's a fine and private

A. Forsström in *O.L.M.* p. 222. Tickell (1740) made a sea-god warn the Scots against rebellion, on the lines of Nereus in *Odes*, I, 15.

1 Stemplinger, *F.H.L.* p. 29.

2 Nor have other poems which could have been cited, such as Campion's *Rose-cheeked Laura*, Shirley's *The Glories of our Blood and State*, Goldsmith's *Deserted Village*, Tennyson's lines to the Reverend F. D. Maurice. See I. M. O. White in *O.L.M.* pp. 99–103.

place'), and its frank Epicurean realism.[1] Some of the best imitators were also the earliest. Petrarch was in many ways akin to Horace: he was an individualist, he loved glory and poetry, he delighted in the solitude of the country, he despised the vulgar and strove for perfection in his art. True, he was a more ardent spirit; *nil admirandum* could never for a moment have been his motto; and his feeling for Laura was beyond the range of Horace's experience; but he gave modern literature at the outset some perfect examples of poems on the Horatian model. These are not to be found in the main body of his work so much as among the casual pieces.

> Vinse Annibal, e non seppe usar poi
>> Ben la vittoriosa sua ventura;
>> Però, Signor mio caro, aggiate cura
>> Che similmente non avvenga a voi.
>
> L' orsa —[2]

So he addresses Stefano Colonna, just as Horace might have addressed some high-placed Roman.

> La gola e 'l sonno e l' oziose piume
>> Hanno del mondo ogni vertù sbandita—[3]

So might Horace have written in the mood of Odes III, 6 (*Delicta maiorum*).

> Signor, mirate come 'l tempo vola
>> E si come la vita
>> Fugge, e la morte n' è sovra le spalle.
>> Voi siete or qui: pensate alla partita;
>> Che l' alma ignuda e sola
>> Convien ch' arrive a quel dubbioso calle.[4]

The moral drawn by the Christian is different, but the tone and the art are inherited from the Roman.

The lyric poetry of France also was largely founded on Horace, by Ronsard, whose favourite poet he was.

> Plein d'ardeur
> Je façonne un vers dont la grâce

---

1 See further Quiller-Couch, *op. cit.* p. 63.
2 *Sopra vari argomenti*, Sonnet XI. 3 *Ib*. Sonnet I.
4 *Ib*. Canzone IV, 7. 5 Side by side with Pindar.

Epilogue

> Maugré les tristes Sœurs vivra
>   Et suivra
> Le long vol des ailes d'Horace.

So he wrote in an early ode.[1] He was perhaps of a more delicate nature: Horace could not have written *Quand vous serez bien vieille*, and Ronsard would not have written *Parcius iunctas*. But more than Petrarch, Ronsard shared Horace's view of life, and he imitates his model as the latter would have wished, *non desiliens imitator in artum*.

Meditation, restraint, balance, tact, urbanity—few poets have dared to hope that such qualities can make a successful poem. The imitators of Horace's Odes, especially the political, have nearly all strained at the leash, heightening the tone, overcharging the language, deserting their model for what they believed to be Pindar because Pindaric pastiche is easier to write than Horatian. But he may well have influenced many poets who were not consciously imitating him, wherever we find apparently effortless perfection, or commonplaces that seem fresh instead of platitudinous, or humour breaking through seriousness, or mock-solemnity, or calm dignity, or ironical self-revelation, or any other of the traits that are especially his. For almost all poets have been to school with him.

> Digne de l'univers, l'univers pour l'entendre
>   Aime à redevenir Latin.

As a literary critic his fame has been immense and not wholly deserved. He should never have been mentioned in the same breath with Aristotle. He is best and most independent when he is dealing with Latin literature, past and present, and with the taste of his contemporaries, as in the magnificent Epistle to Augustus (II, 1). But it was the Epistle to the Pisos, elevated to the title of 'Ars Poetica', that won him his reputation. Abelard discussed it with his pupils, Dante quoted and used it; it provided mottoes for the manifesto of the French Pléiade, Du Bellay's *Defense et Illustration de la Langue Française*; Queen Elizabeth translated the first 178 lines; Vida in Italy, Opitz in Germany, Boileau in France and Pope in England in turn produced works based upon it which achieved great authority in their countries; Societies like the 'Nil Volentibus Arduum' of Amsterdam

---

1 *Des roses plantées près un blé.*

(1669) and the 'Utile Dulci' of Stockholm (eighteenth century) were founded to spread the principles of Classicism derived from it.[1]

Chief among those principles were the pre-eminence of moral poetry, the proper use of models and the importance of careful art; but there were other *obiter dicta*, such as

denique sit quiduis simplex dumtaxat et unum,

which did not pass unnoticed. Some peoples, like the French, love canons of art, and Academies for their observance, and these found in the Horatian maxims something which neither Aristotle's penetrating study of the nature of tragedy nor Longinus' sensitive appreciation could give them. But no amount of precepts can make a man a poet, and Horace himself, as we have seen, often paid scant attention to his own.[2] What they can do is to counteract bad customs and tendencies; and in this the Horatian Classicism of the eighteenth century was valuable, for it checked the excesses of Baroque poetry on the Continent and Metaphysical poetry in England. Reaction would probably have come just as soon without him, but it would not have been so ordered and self-assured.

I have been speaking only of literature, but Horace's words are current coin far beyond the circles of the lettered. 'What's here?' says Demetrius in *Titus Andronicus*,[3]

'What's here? A scroll, and written round about. Let's see:

Integer uitae scelerisque purus
Non eget Mauris jaculis nec arcu.'

And Chiron replies:

'O, 'tis a verse in Horace; I know it well.
I read it in the grammar long ago.'

And still to-day, we are told,[4] if you pass a country burial-ground in Sweden, you may see bareheaded peasants bending over a grave; and if you approach near enough, you may catch the muttered words of their liturgy, Integer uitae scelerisque purus....

1 The Iberian peninsula alone has produced forty-seven translations of it.
2 Some of the eighteenth-century poets who were born to be *dulces* ruined themselves by trying to be *utiles* out of deference to accepted canons of poetic merit.
3 Act IV, Sc. 2. The grammar was probably Lily's, in which the lines occur twice.   4 A. Forsström in *O.L.M.* p. 236.

INDEX OF PASSAGES IN HORACE CITED

INDEX OF PROPER NAMES

Index of Proper Names

Epicurus, 31, 35 and n., 44 n., 57, 98 n.
Erasmus, 162
Eratosthenes, 103 and n.
Esquiline, 18, 79, 81
Etna, 54
Eton, 172 n.
Euganean Hills, 165
Euhemerus, 32
Euphorbus, 111
Euphorion, 116
Euripides, 24, 32 and n., (54), 115 n., 138 n.
Europe, 166, 169
Eurysaces, 36

Farrington, 24 n., 25 n.
Faunus, 28
Fawdry, ix
Fielding, 168
Figulus, 34
Fischart, 166
Fiske, vii, 59 n., 80 n., 88 n., 96 n., 107 n.
FitzGerald, 43, 173
Flaccus (Alcuin), 160 and n.
Flaccus, Statilius, 147 n.
Flavius, 7
Flemming, 172
Florus, 75 n.
Fontanalia, 28
Forsström, 166 n., 172 n., 176 n.
Fortuna, 15, 26 n.
Foscolo, 167
Fraenkel, 1, 72 n., 89 n.
France, 168, 169 f., 174, 175
France, Anatole, 168
Frank, Tenney, viii, 2 n., 14 n., 107 n., 117 n.
Franke, 13 n.
Frederick the Great, 166
French Revolution, 167
Fry, 2, 3 and n.
Fuscus, 54

Galba, 114 n.
Gardthausen, 9 n.
Germany, 161, 167, 170, 172, 175
Giorgione, 149
Glareanus, 169
Glover, 1 n., 2 n., 118 n., 168
Gnatia, 27
Goldsmith, 173 n.
Gorgias, 114 n., 147

Grant, 87 n., 96 n.
Gray, 36 f., 42 f., 173
Gregory the Great, 159
Gustav III, 166

Hack, 2 n., 104 n.
Hallam, 14 n.
Hannibal, 109 nn.
Hardouin, 164 n.
Hartman, 132 n.
Hazlitt, 19 n.
Headlam, 118 and n., 124 n.
Heermann, 172
Heinsius, 97 n.
Heinze, vii, 4 n., 11 n., 13 nn., 14 n., 15 n., 40 n., 62 n., 68 n., 73 nn., 73 n., 80 n., 109 n., 130 f., 131 n., 142
Henri II, 166
Heraclitus, Ps-., 72 n.
Herculaneum, 14 n., 95
Hercules, 31 ff.
Herennium, Auctor *ad*, 80 n., 87 n., 126, 136 n.
Herescu, 161 n.
Herrick, 149, 165, 167 f.
Hilary of Poitiers, 171 n.
Hölderlin, 170
Holland, 166, (175)
Holmes, Rice, 18 n.
Holyday, 104
Homer, vii, 3 n., 61, 63 n., 103 n., 110 and n., (125 n.), 160
Hood, 157 n.
Hoppe, 164 and n.
Hostius, 165 n.
Housman, A. E., viii, ix, 28 n., 40 f., 116 n., 122 and n., 131 n., 156
Housman, Laurence, 28 n.
Hug, 171 n.
Hugo, V., 102 n.
Hugo of Trimberg, 160 n.
Humanists, 162 f., 167 f.
Hungary, 164 n., 167, 170
Huszti, 167 n., 170 n.

Ibycus, 128 n., 131
Ilissus, 54
Immisch, 17 n., 21 n., 90 n., 95 and n., 96 and nn., 97 nn., 106
Ingolstadt, 169
Isidore of Seville, 171 n.
Isocrates, 76 n., 100, 106 and n.
Italy, 11, 67, 83, 98, 170, 172, 175

Index of Proper Names

Index of Proper Names

Index of Proper Names

Index of Proper Names

Mr Wilkinson writes primarily for students of the classics who are not Horatian specialists. His book falls easily within the scope of those who can read any Latin at all—and even of those who cannot, for most passages quoted are also translated.

Horace, for Mr Wilkinson, is the poet of the Odes and Epodes—the incomparable genius of the lyric form, and a sympathetic and engaging character into the bargain. He is especially concerned with Horace as the poetic craftsman. Like most Roman poets, Horace was not inventive in subject-matter: he generally wrote about what we now recognize as the eternal platitudes. But the manner of his writing, his mastery of form, rhythm and cadence, are what have charmed and captivated his readers for centuries. This is the aspect of Horace which Mr Wilkinson studies, with much grace and insight, with profound and liberal scholarship, and with a readily communicated affection.

'His gripping and discriminating book...is the best I have read on Horace's Odes.'